Commodities For Dummies Cheat Sheet

S0-AEB-611

Major Commodities Exchanges

- **New York Mercantile Exchange** (NYMEX): www.nymex.com

  Aluminum, Coal, Copper, Crude Oil, Electricity, Gasoline, Gold, Heating Oil, Natural Gas, Palladium, Platinum, Propane, Silver

- **Chicago Mercantile Exchange** (CME): www.cme.com

  Butter, Milk, Feeder Cattle, Frozen Pork Bellies, Lean Hogs, Live Cattle, Lumber

- **Chicago Board of Trade** (CBOT): www.cbot.com

  Corn, Ethanol, Gold, Oats, Rice, Silver, Soybeans, Wheat

- **London Metals Exchange** (LME): www.lme.com

  Aluminum, Copper, Lead, Nickel, Tin, Zinc

- **New York Board of Trade** (NYBOT): www.nybot.com

  Cocoa, Coffee, Cotton, Ethanol, Frozen Concentrated Orange Juice, Sugar

- **Intercontinental Exchange** (ICE): www.theice.com

  Coal, Crude Oil, Electricity, Natural Gas

Main Regulatory Organizations

- **Commodity Futures Trading Commission** (CFTC): www.cftc.gov

- **National Futures Association** (NFA): www.nfa.futures.org

- **National Association of Securities Dealers** (NASD): www.nasd.com

- **Securities and Exchange Commission** (SEC): www.sec.gov

Amine's Top Investment Rules

- **Due diligence — just do it!** You need to know the ins and outs of any investment you're going to make. The best way to do so is to find out as much as possible about your target investment. Researching a potential investment is an absolute necessity if you're going to design a strategy that takes advantage of the market fundamentals. If you want to be a successful investor, mastering the due diligence process is key.

- **Be creative:** Too often, many investors fall into the habit of group think. One way to differentiate yourself from the average investor is by thinking outside the proverbial box and considering investments that may not be part of the main stream. For example, consider lesser-known commodities such as uranium and orange juice — which, by the way, are a great investments.

- **Be disciplined:** Investing can be a fun activity. However, you need to approach it with a lot of discipline. Markets can and do move very quickly, so knowing how to adapt to these changes is critical to surviving and thriving in the commodities arena.

- **Don't ride the highs too high and the lows too low:** As a trader and investor in commodities, you're going to have great days and you're going to have horrible days. Even the greatest of the greatest have suffered huge losses at some point. Make sure to stay psychologically fit and composed, so that you don't lose focus when things are going your way and you don't get discouraged when they're not.

Commodities For Dummies®

Best Ways to Invest in Commodities

I look at the best investment vehicles to access the commodities markets in Chapter 6. Here is a snapshot of some of these vehicles:

- **Commodity Trading Advisor** (CTA): The CTA is registered with the CFTC and the NFA and can trade futures contracts on your behalf.

- **Commodity Pool Operator** (CPO): The CPO is allowed to "pool" client accounts into one big trading account. All clients share in the profits and losses of the account.

- **Futures Commission Merchant** (FCM): The FCM is like a stock broker except she's licensed to place orders on behalf of clients in the futures markets. If you want direct access to futures trading, then opening an account with an FCM is your best bet.

- **Exchange Traded Fund** (ETF): A number of ETFs now track commodities. Some track individual commodities such as oil and gold, while others track a basket of commodities. ETFs allow you to invest in the futures markets — and to buy the market, so to speak — without having to open a futures trading account.

- **Commodity Mutual Fund:** Because of the increasing popularity of commodities as an asset class, a number of mutual funds now offer funds specialized in the trading of commodities. Make sure to watch out for hidden fees.

- **Equity stakes in commodity companies:** If you like trading stocks, then one way to play the commodities boom is to invest in the stock of companies involved in the production, transformation, and distribution of commodities. Some of these companies are involved in specific commodity sub-asset classes such as energy and metals.

- **Commodity Index**: A commodity index tracks the performance of a number of commodity futures contracts. The commodity index is a good way to not only measure the performance of the commodities markets as a whole, but also provide you with the opportunity to "buy the market."

- **Master Limited Partnership** (MLP): MLPs are publicly traded partnerships. They provide you with the advantage of investing in a publicly traded security in the form of a private partnership. They offer tax advantages and invest primarily in commodity infrastructure such as pipelines and storage facilities.

- **Emerging Markets Funds:** Some of the main beneficiaries of the commodities boom are the countries that have large deposits of these natural resources. As the demand for crude oil, gold, and other important commodities increases, these countries stand to gain. One way to take advantage of this is to invest in emerging market funds with exposure to companies that do business in these countries.

For Dummies: Bestselling Book Series for Beginners

Commodities
FOR
DUMMIES®

Commodities
FOR
DUMMIES®

by Amine Bouchentouf

Wiley Publishing, Inc.

Commodities For Dummies®

Published by
Wiley Publishing, Inc.
111 River St.
Hoboken, NJ 07030-5774
www.wiley.com

Copyright © 2007 by Wiley Publishing, Inc., Indianapolis, Indiana

Published by Wiley Publishing, Inc., Indianapolis, Indiana

Published simultaneously in Canada

For general information on our other products and services, please contact our Customer Care Department within the U.S. at 800-762-2974, outside the U.S. at 317-572-3993, or fax 317-572-4002.

For technical support, please visit www.wiley.com/techsupport.

Wiley also publishes its books in a variety of electronic formats. Some content that appears in print may not be available in electronic books.

Library of Congress Control Number: 2006934824

ISBN-13: 978-0-470-04928-0
ISBN-10: 0-470-04928-6

Manufactured in the United States of America

10 9 8 7 6 5 4 3 2 1

1O/RT/RR/QW/IN

WILEY

About the Author

Amine Bouchentouf is President and Chief Executive Officer of Renaissance Investment Advisors LLC. Renaissance is an international financial advisory firm headquartered in New York City, which provides long-term strategic advice to individuals, institutions, and governments around the world.

Amine is a world-renowned market commentator and analyst and has appeared in media in the United States, Great Britain, France, the United Arab Emirates, and Brazil. He is a member of the National Association of Securities Dealers and the Authors Guild and is also involved with the Council on Foreign Relations. He offers regular market intelligence briefings through the Web site www.commodities-investor.com.

Amine holds a degree in Economics from Middlebury College. In his spare time he enjoys playing golf, traveling, and socializing with friends. This is his third book.

Dedication

This book is dedicated to my most steadfast supporters — my family. You have always been there for me when I needed you and have always supported me in every endeavor I decide to undertake. I would not have been able to accomplish half the things I've done without your tremendous support, and for that I am deeply grateful.

Author's Acknowledgments

I was completely thrilled when Wiley approached me about working on a second book for the *For Dummies* series. I knew right off the bat that this was going to be a very ambitious project that would require a lot of focus. The challenges in writing a book of this scope were numerous and enormous. First, both Wiley and I sought to create the most comprehensive guide on the subject available to investors. I believe we succeeded because *Commodities For Dummies* covers over 30 commodities; besides the *Commodity Research Bureau Yearbook*, no other introductory book includes coverage of so many commodities. Second, Wiley and I also wanted to bring this book to market sooner rather than later. Working pretty much around the clock, seven days a week, I was able to hand in the manuscript in four months (five months total when editing and reviewing are factored in).

Every author who takes on a project of this size realizes very quickly that the undertaking cannot possibly be done alone. Despite romantic clichés about writers locked up in attics writing feverishly and not communicating with the outside world for months on end, one quickly realizes that writing a book of this kind is really a team sport. Fortunately, I had the pleasure of working with a wonderful team of dedicated professionals, both in publishing and in finance.

First, I'd like to acknowledge the first-rate editorial team at Wiley for their input and assistance through every stage of this process. Every writer hopes for nothing more than to have a team of editors who will support their general creative vision, and I was extremely fortunate to have been able to follow through on my vision for the book — from the drafting of the Table of Contents down to the inclusion of technical charts and figures — with the guidance of a knowledgeable group of editors. Specifically, I'd like to thank Laura Peterson Nussbaum, my project editor, for providing valuable insight through every step of the way. I'd also like to express thanks to Stacy Kennedy for helping launch the project early on and for her continuous input throughout the writing period. And I would also like to show my gratitude to the graphics department for helping me express my ideas and illustrate my points with the help of charts, graphs, and other helpful visuals. Finally, I would like to thank Noel Jameson who served as technical editor.

Because the financial markets in general, and the commodities markets in particular, are so broad and deep, getting insight on all the different aspects of the markets is absolutely critical. I was very fortunate that I could turn to some of the sharpest minds in finance for their insight on the markets. I'd like to thank Dr. Scott Pardee at Middlebury College for providing me with cutting-edge analysis on the cyclicality of the markets. I'd also like to acknowledge the contributions of Ray Strong at Goldman Sachs regarding all aspects of the energy markets. Thanks to Karen Treanton at the International Energy Agency in Paris for providing me with all the vital statistical information on the energy industry. I would like to express my appreciation to John D. Phillips and Neil McMahon at Alliance Bernstein for their world-class research. Kevin Rich at Deutsche Bank shared with me his knowledge of managed funds, and thanks to everyone at the NYMEX for their support — Jim Newsome, Madeline Boyd, Sam Glasser, Linda Rapacki, and Jenifer Semenza. Additional thanks goes to Frank Ahmed at Bear Stearns and Richard Adler for their general guidance. I also need to acknowledge the contributions of Elisa Castro, Heather Balke, and, of course, my agent Mark Sullivan.

Finally, I'd like to express my gratitude to my family, whose support was instrumental throughout this process.

Publisher's Acknowledgments

We're proud of this book; please send us your comments through our Dummies online registration form located at www.dummies.com/register/.

Some of the people who helped bring this book to market include the following:

Acquisitions, Editorial, and Media Development

Project Editor: Laura Peterson Nussbaum

Acquisitions Editor: Stacy Kennedy

Technical Editor: Noel Jameson

Editorial Manager: Michele Hacker, Carmen Krikorian

Editorial Assistants: Erin Calligan, Joe Niesen, David Lutton, Leann Harney

Cover Photo: © Markusson Photo/Getty

Cartoons: Rich Tennant (www.the5thwave.com)

Composition Services

Project Coordinator: Erin Smith

Layout and Graphics: Lavonne Cook, Brooke Graczyk, Clint Lahen, Barbara Moore, Barry Offringa, Lynsey Osborn, Heather Ryan, Alicia South

Anniversary Logo Design: Richard Pacifico

Proofreaders: Melanie Hoffman, Jessica Kramer

Indexer: Techbooks

Publishing and Editorial for Consumer Dummies

Diane Graves Steele, Vice President and Publisher, Consumer Dummies

Joyce Pepple, Acquisitions Director, Consumer Dummies

Kristin A. Cocks, Product Development Director, Consumer Dummies

Michael Spring, Vice President and Publisher, Travel

Kelly Regan, Editorial Director, Travel

Publishing for Technology Dummies

Andy Cummings, Vice President and Publisher, Dummies Technology/General User

Composition Services

Gerry Fahey, Vice President of Production Services

Debbie Stailey, Director of Composition Services

Contents at a Glance

Table of Contents

Introduction

· ·

Commodities, as an asset class, are going through a transformational period. What was long regarded as an inferior asset class is quickly moving to the investing mainstream. The reason? Good performance. Investors like to reward good performance, and commodities have performed very well lately. For instance, while I was writing this book, gold prices reached an all-time high; copper prices hit a 25-year high; oil companies, led by Exxon Mobil, posted some of the best quarterly and yearly performances in the history of corporate America; and a plethora of new investment vehicles, from Exchange Traded Funds (ETFs) to Master Limited Partnerships (MLPs), have been introduced to satisfy investor demand to invest in this asset class. I expect commodities to maintain this solid performance in the medium to long term, for reasons I outline throughout the book.

As commodities have been generating more interest, there's a large demand for a product to help average investors get a grip on the market fundamentals. Commodities as an asset class have been plagued by a lot of misinformation, and it's sometimes difficult to separate fact from fiction from outright fantasy. The aim of *Commodities For Dummies* is to help you figure out what commodities are all about and, more importantly, to help you develop an intelligent investment strategy to profit in this market.

About This Book

My aim in writing *Commodities For Dummies* is to offer you a comprehensive guide to the commodities markets and show you a number of investment strategies to help you profit in this market. You don't have to invest in just crude oil or gold futures contracts to benefit. You can trade ETFs, invest in companies that process commodities such as uranium, buy precious metals ownership certificates, or invest in Master Limited Partnerships. The commodities markets are global in nature and so are the investment opportunities. My aim in this book is to help you uncover these global opportunities and to provide you with the investment ideas and tools to help you unlock and unleash the power of the commodities markets. And, best of all, I do all this in plain English!

Anyone who's been around commodities, even for a short period of time, realizes that folks in the business are prone to engage in linguistic acrobatics. Words like *molybdenum, backwardation,* and *contango* are thrown around like "hello" and "thank you". Sometimes, these words seem intimidating and confusing. Don't be intimidated. Language is a powerful thing, after all, and getting a grip on the concepts behind the words is critical, especially if you want to come out ahead in the markets. That's why I use everyday language to explain even the most abstract and arcane concepts.

Here are some of the trading and investing ideas you will discover in the book:

- ✔ **Get more bang for your buck by investing through Master Limited Partnerships, investment vehicles used by only the most sophisticated investors.** *Master Limited Partnerships* (MLPs), which invest in energy infrastructure such as pipelines and storage facilities, are a unique investment because they trade publicly, like a corporation, but they offer the tax benefits of a partnership. Unlike corporations, which are subject to double taxation (on the corporate and shareholder level), MLPs are able to pass through their income to shareholders *tax free*, who are then responsible for taxes only on the individual level. Because MLPs' primary mandate is to distribute practically all their cash flow directly to shareholders, you can't afford not to invest in these hybrid vehicles. Find out how in Chapter 6.

- ✔ **Capitalize on the increasing popularity of nuclear power by investing in uranium, an investment grade material.** The use of nuclear power to generate electricity is on the rise. As a result, the price of uranium, the primary fuel used in nuclear power plants, has been in an extended — albeit quiet — bull market for over a decade, *quadrupling* from $10 in 1994 to $40 in 2006. Find out which companies mine this unique commodity and how to profit from this trend in Chapter 13.

- ✔ **Benefit from the commodity trading craze without trading a single futures contract.** As more investors flock towards the commodities markets, the exchanges that provide futures contracts, options, and other derivatives to commodity traders have seen their business expand exponentially. The *Chicago Mercantile Exchange* (NYSE: CME), one of the largest commodity exchanges, has seen its stock price rise from $40 since its 2003 IPO to almost $500 in 2006 — performing even better than Google! (See Chapter 8 for more on how to capitalize on the success of exchanges.)

- ✔ **Capitalize on the relationship between digital cameras and the silver markets.** You may be surprised to find out that the photographic industry is a major consumer of silver, accounting for almost 20 percent of total silver consumption. That is because traditional cameras use silver halide, a silver and halogen compound, to create photographic film.

However, the introduction of digital cameras, which don't require silver halide, has meant that demand for silver in photography has decreased. Find out how to profit from this by betting against the price of silver, using a trading technique known as *going short*, which I cover in Chapter 9. (Turn to Chapter 15 for more on the silver markets.)

✔ **Generate a gushing stream of dividend income by investing in oil tanker stocks.** It's one of the best kept secrets on Wall Street, but oil tanker stocks provide some of the highest dividend yields in the market. Average dividend yields for some of the industry's top performers are well over 12 percent, higher than even diversified and electric utilities (which I cover in Chapter 13). Frontline (NYSE: FRO), a seaborne transporter of crude oil that operates routes between the Persian Gulf and Asia, offers a $6.00 dividend per share. For a stock that trades within a narrow $40 range, that's a dividend yield of 15 percent. (Check out Chapter 14 for more on Frontline and other companies.)

Conventions Used in This Book

To help you make the best use of this book, I use the following conventions:

✔ *Italics* are used for emphasis and to highlight new words or terms.

✔ **Boldfaced text** is used to indicate key words in bulleted lists or the action parts of numbered steps.

✔ `Monofont` is used to make Web addresses stand out for your ease.

Foolish Assumptions

In writing *Commodities For Dummies*, I have made the following assumptions about you:

✔ You have some previous investing experience but are looking to diversify your holdings.

✔ You're familiar with commodities trading but want to brush up on your knowledge.

✔ Your traditional investments (stocks/bonds/mutual funds) have not performed according to your expectations, and you're looking for alternatives to maximize your returns.

✔ You're a new investor or someone with minimal trading experience, and you're interested in a broad-based investment approach that includes commodities and other assets.

- ✔ You understand the attractiveness of commodities and want a comprehensive and easy-to-use guide to help you get started.

- ✔ You're skeptical about the benefits of commodities but want to read about them anyway. Please do, I'm confident this book will change your mind!

- ✔ You have little or no investment experience but are eager to find out more about investing. This book not only explores investing in commodities but also includes explanations of general investing guidelines that can be applied to any market.

How This Book Is Organized

I've organized the book in a way that helps you look up essential information and analysis on the world's most important commodities and trading techniques. The first two parts of the book cover general portfolio construction methodologies and investment strategies to help you incorporate commodities in your financial life. Parts III, IV, and V then cover each specific commodity sub-asset class: energy, metals, and agricultural products. Finally, the last two parts of the book include the legendary *For Dummies* Part of Tens chapters along with a useful appendix to help you look up the technical terms discussed throughout the book.

Part 1: Commodities: Just the Facts

The first part of *Commodities For Dummies* gives you good, old general investing principles. Whether you're an experienced trader or a new investor, having a good grasp on basic portfolio allocation methods is crucial for your success. Find out how to create and design an investing road map that's specifically tailored to your financial needs and goals. You also discover how commodities stack up against other investment vehicles, such as stocks and bonds.

In addition, I explain and dispel some of the common misconceptions regarding the commodities markets, particularly relating to risk and volatility issues. I also include a whole chapter on identifying, managing, and overcoming risk, which may be the single most important issue you face as an investor. The fact of the matter is that any investment entails a certain degree of risk — overcoming that risk is what separates successful investors from the rest. Find out how you too can successfully minimize risk and maximize your returns with the help of commodities.

Part II: Getting Started

Get the lowdown on the best investment methods you have at your disposal to invest in commodities. I analyze the pros and cons of investing through the futures markets, the equity markets, ETFs, and mutual funds. In addition, I examine the role of the market regulators so you can know your rights as an investor as well as specific trading techniques and analyses, such as technical and fundamental analysis. Read this part to find out how to start trading commodities.

Part III: The Power House: How to Make Money in Energy

Energy is the largest sub-asset class in the commodities universe. Crude oil, for example, is the most widely traded commodity in the world today. Natural gas, coal, and nuclear power are also major commodities. In addition, I uncover investment opportunities in the alternative energy space (wind and solar power) and examine the companies responsible for providing energy to the world.

Part IV: Pedal to the Metal: Investing in Metals

Metals are grouped using two criteria: whether they contain iron and, more importantly, their ability to resist corrosion. Metals that contain iron are called *ferrous metals* and these include metals such as zinc. *Non-ferrous metals,* such as gold, silver, and platinum, do not contain iron. On the corrosion side, the metals that don't corrode easily are usually the precious metals: gold, silver, platinum, and palladium. Base metals, like copper, nickel, and zinc are major industrial metals. As you can tell, you'll find out everything you ever wanted to know about metals in this part.

Part V: Going Down to the Farm: Trading Agricultural Products

There is nothing more fundamental to human life than food. In this part, find out how you can nourish and grow your portfolio by investing in this most basic commodity. Some of the most commonly traded agricultural products include coffee, sugar, and orange juice. I help you decipher the seasonal nature of the business, analyze import/export activities, and consider potential obstacles so that you can design and execute a rock-solid investment approach. Some of the commodities I discuss in this part include orange juice, cocoa, feeder cattle, soybeans, and wheat.

Part VI: The Part of Tens

The legendary *For Dummies* Part of Tens chapters provide you with tips on how to become a better investor and trader. Follow the ten time-tested rules that successful commodities investors have used to make substantial profits in this area. You also get acquainted with ten of the best resources to help you become a successful commodities investor.

Part VII: The Appendix

The appendix includes a detailed glossary covering all the major technical terminology covered in these pages. Investing in commodities can get fairly technical, so understanding the concepts behind the words is critical for your success as an investor.

Icons Used in This Book

One of the pleasures of writing a *For Dummies* book is that you get to use all sorts of fun, interactive tools to highlight or illustrate a point. Here are some icons that I use throughout the book:

I use this icon to highlight information that you want to keep in mind or that is referenced in other parts of the book.

When you see this icon, make sure you read the accompanying text carefully because it includes information, analysis, or insight that will help you successfully implement an investment strategy.

I explain information that is of a technical nature with this icon. The commodities markets are complex, and the vocabulary and concepts are quite tricky. You can skip these paragraphs if you're just wanting a quick overview of the commodities world, but make sure to read them before seriously investing. They allow you to get a better grasp of the concepts discussed.

Investing can be an extremely rewarding enterprise, but it can also be a hazardous endeavor if you're not careful. I use this icon to warn you of potential pitfalls. Make sure you remain alert for these icons because they contain information that will help you avoid losing money.

Sometimes, a potential investment requires a little extra research. Make sure that when you see this icon, you get ready to analyze the investment with a fine-toothed comb. This icon lets you know that extensive due diligence is in order.

Where to Go from Here

I've organized this book in a way that provides you with the most accurate and relevant information related to investing in general and commodity investing in particular. The book is modular in nature, meaning that while it reads like a book from start to finish, you can read one chapter or even a section at a time without needing to read the whole book to understand the topic that's discussed.

If you're a true beginner, however, I recommend that you read Parts I and II carefully before you start skipping around in the chapters on particular commodities.

Part I
Commodities: Just the Facts

The 5th Wave   By Rich Tennant

In this part . . .

The chapters in this part give you everything you wanted to know about commodities. I introduce the commodities markets and go through some of the individual commodities and how they interact with each other. I also look at how commodities as an asset class compares to other assets such as stocks and bonds.

Chapter 1

Investors, Start Your Engines! An Overview of Commodities

....

....

*T*he commodities markets are broad and deep, presenting both challenges and opportunities. Investors are often overwhelmed simply by the number of commodities that are out there: You have over 30 tradable commodities to choose from. (I cover almost all of them — 32 to be exact — more than any other introductory book on the topic.) How do you decide whether to trade crude oil or gold, sugar or palladium, natural gas or frozen concentrated orange juice, soybeans or aluminum? What about corn, feeder cattle, and silver — should you trade these commodities as well? And if you do, what is the best way to invest in them? Should you go through the futures markets, through the equity markets, or by buying the physical stuff (such as silver coins or gold bullion)? And do all commodities move in tandem or do they perform independently of each other?

With so many variables to keep track of and options to choose from, just getting started in commodities can be daunting. Have no fear — this book provides you with the actionable information, knowledge, insight, and analysis to help you grab the commodities market by the horns. A lot of myths and fantasies about commodities are out there, and I set out to shatter some of these myths and, in the process, clear the way to help you identify the real money-making opportunities.

For example, a lot of folks equate (incorrectly) commodities exclusively with the futures markets. There is absolutely no doubt that the two are inextricably linked — the futures markets offer a way for commercial users to hedge against commodity price risks and a means for investors and traders to profit from this price risk. However, the futures market is only one planet in the commodities universe.

The equity markets are also deeply involved in commodities. Companies such as Exxon Mobil (NYSE: XOM) focus exclusively on the production of crude oil, natural gas, and other energy products; Anglo-American PLC (NASDAQ: AAUK) focuses on mining precious metals and minerals across the globe; and Starbucks (NASDAQ: SBUX) offers investors the opportunity to get access to the coffee markets. Ignoring these companies that process commodities is not only narrow-minded, it's also a bit foolish because they provide exposure to the very same commodities traded on the futures market.

In addition to the futures and equity markets, a number of investment vehicles exist that allow you to access the commodities markets, such as Master Limited Partnerships (MLPs), Exchange Traded Funds (ETFs), and commodity mutual funds (all covered in Chapter 6). So while I do focus on the futures markets, I also examine investment opportunities in the equity markets and beyond.

The commodities universe is large, and investment opportunities abound. In this book, I help you explore this universe inside and out, from the open outcry trading pits on the floor of the New York Mercantile Exchange to the labor-intensive cocoa fields of the Ivory Coast; from the vast palladium mining operations in northeastern Russia to the corn-growing farms of Iowa; from the Ultra Large Crude Carriers that transport crude oil across vast oceans to the nickel mines of Papua New Guinea; from the sugar plantations of Brazil to the steel mills of China.

By exploring this fascinating universe, not only do you get insight into the world's most crucial commodities — and get a glimpse of how the global capital markets operate — but you find out how to capitalize on this information to generate profits.

First Things First

Just what, exactly, are commodities? Put simply, commodities are the raw materials humans use to create a livable world. Humans have been exploiting the Earth's natural resources since the beginning of time. They use agricultural products to feed themselves, metals to build weapons and tools, and energy to sustain themselves. These — energy, metals, and agricultural products — are the three classes of commodities, and they are the essential building blocks of the global economy.

Commodities throughout history

The history of commodities tells the story of civilization itself. Ever since man first appeared on Earth, his existence has been defined by a perpetual and brutal quest for the control over the world's natural resources. Civilizations rise and fall, nations prosper and perish, and societies survive and subside based on their ability to harness energy, develop metals, and cultivate agricultural products — in short, on their capacity to control commodities. It's interesting to note that prehistoric times are still defined today by the subsequent stages of man's mastery of the metals production process: the stone age, the bronze age, and the iron age. Nations that have been able to achieve mastery over natural resources have survived, while those that failed have faced extinction. This sobering reality has led to some of the most epic clashes among civilizations.

History reveals that the most devastating battles have been fought over crude oil, gold, uranium, and other precious natural resources (all covered in this book). When Francisco Pizarro's first expedition to South America in 1524 led him to the discovery of vast amounts of gold deposits, his conquistadors proceeded to wipe out the whole Inca civilization that stood between them and the gold. As a matter of fact, it is probably unlikely that Christopher Columbus would have come across to the North American continent in the first place were it not for an unquenchable desire to find the shortest and most secure route to transport spices and other commodities from India to Europe.

A few centuries later, this continuous quest for commodities also resulted in the deadly South African Boer Wars at the end of the 19th century, which pitted the British Empire's armed forces against local fighters in a bloody battle over South Africa's precious metals and minerals. The 20th century, which heralded a new historical phase — the hydrocarbon age, shortly followed by the nuclear age — marks a turning point in humans' ability to utilize and exploit the Earth's raw materials and the extent to which they would go to preserve this control. The Persian Gulf War of 1991, which at its essence was an effort to stabilize global oil markets after the Iraqi invasion of oil-rich Kuwait in the oil-rich Middle East, is another manifestation of this historical reality. To this day, access to the world's vast deposits of oil, gold, copper, and other resources is taken into account by the various international players in the geopolitical world. Commodities have thus determined the fate and wealth of nations throughout history and will continue to do so in the future.

For the purposes of this book, I present 32 commodities that fit a very specific definition, which I define in the following bulleted list. For example, the commodities I present must be raw materials. I don't discuss currencies — even though they trade in the futures markets — because they're not a raw material; they can't be physically used to build anything. In addition, the commodities must present real money-making opportunities to investors.

All the commodities I cover in the book have to meet the following criteria:

✔ **Tradability:** The commodity has to be tradable, meaning there needs to be a viable investment vehicle to help you trade it. For example, I include a commodity if it has a futures contract assigned to it on one of the major exchanges, or if a company processes it, or if there's an ETF that tracks it.

Uranium, which is an important energy commodity, isn't tracked by a futures contract, but several companies specialize in mining and processing this mineral. By investing in these companies, you get exposure to uranium.

✔ **Deliverability:** All the commodities have to be physically deliverable. I include crude oil because it can be delivered in barrels, and I include wheat because it can be delivered by the bushel. However, I don't include currencies, interest rates, and other financial futures contracts because they're not physical commodities.

✔ **Liquidity:** I don't include any commodities that trade in illiquid markets. Every commodity in the book has an active market with buyers and sellers constantly transacting with each other. Liquidity is critical because it gives you the option of getting in and out of an investment without having to face the difficulty of trying to find a buyer or seller for your securities.

Going for a Spin: Choosing the Right Investment Vehicle

The two most critical questions you should ask yourself before getting started in commodities are the following: What commodity should I invest in? How do I invest in it? I will answer the second question first and then examine which commodities to choose.

The futures markets

In the futures markets, individuals, institutions, and sometimes governments transact with each other for price hedging and speculating purposes. An airline company, for instance, may want to use futures to enter into an agreement with a fuel company to buy a fixed amount of jet fuel for a fixed price for a fixed period of time. This transaction in the futures markets allows the airline to hedge against the volatility associated with the price of jet fuel. Although commercial users are the main players in the futures arena, the futures markets are also used by traders and investors who profit from price volatility through various trading techniques.

Follow the money

While commodities have allowed nations to survive and thrive, they have also provided individuals with tremendous wealth accumulation possibilities. Some of the world's most enduring fortunes have been built around commodities. Mayer Rothschild, patriarch of the European Rothschild banking family, made a fortune during the Napoleonic Wars by storing and distributing gold bullion to fund the British side of the war effort.

Andrew Carnegie, the self-made industrialist and founder of the eponymous steel company that eventually became U.S. Steel, consolidated the American steel industry and, in the process, became the second-richest man of his time, behind only John D. Rockefeller, Sr. And what better illustration of the power of commodities as wealth-building vehicles than John Rockefeller himself, whose impact on the global oil industry through the creation of the Standard Oil Company is still felt today. (See Daniel Yergin's

The Prize: The Epic Quest for Oil, Money and Power.) Abdel-Aziz Al-Saud, Saudi Arabia's first monarch, consolidated and created an entire nation through the control of crude oil and natural gas riches.

To this day, individuals involved in commodities have been able to generate tremendous wealth. Legendary oil man T. Boone Pickens, for instance, made $1.4 Billion in 2005 betting on the price of oil and natural gas; and Lakshmi Mittal, the Indian-born steel magnate, became the world's fourth-richest person in 2004 as a result of his business activities in the steel industry. It is clear that those individuals who have the foresight of investing in commodities have profited very handsomely from this enterprise. While you may not be able to build as much wealth as Rockefeller or Al-Saud, I'm confident that you can benefit by opening up to investing in commodities.

One such trading technique is *arbitrage,* which takes advantage of price discrepancies between different futures markets. For example, you purchase and sell the crude oil futures contract simultaneously in different trading venues for the purpose of capturing price discrepancies between these venues. This is an arbitrage trade. I take a look at some arbitrage opportunities in Chapter 9.

The futures markets are administered by the various commodity exchanges, such as the Chicago Mercantile Exchange (CME) or the New York Mercantile Exchange (NYMEX). I discuss the major exchanges, the role they play in the markets, and the products they offer in Chapter 8.

Investing through the futures markets requires a good understanding of futures contracts, options on futures, forwards, spreads, and other derivative products. I examine these products in depth in Chapter 9.

The most direct way of investing in the futures markets is by opening an account with a *Futures Commission Merchant* (FCM). The FCM is very much like your traditional stock brokerage house (such as Schwab, Fidelity, or Merrill Lynch), except that it's allowed to offer products that trade on the futures markets. Here are some other ways to get involved in futures:

- ✔ **Commodity Trading Advisor (CTA):** The CTA is an individual or company licensed to trade futures contracts on your behalf.

- ✔ **Commodity Pool Operator (CPO):** The CPO is similar to a CTA except that the CPO can manage the funds of multiple clients under one account. This provides additional leverage when trading futures.

- ✔ **Commodity Indexes:** A commodity index is a benchmark, similar to the Dow Jones Industrial Average or the S&P 500, which tracks a basket of the most liquid commodities. You can track the performance of a commodity index, which allows you in effect to "buy the market". A number of commodity indexes are available, such as the *Goldman Sachs Commodity Index* or the *Reuters/Jefferies CRB Index,* which I cover in Chapter 7.

These are only a few ways to access the futures markets. Make sure to read Chapters 5 and 6 for additional methods.

The futures markets are regulated by a number of organizations, such as the Securities and Exchange Commission (SEC) and the Commodity Futures Trading Commission (CFTC). These organizations monitor the markets to prevent market fraud and manipulation and to protect investors from such activity. Check out Chapter 8 for an in-depth analysis of the role these regulators play and how to use them to protect yourself from market fraud.

Trading futures is not for everyone. By their very nature, futures markets, contracts, and products are extremely complex and require a great deal of mastery even by the most seasoned investors. If you don't feel you have a good handle on all the concepts involved in trading futures, then don't simply jump into futures or you could lose a lot more than your principal (because of the use of leverage and other characteristics unique to the futures markets). If you're not comfortable trading futures, don't sweat it. You can invest in commodities in multiple other ways.

If you are ready to start investing in the futures markets, you need to have a solid grasp of *technical analysis,* which I discuss in depth in Chapter 10.

The equity markets

Although the futures markets offer the most direct investment gateway to the commodities markets, the equity markets also offer access to these raw materials. You can invest in companies that specialize in the production, transformation, and distribution of these natural resources. If you're a stock investor familiar with the equity markets, then this may be a good route for you to access the commodities markets. The only drawback of the equity markets is that you have to take into account external factors, such as management competence, tax situation, debt levels, and profit margins, which have nothing to do with the underlying commodity. That said, investing in companies that process commodities still allows you to profit from the commodities boom.

Publicly traded companies

The size, structure, and scope of the companies involved in the business are varied, and I cover most of these companies throughout the book. I offer a description of the company, including a snapshot of its financial situation, future growth prospects, and areas of operation. I then make a recommendation based on the market fundamentals of the company.

Here are the types of companies you'll encounter in the book:

- **Integrated Energy Companies:** These companies, such as Exxon Mobil (NYSE:XOM) and Chevron (NYSE: CVX), are involved in all aspects of the energy industry, from the extraction of crude oil to the distribution of Liquefied Natural Gas (LNG). They give you broad exposure to the energy complex (see Chapter 11).

- **Diversified Mining Companies:** A number of companies focus exclusively on mining metals and minerals. Some of these companies, such as Anglo-American PLC (NASDAQ: AAUK) and BHP Billiton (NYSE: BHP), have operations across the spectrum of the metals complex, mining metals that range from gold to zinc. I look at these companies in Chapter 18.

- **Electric Utilities:** Utilities are an integral part of modern life because they provide one of life's most essential necessities: electricity. They're also a good investment because they have historically offered large dividends to shareholders. Read Chapter 13 to figure out whether these companies are right for you.

This list is only a small sampling of the commodity companies I cover in these pages. I also analyze highly specialized companies, such as coal mining companies (Chapter 13), oil refiners (Chapter 14), platinum mining companies (Chapter 15), and purveyors of gourmet coffee products (Chapter 19).

Master Limited Partnerships

Master Limited Partnerships (MLPs) invest in energy infrastructure such as oil pipelines and natural gas storage facilities. I'm a big fan of MLPs because they're a *publicly traded partnership*. This means they offer the benefit of trading like a corporation on a public exchange, while offering the tax advantages of a private partnership. MLPs are required to transfer all cash flow back to shareholders, which makes them an attractive investment. I dissect the structure of MLPs in Chapter 6 and introduce you to some of the biggest names in the business so you can take advantage of this unique investment.

Managed funds

Sometimes it's just easier to have someone else manage your investments for you. Luckily, you can count on professional money managers that specialize in commodity trading to handle your investments.

Here are a few options:

- ✔ **Mutual funds:** If you've previously invested in mutual funds and are comfortable with them, look into adding a mutual fund that gives you exposure to the commodities markets. A number of funds are available that invest solely in commodities. I examine these commodity mutual funds in Chapter 6.

- ✔ **Exchange Traded Funds (ETFs):** ETFs are an increasingly popular investment because they are managed funds that offer the convenience of trading like stocks. A plethora of ETFs that track everything from crude oil and gold to diversified commodity indexes, have appeared in recent years. Find out how to benefit from these vehicles in Chapter 6.

If you have a pet or a child, sometimes you hire a pet sitter or baby sitter to look out after your loved ones. Before you hire this individual, you interview them, check their references, and examine their previous experience. Once you're satisfied with their competency, you entrust them with the responsibility of looking out after your cat, daughter, or both. Same thing applies when you're shopping for a money manager, or money sitter. If you already have a money manager you trust and are happy with, then stick with him. If you're looking for a new investment professional to look out after your investments, you need to investigate her as thoroughly as possible. In Chapter 6, I examine the selection criteria you should use when shopping for a money manager.

Physical attractiveness

The most direct way of investing in certain commodities is by actually buying them outright. Precious metals such as gold, silver, and platinum are a great example of this. As the price of gold and silver has skyrocketed recently, you may have seen ads on TV or in newspapers from companies offering to buy your gold or silver jewelry. As gold and silver prices increase in the futures markets, they also cause prices in the spot markets to rise (and vice versa). You can cash in on this trend by buying coins, bullion, or even jewelry. I present this unique investment strategy in Chapter 15.

This investment strategy is only suitable for a limited number of commodities, mostly precious metals like gold, silver, and platinum. Unless you own a farm, keeping live cattle or feeder cattle to profit from price increases doesn't make much sense. And I won't even mention commodities like crude oil or uranium!

Checking Out What's on the Menu

I cover 32 commodities in the book. Here is a listing of all the commodities you can expect to encounter while going through these pages.

While the book is modular in nature, I list the commodities in this list in order of their appearance in the text.

Energy

Energy has always been indispensable for human survival and also makes for a great investment. Energy, whether fossil fuels or renewable energy sources, has attracted a lot of attention from investors as they seek to profit from the world's seemingly unquenchable thirst for energy. I present in this book all the major forms of energy, from crude oil and coal to electricity and solar power, and show you how to profit in this arena.

- **Crude oil:** Crude oil is the undisputed heavyweight champion in the commodities world. There are more barrels of crude oil traded every single day (85 million and growing) than any other commodity. Accounting for 40 percent of total global energy consumption, it provides some terrific investment opportunities.

- **Natural gas:** Natural gas, the gaseous fossil fuel, is often overshadowed by crude oil. It is nevertheless a major commodity in its own right, which is used for everything from cooking food to heating houses during the winter. I also take a look at the prospects of Liquefied Natural Gas (LNG).

- **Coal:** Coal accounts for over 20 percent of total world energy consumption. In the United States, the largest energy market, 50 percent of electricity is generated through coal. Because of abundant supply, coal is making a resurgence.

- **Uranium/Nuclear power:** Because of improved environmental standards within the industry, nuclear power use is on the rise. I show you how to develop an investment strategy to capitalize on this trend.

✔ **Electricity:** Electricity is a necessity of modern life, and the companies responsible for generating this special commodity have some unique characteristics. I examine how to start trading this electrifying commodity.

✔ **Solar power:** Due to a number of reasons that range from environmental to geopolitical, demand for renewable energy sources such as solar power is increasing.

✔ **Wind power:** Wind power is getting a lot of attention from investors as a viable alternative source of energy.

✔ **Ethanol:** Ethanol, which is produced primarily from corn or sugar, is an increasingly popular fuel additive that offers investment potential.

There are other commodities in the energy complex, such as heating oil, propane and gasoline. Although I do provide insight into some of these other members of the energy family, I focus a lot more on the resources I mentioned in the previous list.

Metals

Metallurgy has been essential to human development since the beginning of time. Societies that have mastered the production of metals have been able to thrive and survive. Similarly, investors that have incorporated metals into their portfolios have been able to generate significant returns. I cover all the major metals, from gold and platinum to nickel and zinc.

✔ **Gold:** Gold is perhaps the most coveted resource on the planet. For centuries, people have been attracted to its quasi-indestructibility and have used it as a store of value. Gold is a good asset for hedging against inflation and also for asset preservation during times of global turmoil.

✔ **Silver:** Silver, like gold, is another precious metal that has monetary applications. The British currency, the pound sterling, is still named after this metal. Silver also has applications in industry (such as electrical wiring) that places it in a unique position of being coveted for both its precious metal status and its industrial uses.

✔ **Platinum:** Platinum, the rich man's gold, is one of the most valuable metals in the world, used for everything from jewelry to the manufacturing of catalytic converters.

✔ **Steel:** Steel, which is created by alloying iron and other materials, is the most widely used metal in the world. Used to build everything from cars to buildings, it's a metal endowed with unique characteristics and offers good investment potential.

✔ **Aluminum:** Perhaps no other metal has the versatility of aluminum; it's lightweight, yet surprisingly robust. These unique characteristics mean that it's a metal worth adding to you portfolio, especially since it's the second most used metal (right behind steel).

✔ **Copper:** Copper, the third most widely used metal, is the metal of choice for industrial uses. Because it's a great conductor of heat and electricity, its applications in industry are wide and deep, which makes this base metal a very attractive investment.

✔ **Palladium:** Palladium is part of the platinum group of metals and almost half of the palladium that's mined goes towards building automobile catalytic converters. As the number of cars with these emission-reducing devices increases, the demand for palladium will increase as well, which makes this an attractive investment.

✔ **Nickel:** Nickel is a ferrous metal that is in high demand because of its resistance to corrosion and oxidation. Steel is usually alloyed with nickel to create stainless steel, which assures that nickel will have an important role to play for years to come.

✔ **Zinc:** The fourth most widely used metal in the world, zinc is sought after for its resistance to corrosion. It is used in the process of galvanization, where zinc coating is applied to other metals, such as steel, to prevent rust.

Agricultural products

Food is the most essential element of human life, and the production of food presents solid money-making opportunities. In *Commodities For Dummies*, you find out how to invest in the agricultural sector in everything from coffee and orange juice to cattle and soybeans.

✔ **Coffee:** Coffee is the second most widely produced commodity in the world, in terms of physical volume, behind only crude oil. Folks just seem to love a good cup of coffee, and this provides good investment opportunities.

✔ **Cocoa:** Cocoa production, which is dominated by a handful of countries, is a major agricultural commodity, primarily because it is used to create chocolate.

✔ **Sugar #11:** Sugar is a popular food sweetener and it can be a sweet investment as well. Sugar #11 represents a futures contract for global sugar.

- ✔ **Sugar #14:** Sugar #14 is specific to the United States and it is a widely traded commodity.

- ✔ **Frozen Concentrated Orange Juice — Type A:** FCOJ-A, for short, is the benchmark for North American orange juice prices, as it's grown in the hemisphere's two largest regions: Florida and Brazil.

- ✔ **Frozen Concentrated Orange Juice — Type B:** FCOJ-B, like FCOJ-A, is a widely traded contract that represents global orange juice prices. This contract gives you exposure to orange juice activity on a world scale.

- ✔ **Corn:** Corn's use for culinary purposes is perhaps unrivaled by any other grain, which makes this a potentially lucrative investment. Check out how to trade it in Chapter 20.

- ✔ **Wheat:** According to archaeological evidence, wheat is one of the first agricultural products grown by man. It is an essential staple of human life and makes for a great investment.

- ✔ **Soybeans:** Soybeans have many applications, including as feedstock and for cooking purposes. The soybean market is a large market and presents some good investment opportunities.

- ✔ **Soybean oil:** Soybean oil, also known as vegetable oil, is derived from the actual soybeans. It's used for cooking purposes and has become popular in recent years due to the health-conscious dietary movement.

- ✔ **Soybean meal:** Soybean meal is another derivative of soybeans that's used as feedstock for poultry and cattle. It may not sound sexy, but it can be a good investment.

- ✔ **Live cattle:** For those involved in agriculture, using the live cattle futures contract to hedge against price volatility is a good idea.

- ✔ **Feeder cattle:** While the live cattle contract tracks adult cows, the feeder cattle contract is used to hedge against the risk associated with growing calves. This area is not widely followed in the markets, but it's important to figure out how this market works.

- ✔ **Lean hogs:** They may not be the sexiest commodity out there, but lean hogs are an essential commodity, which makes them a good trading target.

- ✔ **Frozen pork bellies:** Frozen pork bellies are essentially nothing more than good old bacon. This is a cyclical industry subject to wild price swings, which provides unique arbitrage trading opportunities.

Benefiting from Commodities Creatively

While I was researching this book, I came across a number of colorful characters, both in-person and in historical accounts. One such character was Samuel Brannan, who lived during the 1848 California Gold Rush. The story of Sam Brannan is not well known but it is astonishing nevertheless and provides insight into how to approach the markets.

Sam was the third person to find out that gold had been discovered in California. The first two people with this knowledge — John Sutter and James Marshall — wanted, for obvious reasons, to keep this discovery secret. Sam Brannan, who eventually profited so much from the gold rush that he became California's first millionaire, got rich without digging a single hole or prospecting for a single nugget of gold. How did he do this? By selling shovels!

When Sam, who owned a convenience store in Sutter's Fort near the gold deposits, heard that gold had been discovered, he quietly went around northern California and bought all the shovels, picks, and pans he could get his hands on. After he cornered this market, he literally went around town screaming at the top of his lungs, "We found gold! We found gold!" Once word spread that gold had been discovered, a swarm of people came to northern California, all wanting to dig for gold, and Sam was the only man in town to sell them the shovels.

Sam Brannan's story shows that you can profit from the current commodities boom — which is similar to the California Gold Rush in more ways than one — by being creative. You don't have to invest in just crude oil or gold futures contracts to benefit. You can trade ETFs, invest in companies that process commodities such as uranium, buy precious metals ownership certificates, or invest in Master Limited Partnerships. The commodities markets are global in nature, and so are the investment opportunities. My aim in this book is to help you uncover these global opportunities and to provide you with the investment ideas and tools to help you unlock and unleash the power of the commodities markets.

Chapter 2

Earn, Baby, Earn! Why You Should Invest in Commodities

· ·

In This Chapter

▶ Looking at recent performance

▶ Profiting from global economic trends

▶ Examining the unique characteristics of commodities

▶ Investing in commodities across the business cycle

· ·

Commodities have traditionally been considered the black sheep in the family of asset classes — no one wanted anything to do with them. This traditional lack of interest (which no longer applies, by the way) has generated a lot of misinformation about commodities. As a matter of fact, probably no other asset class has suffered through so much misunderstanding and misconception.

A lot of investors are, quite frankly, scared of venturing into the world of commodities. For one thing, it seems that every time the word "commodities" is uttered, someone pops up with a horrible story about losing their entire life savings trading soybeans, cocoa, or some other exotic commodity.

Even though this negative perception is rapidly changing, commodities are still often misunderstood as an investment. I actually know some investors who invest in commodities (and who have made money off them) but who don't understand the fundamental reasons why commodities are such a good long-term investment. (Yikes!)

In this chapter, I show you why commodities are an attractive investment and why many investors are becoming more interested in this asset class. I also give you the goods on a number of global trends that are responsible for the recent run-up in commodity prices. Those who are able to spot these trends are going to do extremely well. And those who don't, well, I wouldn't want to be in their shoes!

You Can't Argue with Success

In recent years, commodities as an asset class have received a lot of attention from the investor community. Many investors are turning to commodities because they are disappointed with the returns that other investments have offered and, more importantly, because commodities have performed extremely well recently. Take a look at Figure 2-1, which shows the recent performance of the Reuters/Jefferies CRB Index, an index that tracks a basket of commodities.

Figure 2-1:
Performance
of the
Reuters/
Jefferies
CRB Index
from 1997
to 2006.

As you can see from Figure 2-1, the performance of commodities as an asset class has been phenomenal in recent years. And it's not just commodities as an asset class that have done well; individual commodities such as crude oil and gold have also done well recently. For example, the price of crude oil on the New York Mercantile Exchange (NYMEX) as shown in Figure 2-2 has increased from $20 per barrel in 2001 to over $70 in 2006, an increase of 350 percent!

Figure 2-2:
The price of WTI Crude Oil (NYMEX) between 1997 and 2006 (Dollars per Barrel).

The price of gold, another key commodity, has also increased dramatically in recent years. While I was writing this book, gold actually hit a 26-year high when it reached $730 a troy ounce in May 2006. Check out gold's recent performance in Figure 2-3, as measured in the futures market.

Many investors, intrigued by the eye-popping performance of commodities, want in on the action. However, a majority of investors are pouring into commodities without knowing why commodities are performing well — and this is a recipe for disaster.

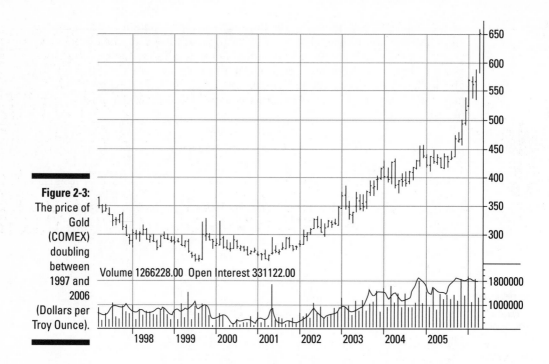

Figure 2-3:
The price of
Gold
(COMEX)
doubling
between
1997 and
2006
(Dollars per
Troy Ounce).

Never invest in something you don't understand. If you hear someone on TV or the radio mention an investment, make sure you perform your due diligence to get the ins and outs of the potential investment. (I talk about due diligence in Chapter 3.) Not understanding an investment before you invest in it is one of the easiest ways to lose money.

In this chapter, I go through the reasons why commodities have been doing so well so that you have an investment framework to follow in your own portfolio. I also argue that the recent run-up in commodities is only the tip of the iceberg — most of the gains still to come!

The 21st Century Is the Century of Commodities

Since the fall of 2001, commodities have been running faster than the bulls of Pamplona. The *Reuters/Jefferies CRB Index* (a benchmark for commodities) nearly doubled between 2001 and 2006. During this period oil, gold, copper, and silver all hit all-time highs (although not adjusted for inflation). Other commodities also reached levels never seen before in trading sessions.

Many investors wondered, what is going on? How come commodities are doing so well when other investments, such as stocks and bonds, aren't performing? I believe that what you and I are witnessing is a long-term cyclical bull market in commodities. Because of a number of fundamental factors (which I go through in the following sections), commodities are poised for a rally that will last well into the 21st century — and possibly beyond that. It's a bold statement, I know. But the facts are there to support me.

Although I'm bullish on commodities for the long term, I have to warn you that there are going to be times when commodities don't perform well at all. This is simply the nature of the commodity cycle. Furthermore in the history of Wall Street, no asset has ever gone up in a straight line. There are always minor (and, occasionally, major) pullbacks before the asset makes new highs — if in fact it does make new highs.

A case in point is that during the first few months of 2006, commodities outperformed every asset class, with some commodities breaking record levels. Gold hit a 25-year high and so did copper. Then during the week of May 15, commodities saw a big drop. The Reuters/Jefferies CRB Index fell over 5 percent that week, with gold and copper dropping 10 and 7 percent, respectively.

Many commentators went on the offensive and started bashing commodities. "We are now seeing the beginning of the end of the rally in commodities," said one analyst. "Is this the end of commodities?" ran a newspaper headline. An endless number of commentators hit the airwaves claiming that this is a speculative bubble about to burst. A respected economist even compared what was happening to commodities to the dot com bubble: "There is no fundamental reason why commodity prices are going up." Nothing could be further from the facts. A couple of weeks after this minor pullback, some of these commodities that were being compared to highly leveraged tech stocks had regained most, if not all, of their lost ground.

There's a story behind the rise in commodities — and it's a pretty compelling one.

Ka-boom! Capitalizing on the global population explosion

The 21st century is going to experience the largest population growth in the history of humankind. The United Nations estimates that the world will add a little fewer than 1 billion people during *each* of the first five decades of the 21st century. This means that the global population will grow to about 9 billion people by 2050 (as of 2006, there are approximately 6.5 billion people on the planet).

Also, consider the following statistic: According to the UN, the average number of years it takes to add 1 billion people has shrunk from an average of 130 years in the 19th century to approximately 13 years in the 21st century! This means the rate at which the human population is increasing has reached exponential levels. Check out Figure 2-4 for the expected population growth in the 21st century.

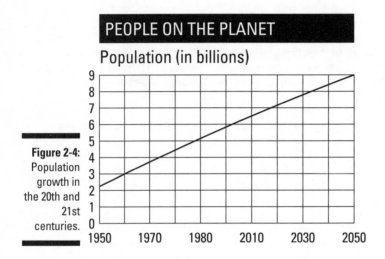

PEOPLE ON THE PLANET

Population (in billions)

Figure 2-4: Population growth in the 20th and 21st centuries.

So how is this relevant to commodities? Put simply, significant population growth translates into greater global demand for commodities. Humans are the most voracious consumers of raw materials on the planet — and the only ones who pay for them. As the number of humans in the world increases, so will the demand for natural resources. After all, people need food to eat, houses to live in, and heat to stay warm during the winter — all this requires raw materials. This large population growth is a key driver for the increasing demand for commodities, which will continue to put upward pressures on commodity prices.

Brick by brick: Profiting from urbanization

Perhaps even more significant than population growth is the fact that it is accompanied by the largest urbanization movement the world has ever seen. In the early 20th century, according to the UN, less than 15 percent of the world's population lived in cities; by 2005 that number jumped to 50 percent — and shows no sign of decreasing. As a matter of fact, 60 percent of the world's population is expected to live in urban areas by the year 2030.

The number of large metropolitan areas with 5 million or more people (mega cities) is skyrocketing and will continue to for much of the century. In Figure 2-5, I list the number of cities expected to have 5 million inhabitants by 2015. When you compare that with the growth in the number of cities with 5 million people from 1950 to 2000, you quickly realize how staggering this growth really is.

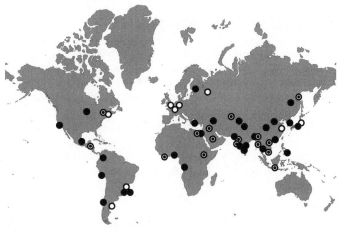

Figure 2-5:
The number of cities with 5 million inhabitants in 1950, 2000, and 2015 (projected).

Size of Urban Population
○ 5 million and over since 1950
● 5 million and over since 2000
◉ 5 million and over since 2015 (projected)

Urbanization is highly significant for commodities because people who live in urban centers consume a lot more natural resources than those who live in rural areas. In addition, more natural resources are required to expand the size of cities as more people move to them (rural to urban migration) and are having more kids (indigenous urban population growth). More natural resources are required for the roads, cars, and personal appliances that are staples of city life.

Industrial metals such as copper, steel, and aluminum are going to be in high demand to construct apartment buildings, schools, hospitals, cars, and so on. Investing in industrial metals is therefore one possible way to play the urbanization card. Make sure to read Chapter 16 for more information on these metals.

As you can see from the map in Figure 2-5, the largest urbanization is taking place in the developing world, particularly in Asia. As more Asians move from the countryside to large urban areas, expect to see huge demand from that part of the world for raw materials to fuel this growth.

One way to profit from Asian urbanization is to invest in indigenous Asian companies and countries that process natural resources. I present this investment strategy in Chapter 5.

Full steam ahead! Benefiting from industrialization

The first industrial revolution, which took place in the 19th century, was a major transformational event primarily confined to Western Europe and North America. Major industrialization did not spread to other corners of the globe until parts of the 20th century, and even then only sporadically.

A new wave of industrialization is taking place in the 21st century and it may be the most important one in history. This wave is transforming a large number of developing countries into more industrialized countries, and this transformation is fueled by raw materials.

The BRIC countries

Although a number of developing countries are on the fast track to industrialization, four countries in particular need to be singled out as the frontrunners in this movement — Brazil, Russia, India, and China (known as the *BRIC countries*).

The BRIC countries, which are now on a path towards full industrialization, are scouring the globe to secure supplies of key natural resources such as oil, natural gas, copper, and aluminum — the raw materials necessary for a country to industrialize. (See the sidebar "It's déjà vu all over again: The great game 21st century style.")

As demand from the BRIC countries for natural resources increases, expect to see increasing upward price pressures on commodities.

China

Although all four of the BRIC countries are rapidly transforming themselves, no other country is doing so as rapidly and dramatically as China. Actually, it is only very fitting that the saying "May you live in interesting times" is said to be an old Chinese proverb. The 21st century is undoubtedly going to be an interesting century, and China is going to play an increasingly important role in global economic affairs.

China's GDP has increased by 9 percent each year from 2000 to 2006. To sustain this growth, China has been consuming all sorts of commodities. Some of the highs that commodities such as oil, natural gas, cement, copper, and aluminum have experienced between 2003 and 2006 are a direct result of increased demand from China.

For example, in 2004 China gobbled up half the cement, one-third of the steel, one-quarter of the copper, and one-fifth of the aluminum produced in the world. In 2003, China overtook Japan to become the second largest consumer of crude oil — right behind the United States. (For more information on global oil consumption, make sure you read Chapter 11.) In Figure 2-6 you can see the expected Chinese consumption of crude oil for the first quarter of the century.

Figure 2-6:
China is expected to increase its consumption of crude oil products to approximately 12 Million Barrels a day by 2025. Source: Energy Information Administration.

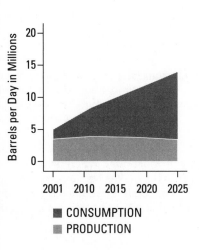

China is going to have a tremendous impact on the global economy in the 21st century and is expected to be the largest consumer of commodities in the world. For more information on China's emergence as a global economic power and the transformation of the economic playing field that this entails, I recommend the following titles:

- *The World Is Flat* by Thomas Friedman
- *Three Billion New Capitalists* by Clyde Prestowitz
- *The Silk Road to Riches* by Yiannis Mostrous
- *The End of Poverty* by Jeffrey Sachs
- *China, Inc.* by Ted Fishman
- *The Next Global Stage* by Kenichi Ohmae

It's All about Me! Why Commodities Are Unique

As an asset class, commodities have unique characteristics that separate them from other asset classes and make them attractive, whether as independent investments or as part of a broader based investment strategy. I go through these unique characteristics in the following sections.

Inelasticity

In economics, *elasticity* seeks to determine the effects of price on supply and demand. The calculation can get pretty technical but, essentially, elasticity quantifies how much supply and demand will change for every incremental change in price.

Goods that are elastic tend to have a high correlation between price and demand, which is usually inversely proportional: When prices of a good increase, demand tends to decrease. This makes sense because you're not going to pay for a good that you don't need if it becomes too expensive. Capturing and determining that spread is what elasticity is all about.

Inelastic goods, however, are goods that are so essential to consumers that changes in price tend to have a limited effect on supply and demand. Most commodities fall in the inelastic goods category because they are essential to human existence. There is no way around this.

For instance if the price of ice cream were to increase by 25 percent, chances are you're going to stop buying ice cream. Why? Because it's not a necessity, but more of a luxury. However, when the price of unleaded gasoline at the pump increases by 25 percent (as it has actually done during 2003–2006), you're definitely not happy about the price increase, but you still go out there and fill up your tank. The reason? Gas is a necessity — you need to fill up your car in order to go to work, school, run errands, and so on.

The demand for gasoline isn't absolutely inelastic, however — you won't keep paying for it regardless of the price. A point will come when you decide that it's simply not worth it to keep paying the amount you're paying at the pump; and so you begin looking for alternatives. (Please read Chapter 13 for more information on alternative energy sources.) But the truth remains that you're willing to pay more for gasoline than for other products you don't need (such as ice cream); that's the key to understanding price inelasticity.

It's déjà vu all over again: The great game 21st century style

During parts of the 19th and 20th centuries, the global powers of the time were embroiled in a strategic geopolitical contest over control of the world's precious natural resources, commonly referred to as "the great game." The 21st century is experiencing a new great game, where the stakes are higher and the competition fiercer. The world's industrialized and rapidly industrializing countries are prowling the investment landscape in search of secure energy and raw material sources.

China, in particular, is becoming one of the most aggressive players on the world stage when it comes to securing energy sources. As natural resources such as oil become more scarce, expect more countries and companies to act more aggressively to secure whatever supplies are left. Because demand for raw materials is fairly inelastic (please see the "Inelasticity" section) and supply is limited, there is double upward pressure from both the demand and supply sides of the equation. (Yet another reason to be bullish on commodities.)

For now, the pie is large enough that most of the global players are able to participate and get something out of this contest. To profit as an investor, keep your eye out for new companies that are making deals overseas to secure raw materials. The companies that are able to do so efficiently and aggressively will generally tend to produce higher revenues and cash flows — key ingredients to the success of any company. You should keep a particular close eye on companies from emerging China, India, South Korea, and Russia as well as the traditional players from the United States, Great Britain, Australia, Europe, and Japan, which have the technological and capital resources to close in on some big deals. (For more on how to identify and evaluate these kinds of companies, flip on over to Chapter 14.)

Most commodities are fairly inelastic because they are the raw materials that allow us to live the lives we strive for; they allow us to maintain a decent (and, in some cases, extravagant!) standard of living. Without these precious raw materials, you wouldn't be able to heat your home in the winter; actually, without cement, copper, and other basic materials, you wouldn't even have a house to begin with! And then of course, there's the most essential commodity of all: food. Without food we would not exist.

Because of the absolute necessity of commodities, you can be sure that as long as there are humans around, there is going to be a demand for these raw materials.

Is it safe in here? Commodities as a safe haven

During times of turmoil, commodities tend to act as safe havens for investors. Certain commodities, such as gold and silver, are viewed by investors as reliable stores of value. And so investors flock to these assets when times aren't good. When currencies slide, when nations go to war, when global pandemics break out, you can rely on gold, silver, and other commodities to provide you with financial safety.

For example, after the horrible acts of September 11, 2001, the price of gold jumped as investors sought safety in the metal. You can see a clear spike in the price of gold in Figure 2-7 right after September 11.

Figure 2-7:
Investors turn to gold for safety during and right after the tragic events of September 11, 2001 (Prices as measured by the London Gold Fix).

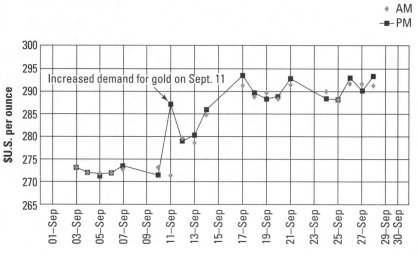

It's a good idea to have part of your portfolio in gold and other precious metals so that you can protect your assets during times of turmoil. Please turn to Chapter 15 for more on investing in precious metals.

Hedge-hogging galore! Commodities as a hedge against inflation

One of the biggest things you need to watch out for as an investor is the ravaging effects of inflation. Inflation can devastate your investments, particularly paper assets such as stocks. (I discuss inflation and other risks in

Chapter 3.) The central bankers of the world — smart people all — spend their entire careers trying to tame inflation, but despite their efforts, inflation can easily get out of hand. This is why you need to protect yourself against this economic enemy.

Ironically, one of the only asset classes that actually *benefits* from inflation is, you guessed it, commodities. Perhaps the biggest irony of all is that increases in the prices of basic goods (commodities such as oil and gas) actually contribute to the increase of inflation.

As you can see in Figure 2-8, for example, there's a positive correlation between gold and the inflation rate. During times of high inflation, investors load up on gold because it is considered a good store of value.

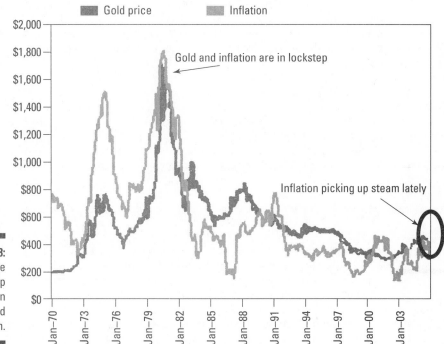

Figure 2-8:
The relationship between gold and inflation.

One way to not only protect yourself from inflation, but also to actually profit from it, is to invest in gold. I discuss the inflation hedging opportunities that gold provides in Chapter 15.

Could you hurry up, please! Bringing new sources online takes time

The business of commodities is a time and capital intensive business. Unlike investments in high tech companies or other "new economy" investments (such as e-commerce), bringing commodity projects online takes a lot of time.

For example, it can take up to a decade to bring new sources of oil online. First a company must identify potentially promising areas to explore for oil. Once an area is located, the company then has to actually start drilling and prospecting for the oil. If it's lucky, this process of discovering significantly recoverable sources of oil will only take three to five years. The company must then develop infrastructure and bring in machinery to extract the oil, which must then be transported to a refining facility to be transformed into consumable energy products such as gasoline or jet fuel. After it goes through the lengthy refining stage it must finally be transported to consumers!

So what does this all mean to you as an investor? When you're investing in commodities, you have to think long term! If you're used to investing in tech stocks or if you're an entrepreneur involved in e-commerce, you need to radically change the way you think about investing when you approach commodities. If you're able to recognize the long-term nature of commodities, you're on your way to becoming a successful commodities investor.

Sell in May and go away? Definitely nay!

You may have heard the saying "sell in May and go away." This is a Wall Street adage referring to stocks. The thinking goes that because the stock market doesn't perform well during the summer months, you should sell your stocks and get back into the game in the fall.

This adage does not apply to commodities because commodities move in different cycles than stocks. Some commodities perform really well during the summer months. For example, because summer is the heavy driving season, there is an increase in demand for gasoline products. Thus, all things equal, unleaded gasoline tends to increase in price during the summer.

I discuss the cyclical nature of commodities in the following section. For a more in-depth comparison between the performance of commodities and other assets, please go to Chapter 4.

Constructing the BTC pipeline

A good example of the capital and time intensive aspect of commodity projects is the construction of the *Baku-Tbilisi-Ceyhan* oil pipeline that links a large Azerbaijan offshore oil field located in the Caspian Sea (the Azeri-Chirag-Guneshi oil field) to the Turkish port city of Ceyhan in the Mediterranean Sea.

Talks about building a pipeline to deliver Azerbaijan's 32 Billion Barrels of oil to consumer markets started in 1996. Many Western countries and energy companies supported the project because the pipeline would tap into a vast new source of oil (thereby lowering dependence on the volatile Persian Gulf region) and would pass through Azerbaijan, recently independent Georgia, and democratic Turkey (thereby bypassing the Russians and the Iranians).

The project faced immediate opposition because of strategic geopolitical maneuvering; in other words, the Russians were not happy that a pipeline would be built in what they considered their "backyard." Environmentalists also quickly expressed their discontent, fearing the pipeline would disturb precious environmental and ecological zones.

Talks among the various interested parties stretched from 1996 until 1999, when a mutually agreed upon solution was reached, and the project received the green light. Planning for the construction of the pipeline then began, but actual construction didn't begin until late 2002. The pipeline construction finished in 2006, and oil started flowing from the Caspian Sea to the Mediterranean Sea on May 28, 2006.

So all in all, it took about ten years to create, design, and execute this project, which has cost $4 Billion and employed thousands of workers. The BTC pipeline is a good example of how long it can take to bring new sources of energy and other precious commodities to consumer markets. And I'm not even counting the decades it took of prospecting and exploring the Caspian Sea to discover the oil in the first place!

The point is that the world in 2006 is in serious need of oil and other raw materials to fuel global economic growth. However, the projects that are now being developed will take a number of years before they are able to produce. Make sure you consider these factors before you invest in commodities.

Time to Get Down to Business: Commodities and the Business Cycle

Commodities are cyclical in nature. Returns on commodity investments are not generated in a vacuum — they are influenced by a number of economic forces. In other words, the performance of commodities, like that of other major asset classes, is tied to general economic conditions. Because economies move in cycles, constantly alternating between expansions and recessions, commodities react according to the current economic phase.

The performance of commodities as an asset class is going to be different during economic expansions than during recessions.

As a general rule, commodities tend to do well during periods of late expansions and early recessions. The reason is that as the economy slows, key interest rates are decreased in order to stimulate economic activity — this tends to help the performance of commodities. Stocks and bonds, on the other hand, do not perform as well during recessions. This means that as an investor seeking returns across all phases of the business cycle, opening up to commodities will allow you to generate returns during good and bad economic times.

Make sure to read Chapter 3 for a comprehensive comparison between the performance of commodities and other asset classes. Also please turn to Chapter 5 for an overview of the benefits of diversification.

The study of cycles, whether for commodities, stocks or other assets, is not an exact science. I don't recommend you use cycles as the foundation of a trading or investment strategy. Rather, try to use the study of cycles to get a sense of what historical patterns have indicated. This should help you get a better sense of where an asset class is heading.

While the historical pattern of commodities tends to show better performance during late expansions and early recessions, this in no way guarantees that commodities will keep following this pattern. Actually, during the latest commodity bull market, commodities have acted independently of the business cycle. This could be attributed to the fact that this commodity bull market, for the reasons outlined in the section "The 21st Century Is the Century of Commodities," is a different beast than previous cycles.

Chapter 3

Is Investing in Commodities Only for the Brave?

In This Chapter

▶ Understanding leverage

▶ Checking out the real risks

▶ Managing risk

. . . .

Commodities have a reputation for being a risky asset. Many investors are simply scared of investing in this asset class. This fear is largely unfounded because, statistically speaking, there is no greater risk in investing in commodities than there is in investing in stocks.

For whatever reason, investors have shunned this asset class in favor of what they think are more "prudent" investments such as stocks. This is quite baffling because the performance of commodities in recent years has been superior to that of stocks. For example, between 2002 and 2005, the Dow Jones Industrial Average returned a respectable 7 percent. However, the *Dow Jones-AIG Commodity Index,* which tracks a basket of commodities, was up over 21 percent! In fact in 2002 alone, while the Dow Jones Industrial Average had negative returns (–7 percent), the Dow Jones-AIG Commodity Index had returns of 26 percent.

I once attended a lecture with a world-renowned market psychologist who made this simple argument: Investors are afraid of what they don't know. Many investors will prefer to stick with an investment they know even if that investment doesn't perform well for them. For example, during 2000 and 2001, the investing public lost a total of $5 Trillion in stocks (remember the bursting of the dot.com bubble?). And yet you never hear the kinds of warnings about stocks that you hear about commodities. Is this a double standard? You can judge for yourself.

I believe that many investors are afraid of commodities because they don't know too much about them. My aim in this chapter is to shed some light on the issues surrounding commodities so that you can invest with confidence. However, I'm not denying that commodities present some risk — all investments do. So I give you some tools in the following sections to minimize and manage those risks.

Biting Off More Than You Can Chew: The Pitfalls of Using Leverage

In finance, *leverage* refers to the act of magnifying returns through the use of borrowed capital. Leverage is a powerful tool that gives you the opportunity to control large market positions with relatively little upfront capital. However, leverage is the ultimate double-edged sword because both your profits and losses are magnified to outrageous proportions.

If you invest in stocks, you know that you are able to trade on margin. You have to qualify for a margin account but, once you do, you are able to use leverage (margin) to get into stock positions. You can also trade commodities on margin. However, the biggest difference between using margin with stocks and with commodities is that margin requirement for commodities is much lower than margins for stocks, which means the potential for losses (and profits) is much greater in commodities.

If you qualify for trading stocks on margin, you have to have at least 50 percent of the capital in your account before you can enter into a stock position on margin.

The minimum margin requirements for commodity futures vary but are, on average, lower than that for stocks. For example, the margin requirement for soybeans in the Chicago Board of Trade is 4 percent. This means that with only $400 in your account, you can buy $10,000 worth of soybeans futures contracts! If the trade goes your way, you're a happy camper. But if you're on the losing side of a trade on margin, you can lose much more than your principal.

Another big difference between stock and commodity futures accounts is that the balance on futures accounts is calculated at the end of the trading session. This means that if you get a margin call, you need to take care of it immediately.

When you're trading on margin, essentially on borrowed capital, you may get a margin call from your broker requiring you to deposit additional capital in your account to cover the borrowed amount.

Because of the use of margin and the extraordinary amounts of leverage you have at your disposal in the futures markets, you should be extremely careful when trading commodity futures contracts. In order to be a responsible investor, I recommend using margin only if you have the necessary capital reserves to cover any subsequent margin calls you may receive if the market moves adversely. For more on trading futures and margin requirements, run on over to Chapter 9.

Watch Your Step: Understanding the Real Risks behind Commodities

Investing is all about managing the risk involved in generating returns. In this section, I lay out some common risks you face when investing in commodities and some small steps you can take to minimize these risks.

Geopolitical risk

One of the inherent risks of commodities is that the world's natural resources are located in various continents and the jurisdiction over these commodities lies with sovereign governments, international companies, and many other entities. For example, to access the large deposits of oil located in the Persian Gulf region, oil companies have to deal with the sovereign countries of the Middle East that have jurisdiction over this oil.

Negotiations for natural resource extractions can get pretty tense pretty quickly, with disagreements rising over licensing agreements, tax structures, environmental concerns, employment of indigenous workers, access to technology, and many other complex issues.

International disagreements over the control of natural resources are quite commonplace. Sometimes a host country will simply kick out foreign companies involved in the production and distribution of the country's natural resources. In 2006, Bolivia, which contains South America's second largest deposits of natural gas, nationalized its natural gas industry and kicked out the foreign companies involved. In a day, a number of companies such as Brazil's Petrobras and Spain's Repsol were left without a mandate in a country where they had spent billions of dollars in developing the natural gas industry. Investors in Petrobras and Repsol paid the price.

So how do you protect yourself from this geopolitical uncertainty? Unfortunately, there is no magic wand you can wave to eliminate this type of risk. However, one way to minimize it is to invest in companies with experience and economies of scale. For example, if you're interested in investing in an international oil company, go with one with an established international track record. A company like ExxonMobil, for instance, has the scale, breadth, and experience in international markets to manage the geopolitical risk they face. A smaller company without this sort of experience is going to be more at risk than a bigger one. In commodities, size does matter.

Speculative risk

The commodities markets, just like the bond or stock markets, are populated by traders whose primary interest is in making short-term profits by speculating whether the price of a security will go up or go down.

Because speculators, unlike commercial users who are using the markets for hedging purposes, are simply interested in making profits, they will tend to move the markets in different ways. Although speculators provide much-needed liquidity to the markets (particularly in commodity futures markets), they can also tend to increase market volatility, especially when they begin exhibiting what one Alan Greenspan termed "irrational exuberance." Because speculators can get out of control, as they did during the dot.com bubble, always be aware of the amount of speculative activity going on in the markets. The amount of speculative money involved in commodity markets is in constant fluctuation, but as a general rule, most commodity futures markets contain about 75 percent commercial users and 25 percent speculators.

Although I'm bullish on commodities because of the fundamental supply and demand story (which I present in Chapter 2), too much speculative money coming into the commodities markets can have detrimental effects. I anticipate that there will be times when speculators drive the prices of commodities in excess of the fundamentals. If you see too much speculative activity, it's probably a good idea to simply get out of the markets.

If you trade commodities, constantly check the pulse of the markets, finding out as much as possible about who the market participants are so that you can distinguish between the commercial users and the speculators. One source I recommend you check out is the *Commitment of Traders* report which is put out by the Commodity Futures Trading Commission (CFTC). This report is available online at www.cftc.gov/cftc/cftccotreports.htm and gives you a detailed look at the market participants. For more information on the CFTC and other regulatory bodies, check out Chapter 8.

The unraveling of Refco

Refco was one of the largest commodity brokers in the world. In moves not unlike the ones followed by Enron executives, the company's management hid about $400 Million in debts from the public in offshore accounts right before launching an Initial Public Offering (IPO) in order to make itself attractive to public investors. When these losses were uncovered, things got completely out of hand and the company was forced into bankruptcy in 2005. A large number of individual and institutional investors were affected by this unraveling.

Corporate governance risk

As if there weren't enough things to worry about, you should always watch out for plain and simple fraud. Although the Commodity Futures Trading Commission (CFTC) and other regulatory bodies (see Chapter 8) do a decent job of protecting investors from market fraud, there is always the possibility that you will become a victim of fraud. For example, your broker may hide debts or losses in offshore accounts, as was the case with Refco (see sidebar).

One way to prevent being taken advantage of is to be extremely vigilant about where you're putting your money. Make sure that you thoroughly research a firm before you hand over your money. I go through the due diligence process you should follow when selecting managers in Chapter 6. Unfortunately, there are times when no amount of research or due diligence is able to protect you from fraud — it's just a fact of the investment game.

Managing Risk

You cannot completely eliminate risk, but you can sure take steps to help you reduce it. In this section, I go through time-proven and market-tested ways to minimize risk.

Due diligence: Just do it

One way to minimize risk is to research all aspects of the investment you're about to undertake — before you undertake it. Too often, investors won't start doing research until after they invest in commodities contracts or companies.

A large number of investors buy on hype; they hear a certain commodity mentioned in the press, and they buy just because everyone else is buying. Buying on impulse is one of the most detrimental habits you can develop as an investor. Before you put your money in anything, you should find out as much as possible about this potential investment.

Because you have a number of ways you can invest in commodities (which I discuss in Chapter 5), the type of research you perform depends on what approach you take. The following sections go over the due diligence you should perform for each investment methodology.

Commodity companies

One way to get exposure to commodities is to invest in companies that process commodities. Although this is an indirect way to access raw materials, it is a good approach for investors who are comfortable in the equity environment.

Here are a few questions you should ask before you buy the company's stock:

- ✔ What are the company's assets and liabilities?
- ✔ How effective is the management with the firm's capital?
- ✔ Where will the firm generate future growth from?
- ✔ Where does the company actually generate its revenue from?
- ✔ Has the company run into any regulatory problems in the past?
- ✔ What is the company's structure? (Some commodity companies are corporations, while others act as limited partnerships — more on these in Chapter 6.)
- ✔ How does the company compare with competitors?
- ✔ Does the company operate in regions of the world that are politically unstable?
- ✔ What's the company's performance across business cycles?

Of course, these are only a few questions you should ask before making an equity investment. I go through a series of other facts and figures you should gather about commodity companies in Chapter 14 (for energy companies) and Chapter 18 (for mining companies).

You can get the answers to these questions by looking through the company's annual report (Form 10K) and/or quarterly reports (Form 8K).

Managed funds

If you're not a hands-on investor or simply don't have the time to actively manage your portfolio, you may want to choose a manager to do the investing for you. You can choose from a number of different managers, including:

- **Commodity Trading Advisor:** Manager of individual futures accounts
- **Commodity Pool Operator:** Manager of group futures accounts
- **Commodity Mutual Fund:** Manager of mutual funds that invest in commodities

Before you invest with a manager, you need to find out as much as you can about him. Here are a few questions you should ask:

- What is the manager's track record?
- What is her investing style? Is it conservative or aggressive and are you comfortable with it?
- Does he have any disciplinary actions against him?
- What do clients have to say about her? (It's okay to ask a manager to speak to one of her existing clients.)
- Is he registered with the appropriate regulatory bodies? (Please turn to Chapter 8 for information on the regulators.)
- What fees does she charge? (Ask whether there are fees that are not disclosed: Always watch out for hidden fees!)
- How much assets does he have under management?
- What are her after-tax returns? (Make sure you specify *after*-tax returns because many managers only post returns before taxes are considered.)
- Are there minimum time commitments?
- Are there penalties if you choose to withdraw your money early?
- Are there minimum investment requirements?

I go through other qualifying questions you should ask yourself before choosing a manager to invest money for you in Chapter 6.

Futures market

The futures markets play an important role in the world of commodities. They provide liquidity and allow hedgers and speculators to establish benchmark prices for the world's commodities.

If you are interested in investing through commodity futures, you need to ask a lot of questions before you get started. Here are some of these questions:

- ✔ On what exchange is the futures contract traded?
- ✔ Is there an accompanying option contract for the commodity?
- ✔ Is the market for the contract liquid or illiquid? (You want it to be liquid, just in case you were wondering.)
- ✔ Who are the main market participants?
- ✔ What is the expiration date for the contract you're interested in?
- ✔ What is the open interest for the commodity?
- ✔ Are there any margin requirements? If so, what are they?

To find out more about trading futures contracts, as well as options, make sure you read Chapter 9.

Commodity fundamentals

Whether you decide to invest through futures contracts, commodity companies, or managed funds, you need to gather as much information as possible about the underlying commodity itself. This is perhaps the most important piece of the commodities puzzle because the performance of any investment vehicle you choose depends on what the actual fundamental supply and demand story of the commodity is.

Here are a few questions you should ask yourself before you start investing in a commodity, whether it's coffee or copper.

- ✔ Which country/countries hold the largest reserves of the commodity?
- ✔ Is that country politically stable or is it vulnerable to turmoil?
- ✔ How much of the commodity is actually produced on a regular basis? (Ideally you want to get data for daily, monthly, quarterly, and annual basis.)
- ✔ Which industries/countries are the largest consumers of the commodity?
- ✔ What are the primary uses of the commodity?
- ✔ Are there any alternatives to the commodity? If so, what are they and do they pose a significant risk to the production value of the target commodity?
- ✔ Are there any seasonal factors that affect the commodity?
- ✔ What is the correlation between the commodity and comparable commodities in the same category?
- ✔ What are the historical production and consumption cycles for the commodity?

These are only a few questions you should ask before you invest in any commodity. Ideally you want to be able to gather this information before you start trading.

Diversify, diversify, diversify

One of the best ways to manage risk is through diversification. This applies on a number of levels: both diversification among asset classes, such as bonds, stocks, and commodities and also diversification within an asset class, such as diversifying your commodity holdings among energy and metals.

In order for diversification to have the desired effects on your portfolio (to minimize risk), you want to have asset classes that perform differently. One of the benefits of using commodities to minimize your overall portfolio risk is that commodities tend to behave differently than stocks and bonds. For example, as you can see in Figure 3-1, the performance of commodities and equities is remarkably different. This means that when stocks are not doing well, you will at least have your portfolio exposed to an asset class that is performing.

To find out more about how the performance of commodities compares to that of other assets and how this is beneficial to you, check out Chapter 4.

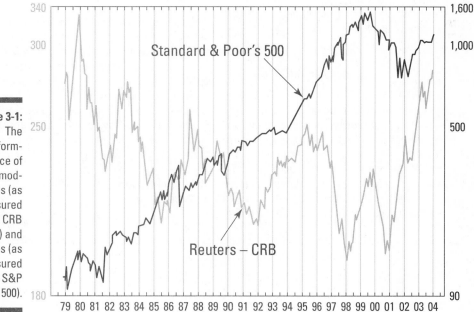

Figure 3-1: The performance of commodities (as measured by the CRB Index) and equities (as measured by the S&P 500).

Managed funds: Another one (or two) bites the dust

While I was writing *Commodities For Dummies,* the prices of certain commodities such as crude oil, natural gas, and gold were in an upward trend line that seemed endless. Of course, every rally eventually comes to an end, either to take a breather before rallying again or to falter and break down completely. Such was the case with natural gas prices during the summer and early fall of 2006. Natural gas prices, which are notoriously volatile because natural gas is hard to store (see Chapter 12), broke down after a six-month rally. Several hedge funds were forced to close down because of their exposure to natural gas futures.

Hedge funds, like a number of other financial institutions, poured billions and billions of dollars into commodities such as natural gas and copper to profit from, and naturally contribute to, the bull market in commodities. Hedge funds generally have a high tolerance for risk and so aren't afraid to enter into highly leveraged positions (through the use of high margin). Two funds that were exposed to heavy losses were caught against the tide trading natural gas futures contracts in the middle of 2006.

The first fund to suffer massive losses was MotherRock Energy Fund, a half billion dollar hedge fund that specializes in energy futures. MotherRock placed huge bets that the price of natural gas was going to drop; they were correct, of course, except that they got their timing wrong — natural gas prices rallied a few more weeks before they dropped. MotherRock's unfortunate timing meant that the fund lost $100

Million in June 2006 and another $100 Million in July 2006. Having lost half its total capital in two months, the fund was forced to shut down.

The second fund that fell victim to wild natural gas price swings was a much-larger, multi-strategy hedge fund based in Greenwich, Connecticut, called Amaranth Advisors. Amaranth, a fund with approximately $10 Billion in assets, invests in various markets, not simply commodities. Its multi-strategy focus allows it to enter any market it believes is promising. The company entered the natural gas market, hoping that its previous successes would allow it to profit in this market as well. Amaranth bet that the prices of natural gas futures would increase; unfortunately for Amaranth (and their investors), natural gas prices decreased and it was caught on the wrong side of the natural gas tide. As a result, Amaranth lost a whopping $3 Billion!

A number of lessons can be gleamed from these hedge fund debacles. First, natural gas futures are extremely volatile. Second, use leverage at your own risk. Third, over-concentration (putting all your eggs in one basket) can be devastating. While these sorts of losses are few and far between, they serve to remind the investor that investing can be very rewarding but can also be dangerous if not done properly. At the end of the day, if you're going to invest using margin in volatile commodities, you need to be ready for both spectacular wins, but also devastating losses.

Chapter 4

Get Ready to Rumble! Commodity Bulls vs. Bears

....

....

Commodities are generating some heated arguments among some of the most sophisticated investors and experts. Some commodity bulls are proclaiming a new era for commodities, while the bears are warning of an impending commodity implosion. You may have heard of the commodities *super cycle theory* on the one hand; and the story about the neighbor who lost his entire life savings trading commodities on the other.

With so many arguments and counter-arguments, claims and counter-claims, how do you decide who is right and who is wrong? More importantly, how do you decide whether to start investing in commodities or not? If you do, are you subjecting yourself to potentially disastrous losses? But if you don't invest, will you lose out on some very lucrative gains? So many questions, so little insight. My aim in this chapter is to deconstruct the arguments of both the commodity bulls and bears in order to allow you to make up your own mind about this crucial issue.

The constant tension between the bulls and bears, not simply in the commodities markets but in other markets as well, is actually good for the markets. If you didn't have both sides, there would be no market: Buyers wouldn't find sellers and sellers wouldn't find buyers. Even though the bulls and the bears are in a constant struggle, they both need each other. This is what makes investing in, and studying, the markets so much fun.

Reasonable doubt

During the California Gold Rush, a number of charlatans emerged trying to sell products to folks intent on finding gold. One fella was selling a bottled ointment that guaranteed the user instant wealth through large discoveries of gold. He promised that whoever poured this ointment on their body, climbed to the top of a mountain, and rolled down the mountain would become rich instantly. He claimed that the ointment was so powerful it would attract all the surrounding gold as the individual rolled down the mountain! As ridiculous as this sounds, this guy sold hundreds of these bottles to gullible customers.

While this is an extreme example, the moral of the story is that there are a lot of people out there who try to sell products that are simply bogus. Avoid these people like the plague. Whoever promises you guaranteed returns in the markets, whether in commodities or elsewhere, either doesn't know what they're talking

about or they're outright crooks. Either way, you don't want to have anything to do with such people.

Investing in general, and in commodities in particular, requires tremendous amounts of focus, discipline, analysis, research, and — sometimes — just plain old luck (although it's unlikely any one on Wall Street will ever admit they got lucky). The bottom line is that a little skepticism is not only a useful trait, it's a necessary trait. I've spent thousands of hours analyzing specific investments and scrutinizing potential investments top to bottom, inside out, and I could never guarantee returns to anyone — it's simply not possible. The best you can do is perform your due diligence before any trade or before committing any capital to an investment. Having all the knowledge and information at your disposal is critical, and the aim of this book is to help you do just that.

Seeing Both the Forest and the Trees

One of the biggest discrepancies between the arguments of the bulls and the bears results from the natural divergence among the performance of the individual commodities themselves. In Chapter 1, I explain that every single commodity has two fundamental qualities that determine its performance: the laws of supply and demand specific to its production and consumption, and its reaction based on the movements of the commodities asset class of which it is a member. In other words, you have to look at commodities — whether it's natural gas, nickel, or cocoa — as individual entities as well as part of a larger asset class. This financial dichotomy, which is sometimes captured by the *alpha* and *beta coefficients* in a portfolio, is worth remembering as you start investing in this market.

In the Capital Asset Pricing Model (CAPM), which describes the relationship between risk and return in a portfolio, the *beta coefficient* is a measure of risk or volatility of a security or portfolio relative to a broader market. In other words, beta measures the performance of the part relative to the whole. On the other hand, the *alpha coefficient* quantifies the performance of a security relative to its ability to generate returns independently of the broader market. I talk about portfolio construction, efficient portfolio theory, and general portfolio allocation methods in Chapter 5 to help you design a portfolio that synchronizes commodities with your other holdings.

In this section, I want to show you that the performance of individual commodities varies dramatically both in relation to other individual commodities as well as relative to a broader market benchmark. For example, take a look at the performance of crude oil, as measured by the West Texas Intermediate (WTI) futures contract on the New York Mercantile Exchange (NYMEX), in Figure 4-1.

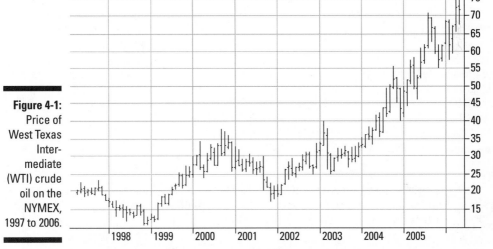

Figure 4-1:
Price of
West Texas
Inter-
mediate
(WTI) crude
oil on the
NYMEX,
1997 to 2006.

No one who looks at this chart can argue that crude oil, as measured by the WTI futures contract, hasn't been in a bull market since at least the beginning of 2002. But what does this mean for the broader market? What about other commodities? Have they performed just as well as crude, which is touted by commodity bulls as a sign of a broader bull market in commodities?

Check out Figure 4-2. It shows the performance of the gold futures contract on the COMEX division of the NYMEX.

As you can see, gold has performed almost as well as — if not better than — crude oil during the same time period. So this means that there's definitely a bull market in commodities, right? Well, not exactly. Figures 4-1 and 4-2 show the performance of crude oil and gold, and only crude oil and gold. It's true that crude oil and gold are perhaps the two most important commodities in the asset class, but are they representative of the whole asset class?

Figure 4-2:
Historical
price levels
of gold on
the COMEX
from 1997 to
2006.

Crude oil is a closely followed commodity because of its importance to the global economy, and gold because of its precious metal status. (I cover crude oil in Chapter 11, and gold in Chapter 15.)

In Figure 4-3, you can see the performance of coffee — another major commodity — as measured by the coffee futures contract on the New York Board of Trade (NYBOT), during same time period, 1997 to 2006.

What's going on here? Not only is coffee not in a rally, it seems to be trading sideways (within a narrow price band). If crude oil and gold are experiencing a rally, then shouldn't there be a bull market in coffee as well? After all, coffee is one of the most important commodities in the world, second only to crude oil in terms of global production figures. Perhaps it's a statistical anomaly.

I'm sure that other commodities have experienced a rally similar to crude oil and gold. Maybe another major commodity, say live cattle, has experienced a rally. Take a look at Figure 4-4 for the recent performance of the Chicago Mercantile Exchange (CME) live cattle futures contract.

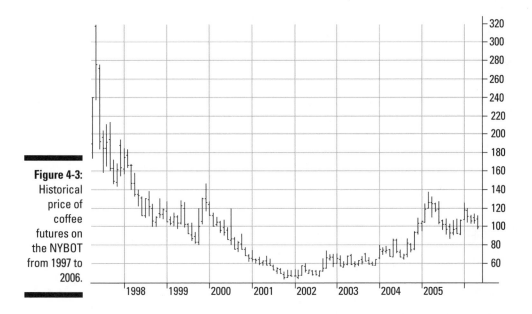

Figure 4-3:
Historical
price of
coffee
futures on
the NYBOT
from 1997 to
2006.

Whoa! No rally in the live cattle futures contract either. As a matter of fact, it doesn't look like there's any correlation between live cattle and coffee either. The performance is so varied that these four representative commodities seem to have no relation to each other. Even their risk profiles seem very different — live cattle is a lot more volatile than the other three.

And this is the point that I want to make: The performance of each individual commodity varies dramatically from the performance of other commodities. If commodities moved in lock step, then the live cattle and coffee markets would be experiencing the same rally as crude oil and gold. But they don't because the markets are a lot more nuanced than that. Always keep this diverging performance among individual commodities in mind, particularly when folks start talking about commodities as an asset class.

However, there are benchmarks that attempt to capture the performance of commodities as an asset class. These benchmarks, known as *commodity indexes,* are similar to the Dow Jones Industrial Average or other market benchmarks that track the performance of a group of securities. Like the commodities markets themselves, these benchmarks are varied in terms of both the commodities they track as well as their construction methodologies. Some indexes are overweight specific sub-asset classes (such as energy), while others follow an equal weight strategy.

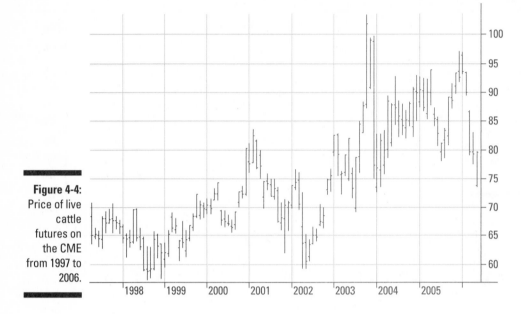

Figure 4-4:
Price of live
cattle
futures on
the CME
from 1997 to
2006.

These indexes, which I discuss extensively in Chapter 7, do their best to provide a "big picture" of what the commodities markets are doing. However, because of the index component selection, construction and rolling methodologies, rebalancing features, and other external variables, these indexes fail to provide a complete picture of what the markets are doing. Take the Reuters/Jefferies Commodity Research Bureau Index, widely viewed as the gold standard of the commodity benchmarks. One quarter of this index tracks the WTI crude oil contract (see Figure 4-1), while other commodities such as coffee account for a much less significant percentage — in the case of coffee only 5 percent. Placing an emphasis on crude oil is reflected in the performance of the benchmark, as you can see in Figure 4-5.

Placing such a great emphasis on crude oil means that the benchmark is more sensitive to price movements in crude than in any other commodity — which is reflected in its performance as you can clearly see by comparing Figures 4-1 and 4-5.

Now, the emphasis on crude oil is justified to a certain extent because crude oil is in fact an important commodity, perhaps the most important commodity both in terms of production and dollar value. However, despite the importance of crude, the benchmarks don't provide a complete picture of what the commodities markets as a *whole* are doing. Part of the reason is that benchmarks track only a few commodities, while they completely fail to include a number of important commodities.

Figure 4-5:
Perform-
ance of the
Reuters/
Jefferies
CRB Index
from 1997 to
2006.

For example, none of the benchmarks include steel, which is the most widely
used metal in the world. Knowing what steel is doing is an important consideration and not including such an important commodity — because there
isn't a futures contract that tracks steel — takes away from the big picture of
what the commodities markets are actually doing.

The bottom line here is that you need to take all the talk about commodities
being in a bull or bear market or about commodities being a risky asset class
with a big grain of salt. Some commodities, such as crude oil and gold, have
clearly been in a bull market, while others such as coffee and live cattle
haven't performed as well. And some commodities, such as live cattle or
frozen pork bellies, are notoriously more volatile than crude oil and other
commodities.

At the end of the day, you need to be able to see both the forest and the
trees. That's why my aim throughout the book is to provide you with the critical information regarding every individual commodity, but also to make sure
to help you tie it with the performance of the broader asset class. Figuring
out what individual commodities are doing is as crucial as knowing what the
broader market is doing.

Ride the Wave? Kondratieff and the Super Cycle Theory

One theory that keeps popping up during debates about commodities between the bulls and the bears is the *super cycle theory*. This theory, which has been made famous by legendary commodities investor Jim Rogers, stipulates that commodities are in a long-term cyclical bull market that began in the late 1990s and will last for 15 years or so. I agree with Rogers — up to a point. I agree with the premise that the fundamentals are there to support and generate a run-up in commodity prices, namely a tight supply coupled with soaring demand. There is no doubt that the fundamentals explain the recent rally in commodities, and I talk about these fundamental reasons — such as population growth, industrialization, urbanization, and project duration — extensively in Chapter 2.

My mid- to long-term outlook for commodities is certainly bullish, but I cannot say with certitude how long this bull market will last. The theory about super cycles is nothing new. Nikolai Kondratieff, a Russian economist working in the 1920s, claimed to have identified patterns of economic boom and bust cycles that stretched across a 50-year period. Kondratieff, the grandfather of the super cycle theories, based this conclusion on historical data he gathered on advanced capitalist societies. Not surprisingly, his theory did not hold up during the next ten years, let alone for the next 50 years.

When confronted with this information, Kondratieff's followers claimed that human life expectancy had increased and therefore the Kondratieff cycle no longer applied. At the end of the day, the whole literature on these super cycles — be they for advanced capitalist societies or commodities — is inconclusive.

At the end of the day, I recommend you analyze every asset you invest in — whether a stock, a particular commodity or a commodity index — based on the fundamental reasons specific to that asset. Super cycle theories should help shed some light on a particular asset but don't rely solely on these broad market theories to guide your investment strategy.

Keeping It Simple: Looking at the Laws of Supply and Demand

The most basic, and fundamental, premise in the study of economics is that price is a function of the interaction between supply and demand. If supply doesn't change and demand increases, prices will increase. When demand remains constant and supply increases, prices go down. It doesn't get any simpler than that. This simple but powerful concept can be used to explain the current commodities boom, as well as the previous commodities downturns — and the future movements of commodity cycles.

As I outlined in the previous section "Kondratieff and the Super Cycle Theory," theories about long-term cycles are more of an economic curiosity than historical fact. At the end of the day, what moves prices are the laws of supply and demand. The current boom in commodities can be explained through this lens. For years — perhaps even decades — the commodities industry was plagued by capital underinvestment in infrastructure. New mines weren't being exploited and new oilfields weren't being discovered. In the late 20th and early 21st century, demand for the world's raw materials began to increase at a rapid clip, driven primarily by the needs of the newly emerging leading developing countries, particularly India and China (see Chapter 2).

While demand from the industrialized world — mostly North America, Europe, Japan, and Australasia — remained constant, and demand from the developing world skyrocketed, prices for the world's commodities increased. One of the characteristics of the commodities world is that bringing new capacity on line takes a long time, often five years and sometimes even decades (Chapter 2). Extracting raw materials from the earth, transforming them into usable goods and then transporting them to consumers is a labor-intensive, technologically driven and time-consuming process. The world was therefore caught by surprise when economic growth around the world spurred an intense and lasting demand for natural resources, which ranged from crude oil and copper to coal and steel.

Faced with surging demand (especially from the leading developing countries) and lagging supply (because of infrastructure underinvestment for decades), prices for commodities went through the roof. And this is the situation the world is facing now: increased demand with limited supply. Will this current supply and demand balance remain static forever? It's unlikely. Already, oil companies are building pipelines to transport oil from hard-to-reach locations to consumers, and mining companies are digging new mines to provide consumers with primary base metals.

As this supply-side crunch subsides, and as demand decreases — and it will eventually — prices for commodities will again decline. When you enter the current commodities market, you should be well aware of the fact that prices are going to come down at some point.

It's sometimes easy to lose track of the fundamental nature of the commodities markets because of all the hype and all the hot money coming in and out of the markets for speculative purposes. But once you clear out all this noise, what remains is clear: The commodities markets, like all other markets, are driven by the fundamental laws of supply and demand. If you remember this basic premise, you will be able to come out ahead in the markets.

Chapter 5

Feel the Love: Welcoming Commodities into Your Portfolio

In This Chapter

▶ Creating a financial road map

▶ Designing a portfolio

▶ Including commodities in your portfolio

▶ Identifying the best ways to invest in commodities

*W*hether you're an experienced investor or a first-time trader, it's important to have a good grasp on how to use your portfolio to improve your overall financial situation. You need to consider factors such as your risk tolerance, tax bracket, and level of liabilities when designing your portfolio. I start off this chapter by going through these basic portfolio management techniques so that you can synchronize your portfolio to your personal financial profile.

In the second half of the chapter, I show you how to actually introduce commodities into your portfolio. I go through basic portfolio allocation methods and include an overview of the benefits of diversification. In the last part of the chapter I list all the different investment methods you have at your disposal to get exposure to commodities, from index funds to Master Limited Partnerships.

If you've ever wondered how to actually include commodities in your portfolio, then you can't afford not to read this chapter!

The Color of Money: Taking Control of Your Financial Life

You invest because you've come to the realization that it's better to have your money working for you than to have it sit in a bank account earning so little interest that you end up losing money when you factor in inflation. Enough of that — you want your money to work for you. Most people end up working for their money all their lives, and they get stuck in a vicious cycle where they become servants to money.

If you're caught in this vicious cycle, you want your relationship with money to go through a 180-degree reversal: Instead of working hard for your money, you should have your money work hard for you! This is how investing allows you to build and, more importantly, to maintain your wealth. (In the following sections I show you how to use commodities to achieve this goal.)

There are a plethora of books that deal with building and maintaining wealth. With such a wide selection, how do you know which ones to choose? Fortunately, I've taken a look at most of them and have come up with a good list of recommendations.

Here are a few books on the topic that I highly recommend you read if you're new at investing:

- *Rich Dad, Poor Dad* by Robert Kiyosaki
- *Personal Finance For Dummies* by Eric Tyson
- *Start Late, Finish Rich* by David Bach
- *The Millionaire Mind* by Thomas Stanley
- *One Up on Wall Street* by Peter Lynch

Building wealth is not easy, but with a little discipline and self-control, it can actually be a very fun and rewarding process.

Often, the accumulation phase isn't the biggest challenge to building wealth; being able to preserve wealth is often more difficult. Here are a couple things you should be aware of that can negatively impact your bottom line:

- **Inflation:** *Inflation,* an increase in prices or in the money supply that can result in a quick deterioration of value, is one of the most detrimental forces you face as an investor. Inflation keeps some of the brightest minds up at night; among them is the Chairman of the Federal Reserve, whose main priority is making sure that the economy doesn't grow so fast that it creates bad inflation. When inflation gets out of control, the currency literally isn't worth the paper it's printed on. This state, known as *hyperinflation,* occurred in Weimar Germany in the 1920s. At its worst, people placed paper money in their stoves to heat themselves during the winter because the money burned longer than wood. Conveniently, one way to protect yourself from inflation is by investing in commodities such as gold and silver. (Make sure to read Chapter 15 for more on using precious metals as a hedge against inflation.)

✔ **Business Cycles:** In the world of investing, nothing ever goes up in a straight line. There is always minor turbulence along the way, and most investments usually experience some drops before they make new highs — that is, if they ever make new highs! The economy moves in the same way, alternating between expansions and recessions. Certain assets that perform well during expansions (such as stocks) don't do so well during recessions. Alternatively, assets such as commodities do fairly well during late expansionary and early recessionary phases of the business cycle. As an investor interested in preserving and growing your capital base, you need to be able to identify and invest in assets that are going to perform and generate returns regardless of the current business cycle. Make sure you check out Chapter 2, where I discuss the performance of commodities across the business cycle.

These and other risks, such as those posed by fraud, the markets, and geopolitics, can be minimized with some due diligence and a few wise decisions. I look at risk as it relates to both commodities and investing in general in Chapter 3.

Looking Ahead: Creating a Financial Road Map

Building wealth through investing takes a lot of time, effort, and discipline — unlike winning the lottery or getting a large inheritance. It takes a conscious and systematic effort to achieve your financial goals. Of course, the first part is identifying and establishing your financial goals. These could be as diverse as amassing enough money to retire by age 50 and travel the world, to gather enough money to pay for college, or to make enough money to pass on to your children or grandchildren. Before you start investing in commodities (or any other asset), sit down and figure out clear financial goals. Every individual has different needs and interests. In the following sections, I outline some key points to help you establish your financial goals.

Once you identify your goals, you can then begin figuring out how to use commodities to achieve these goals. I show you how in the section "Opening Up Your Portfolio to Commodities."

Figuring out your net worth

You need to know where you are before you can determine where you want to go. From a personal finance perspective, you need to know how much you are worth in order to determine how much capital to allocate to investing, living expenses, retirement, and so on.

Your net worth is calculated by subtracting your total liabilities from your total assets. (*Assets* put money in your pocket, while *liabilities* remove money from your pocket.)

Fill in the blanks in Table 5-1 to determine the total value of your assets.

Table 5-1	Total Assets
Assets	*Value*
Cash in all checking and savings accounts	$_____
Cash on hand	$_____
Certificates of Deposits	$_____
Money market funds	$_____
Market value of home	$_____
Market value of other real estate	$_____
Life insurance	$_____
Annuities	$_____
Pension plans 401(k) and/or 403(b)	$_____
IRAs (Individual Retirement Accounts)	$_____
Stocks and other equity	$_____
Bonds and other fixed income	$_____
Mutual funds	$_____

Assets	Value
Commodity investments	$_____
Futures and options	$_____
Other investment assets	$_____
Vehicles (car, boat, etc.)	$_____
Personal belongings (home furnishings, jewelry, etc.)	$_____
TOTAL OF ALL ASSETS	$_____

Assets are only one part of the net worth equation. Once you have calculated your total assets, you need to determine how many liabilities you have. Use Table 5-2 to help you determine your total liabilities.

Table 5-2	Total Liabilities
Liabilities	**Value**
Mortgage(s)	$_____
Car payments	$_____
College loan payments	$_____
Mortgage equity line	$_____
Credit card loans	$_____
Other loans	$_____
TOTAL VALUE OF LIABILITIES	$_____

Once you have determined both your total assets and total liabilities, simply use the following formula to determine your total net worth:

Total Net Worth = Total Assets – Total Liabilities

Determining your net worth on a regular basis is important because it allows you to keep track of the balance between your assets and liabilities. Knowing your net worth will allow you in turn to determine which investment strategy you should pursue.

Based on this simple mathematical formula, the key to increasing your net worth is to increase your assets while reducing your liabilities. Investing helps you increase your assets. Cutting down on living expenses may help you reduce your liabilities.

Identifying your tax bracket

Taxes have a direct impact on how much of your assets you get to keep at the end of the day. It is important to understand the implications that taxes can have on your portfolio.

How much you pay in taxes is based on where you are in the tax bracket. I list in Table 5-3 the individual income tax brackets to help you determine how much you'll end up paying in taxes based on your income.

Table 5-3	2006 Income Tax Rate Schedule (Federal Level)
Taxable Income	*Tax Level*
$0 to $7,550	10%
$7,550 to $30,650	15%
$30,650 to $74,200	25%
$74,200 to $154,800	28%
$154,800 to $336,550	33%
$336,550 to infinity	35%

The tax rate schedule in Table 5-3 is known as Schedule X and applies to you if you are filing your tax return as a single. The Internal Revenue Service (IRS) has a number of different schedules depending on how you are filing your returns.

- ✔ **Schedule Y-1:** Married and filing jointly OR Qualifying widow(er)
- ✔ **Schedule Y-2:** Married filing separately
- ✔ **Schedule Z:** Head of household

Tax rates change depending on which schedule you file under. Visit the IRS Web site at www.irs.gov or talk to your accountant to find out the tax rates under the different schedules. Because tax rates may change on an annual basis, make sure you inquire about these tax issues regularly.

Where you live can also have a big impact on how taxes affect your investments. Did you know that there are a number of states within the continental United States that don't have income taxes? Here are the states that have absolutely no income tax, which means you get to keep more of what you earn!

- ✔ Alaska
- ✔ Florida
- ✔ Nevada
- ✔ New Hampshire
- ✔ South Dakota
- ✔ Tennessee
- ✔ Texas
- ✔ Washington
- ✔ Wyoming

By living in one of these states, you will pay federal income taxes but no state income taxes, so I understand if you start thinking about relocating to one of these states!

Out of the nine states that don't have personal income taxes, Florida does place a tax on intangible personal property. This means that items such as stocks, bonds, and mutual funds are subject to taxes. Also note that New Hampshire and Tennessee both tax income earned on interest and dividends.

Investing in commodities, as in any other asset class, has tax implications. While I'm not an accountant and the aim of this book is not to offer you tax advice, I do recommend you talk to your accountant before you invest in commodities. Knowing the tax implications before you invest will save you a lot of heartache down the road. Make sure to talk to your accountant, who can provide you with appropriate tax advice.

Are you hungry? Determining your risk appetite

Risk is perhaps the single greatest enemy you face as an investor. How wonderful would life be if you could have guaranteed returns without risk? Since that's not possible, and has never been possible, you have to learn how to manage, tame, and minimize risk. While I devote a whole chapter to managing risk related to commodities (see Chapter 3), I do want to briefly discuss general portfolio risk in this section.

Your risk tolerance depends on a number of factors that are unique to you as an individual. The first step in determining your risk tolerance is deciding how much risk you are willing to take on. Although there is no equation or formula to determine risk (it would be nice if there were one), you can use a general rule to identify the percentage of your assets you should dedicate to aggressive investments with an elevated risk/reward ratio.

As a general rule, the younger you are, the higher your percentage of assets should be devoted to higher-risk investments. This makes sense because if you lose a lot you still have a lot of time ahead of you to recoup your losses. When you're older, however, you don't have as much time to get back your investments.

Table 5-4 gives you a simple guideline to help you determine the percentage of assets that should go into investments with higher returns (and risks).

Table 5-4	Percentage of Assets in Growth Investments by Age Group
Age Group	*Percentage in growth investments*
0 to 20	Up to 90%
20 to 30	80% to 90%
31 to 40	70% to 80%
41 to 50	60% to 70%
51 to 64	45% to 60%
65 and over	Less than 45%

This rule is not set in stone, but you can use it to approximate how much of your assets should be placed in investments that have a high risk/reward ratio. If you're investments are working just fine with the percentages you're working with, don't change them! As the saying goes, if it's not broken, don't try to fix it.

This table provides you with a general guideline of the percentage of assets you should earmark for growth investments, such as stocks, commodities, and real estate. This is *not* a percentage of how much of your portfolio you should invest in commodities. I discuss that percentage in the following section.

Making Room in Your Portfolio for Commodities

One of the most common questions I get from investors is, "How much of my portfolio should I have in commodities?" My answer is usually very simple: It depends. You have to take into account a number of different factors to determine how much capital to dedicate to commodities.

Personally, my portfolio may include at any one point anywhere between 35 to 50 percent commodities. However, there are times when it's much lower than that. And there have been times where almost 90 percent of my portfolio was in commodities!

If you're new to commodities, I would recommend starting out with a relatively modest amount, anywhere between 3 and 5 percent to see how comfortable you feel with this new member of your financial family. Test out how commodities contribute to your overall portfolio's performance. If satisfied, I recommend you gradually increase it.

Many investors who like the way commodities anchor their portfolios have about 15 percent exposure to commodities. I find that's a pretty good place to be if you're still getting used to commodities. Although my guess is that once you see the benefits and realize how much value commodities can provide, that number will steadily increase.

In Figure 5-1, I create a hypothetical portfolio that includes commodities along with other asset classes.

Hypothetical Portfolio

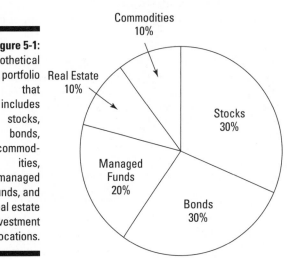

Figure 5-1:
Hypothetical
portfolio
that
includes
stocks,
bonds,
commod-
ities,
managed
funds, and
real estate
investment
allocations.

Having a diversified portfolio is important because it helps reduce the overall volatility of your market exposures. Having unrelated assets increases your chances of maintaining good returns when a certain asset under-performs.

Fully Exposed: The Top Ways to Get Exposure to Commodities

You have several methods at your disposal, both direct and indirect, for getting exposure to commodities. In this section, I go through the different ways you can invest in commodities.

Looking towards the future with commodity futures

The futures markets are the most direct way to get exposure to commodities. Futures contracts allow you to purchase an underlying commodity for an agreed upon price in the future. I talk about futures contracts in depth in Chapter 9. In this section, I list some ways you can play the futures markets.

Modern Portfolio Theory and the benefits of diversification

The idea that diversification is a good strategy in portfolio allocation is the cornerstone of the Modern Portfolio Theory (MPT). MPT is the brainchild of Nobel Prize winning economist Harry Markowitz. In a paper he wrote in 1952 for his doctoral thesis, Markowitz argued that investors should look at a portfolio's overall risk/reward ratio. While this sounds like common sense today, it was a groundbreaking idea at the time.

Up until Markowitz's paper, most investors constructed their portfolios based on a risk/reward ratio analysis of individual securities. Investors chose a security based on its individual risk

profile and ignored how that risk profile would fit within a broader portfolio. Markowitz argued (successfully) that investors could construct more profitable portfolios if they looked at the overall risk/reward ratio of their portfolios.

Therefore, when you are considering an individual security, you should not only assess its individual risk profile, but also take into account how that risk profile fits within your general investment strategy. Markowitz's idea that holding a group of different securities reduces a portfolio's overall volatility is one of the most important ideas in portfolio allocation.

Commodity index

Commodity indexes track a basket of commodity futures contracts. The methodology that each index uses is different and the performance of the index is different from its peers. Commodity indexes are known as passive, long-only investments because they are not actively managed and they can only buy the underlying commodity; they can't short it. (For more on going long and going short, please turn to Chapter 9.)

Here are the five major commodity indexes you can choose from:

- Goldman Sachs Commodity Index (GSCI)
- Reuters/Jefferies Commodity Research Bureau Index (R/J-CRBI)
- Dow Jones-AIG Commodity Index (DJ-AIGCI)
- Rogers International Commodity Index (RICI)
- Deutsche Bank Liquid Commodity Index (DBLCI)

I analyze the components, performance, and construction methodology of each one of these indexes in Chapter 7.

Futures Commission Merchant

Don't be intimidated by the name — a *Futures Commission Merchant* (FCM) is very much like your regular stock broker. However, instead of selling stocks, an FCM is licensed to sell futures contracts, options, and other derivatives to the public.

If you are comfortable trading futures and options contracts, then opening an account with an FCM will give you the most direct access to the commodity futures markets. Make sure you read Chapter 6 to find out the pros and cons of investing through an FCM.

If you're going to trade futures contracts directly, you should have a solid grasp of technical analysis, which I discuss in Chapter 10.

Commodity Trading Advisor

A *Commodity Trading Advisor* (CTA) is an individual who manages accounts for clients who trade futures contracts. The CTA may provide advice on how to place your trades, but may also manage your account on your behalf. Make sure you research the CTA's track record and investment philosophy to make sure it squares with yours.

The CTA may manage accounts for more than one client. However, they are not allowed to "pool" accounts and share all profits and losses among clients equally. (This is one of the main differences between a CTA and a CPO, discussed next.)

Make sure to read Chapter 6 to identify key elements to look for when shopping for a CTA.

Commodity Pool Operator

The *Commodity Pool Operator* (CPO) acts a lot like a CTA except that, instead of managing separate accounts, the CPO has the authority to "pool" all client funds in one account and trade them as if she were trading one account.

There are two advantages of investing through a CPO over a CTA:

- ✔ Because a CPO can pool funds together, she has access to more funds to invest. This provides both leverage and diversification opportunities that smaller accounts don't offer. You can buy a lot more assets with $100,000 than with $10,000.

- ✔ Most CPOs are structured as partnerships, which means the only money you can lose is your principal. In the world of futures, this is pretty good because, due to margin and the use of leverage, you can end up owing a lot more than the principal should a trade go sour. Make sure to read Chapter 9 for more on margin and leverage.

I go through the pros and cons of investing through a CPO in Chapter 6.

Funding your account with commodity funds

If you think that delving into commodity derivatives is not for you, then you can access the commodity markets through funds. If you've invested before, you may be familiar with these two investment vehicles.

Commodity mutual funds

Commodity mutual funds are exactly like your average, run of the mill mutual funds except that they focus specifically on investing in commodities. You have a number of such funds to choose from, although the two biggest ones are the PIMCO and the Oppenheimer funds.

A recent SEC ruling changed the way that mutual funds account for qualifying income, and this has put some pressure on funds, particularly PIMCO, to come up with different accounting methods. Make sure you find out how such rulings affect your investments.

I examine commodity mutual funds in Chapter 6.

Exchange Traded Funds

Exchange Traded Funds (ETFs) have become really popular with investors because they provide the benefits of investing in a fund with the ease of trading a stock. This hybrid instrument is becoming one of the best ways for investors to access the commodities markets.

The world of commodity ETFs is fairly new and is constantly changing. Just during the writing of this book, three new ETFs were launched. Because this is such a dynamic field, I have a section called *ETF Watch* in my Web site www.commodities-investor.com that I encourage you to check out to keep up to date on everything that's happening in the world of ETFs.

You currently have at your disposal ETFs that track baskets of commodities through commodity indexes, as well as ETFs that track single commodities such as oil, gold, and silver. I list some popular commodity ETFs in Table 5-5.

Table 5-5	Commodity ETFs
ETF	*Description*
Deutsche Bank Commodity Index Tracking Fund (DBC)	ETF that tracks the performance of the Deutsche Bank Commodity Index
US Oil Fund (USO)	ETF that mirrors the movements of the WTI Crude oil on the NYMEX
Street Tracks Gold Shares (GLD)	Tracks the performance of gold bullion
iShares COMEX Gold Trust (IAU)	ETF that tracks the performance of gold futures contracts on the COMEX
iShares Silver Trust (SLV)	First ETF that tracks the performance of silver

Make sure you examine all fees associated with the ETF before you invest. (And check out Chapter 6.)

You're in good company: Investing in commodity companies

Another route you can take to get exposure to commodities is to buy stocks of commodity companies. These companies are generally involved in the production, transformation, and/or distribution of various commodities.

This is perhaps the most indirect way of accessing the commodity markets because in buying a company's stock, you're getting exposure not only to the performance of the underlying commodity the company is involved in, but also other factors such as the company's management skills, creditworthiness, and ability to generate cash flow and minimize expenses.

Publicly traded companies

Publicly traded companies can give you exposure to specific sectors of commodities, such as metals, energy, or agricultural products. Within these three categories, you can choose companies that deal with specific methods or commodities, such as refiners of crude oil into finished products or gold mining companies.

If you're considering an equity stake in a commodity company, you should determine how the company's stock performs relative to the price of the underlying commodity that company is involved in.

Although there is no hard rule, I've found that there is a relatively strong correlation between the performance of commodity futures contracts and the performance of companies that use these commodities as inputs.

So investing in the stock of commodity companies actually gives you pretty good exposure to the underlying commodities themselves. However, you want to be extra careful and to perform a thorough due diligence before you invest your money in these companies. I show you some key things you should look for before you invest in such companies in Chapters 14 and 18.

Master Limited Partnerships

Master Limited Partnerships (MLPs) are a hybrid instrument that offers you the convenience of trading a partnership like a stock. You really get the best of both worlds: the liquidity that comes from being a publicly traded entity with the tax protection of being a partnership.

One of the biggest advantages of MLPs is that, as a unit holder, you are only taxed at the individual level. This is different than if you invested in a corporation, where cash back to shareholders (in the form of dividends) is taxed both at the corporate level as well as the individual level. MLPs do not pay any corporate tax! This is a huge benefit for your bottom line.

In order for an MLP to qualify for these tax breaks, it must generate 90 percent of its income from qualifying sources that relate to commodities, particularly in the oil and gas industry.

Some of the popular assets that MLPs invest in include oil and gas storage facilities and transportation infrastructure such as pipelines. I go through MLPs in detail in Chapter 6.

Part II
Getting Started

The 5th Wave   By Rich Tennant

"You may want to talk to Phil – he's one of our more aggressive brokers."

In this part . . .

Whether you're an experienced investor or a beginning trader, having a good grasp of portfolio allocation and design methodology is critical for your success. In this part, you discover the best strategies, trading techniques, and investment vehicles to help you profit in the commodities markets.

Chapter 6

Show Me the Money! Choosing the Right Manager

*I*f you're looking for ways to get involved in commodities, you have the option of hiring a trained professional to do the investing for you. As the number of investors putting their money in this asset class grows, more and more investment vehicles are being developed to satisfy this demand. Currently, a number of money managers offer their services to help you invest in this market.

Of course, whenever you hand over your hard-earned money to a manager, you want to make sure you feel confident about her ability to invest your money wisely. You should consider several criteria before handing over your money to a manager. In this chapter, I look at some of the vehicles you have at your disposal to invest in the commodities markets, and I offer you hands-on information to help you select the most suitable money manager for you.

Mutually Beneficial: Investing in Commodity Mutual Funds

A common way for individuals to invest in commodities is through a mutual fund. It just may be the simplest way for you to get involved in the commodities markets because you're relying on a trained professional to do the investing on your behalf.

A *mutual fund* is a fund managed by an investment professional for the benefit of the fund investors. Mutual funds, by definition, can only follow a specific set of trading techniques. Mutual funds don't engage in sophisticated trading techniques such as arbitrage trades, special situations, long-short strategies, or distressed asset investing. These strategies are conducted primarily by *hedge funds,* which are similar to mutual funds except they can engage in these sophisticated investment strategies. Most mutual funds follow *long-only* strategies, which is an investment policy based on the *buy-and-hold* principle.

There are many different types of mutual funds that have nothing to do with commodities. You can invest in stock funds, bond funds, currency funds, and even country-specific funds. But a number of mutual funds specialize in investing in only commodities or commodity-related products.

Plain vanilla funds are your run-of-the-mill funds. If you've ever invested in a mutual fund, you should have no problems investing in these straightforward funds. How do you get started? You write your check and purchase shares of the mutual funds either through your broker or directly from the fund providers, and voila! Of course, I recommend you ask a number of questions before writing your check. I look at these qualifying questions in the following section.

Plain vanilla funds are actively administered by a fund manager whose responsibility is to allocate capital across various sub-asset classes in order to maximize the fund's returns. Generally speaking, these mutual funds invest in commodity-linked derivative instruments such as futures contracts and options on futures traded on the major commodity exchanges in New York, Chicago, and elsewhere. (Make sure to read Chapter 8 for more information on commodity exchanges.) Others may also invest in companies that process these raw materials, such as energy companies (Chapter 14) and mining companies (Chapter 18).

Riddle me this, riddle me that: Asking the right questions

Before you invest in a mutual fund, you should gather as much information as possible about the fund itself as well as about the mechanics of investing in the fund. You can get answers to these questions directly from the fund manager or the fund's prospectus.

Call the mutual fund company directly and ask for a prospectus. A *prospectus* contains a wealth of information regarding how the fund is managed, what strategies the fund managers use, as well as details on fees and expenses. It's a great way to start gathering information on a prospective fund. And best of all, mutual funds will send you their prospectus for free!

Here are some useful questions to help you zero in on the key points of mutual fund investing:

✔ **What is the fund's investment objective?** Different funds have radically different investment objectives. While one may focus on *capital gains,* another may specialize in *income investing.* Knowing the fund's objective is one of the first pieces of information to look out for.

✔ **What securities does the fund invest in?** This may seem like a straight-forward answer (such as commodities), but a number of funds claim their main investment products are commodities when in reality only a small percentage of the fund is commodities-related. I look at some of these funds in the section "Taking a look at what's out there."

✔ **Who manages the fund?** You want to know as much as possible about the individuals who are going to be managing your hard-earned money. Most money managers in the United States have to be registered with the National Association of Securities Dealers (NASD). You can get information on the manager's personal background by checking the NASD Web site at www.nasdbrokercheck.com. Here are some key points to look for:

- **Experience:** How long has he been a manager?

- **Track record:** What kind of returns has the manager achieved for his clients in the past?

- **Disciplinary actions:** Has this manager been disciplined for a past action? If so, find out more.

- **Registrations and certifications:** Does this manager have all the required registrations with the appropriate financial authorities to trade and invest on behalf of clients?

✔ **What kind of strategy does the fund use?** A fund's strategy relies on a number of factors, including the investing style of the portfolio managers, the fund's objective, and the securities it chooses to invest in. Some funds follow low-risk, steady income strategies, while others have a more aggressive strategy that uses a lot of leverage. Identifying the fund's strategy right away is critical.

✔ **What is the profile of the typical investor in this fund?** The fund will cater to the profile of its investors, which can be anywhere from highly conservative to extremely aggressive. You need to know what kind of individual is likely to invest in this fund and determine whether your risk tolerance squares with that of the other investors.

✔ **What are the main risks of investing in this fund?** Whenever you invest, you take on a certain degree of risk: interest rate risk, credit risk, risk of loss of principal, liquidity risk, hedging risk, and geopolitical risk. For a detailed look at a number of different risks, take a look at Chapter 4.

✔ **What is the fund's track record?** Although past performance does not guarantee future results, it's always important to examine the fund's track record to get a sense of the kinds of returns the managers have achieved for their investors in the past. Most funds will post their performance over a number of different years — take a look particularly at the key periods of the past three, five, and ten years.

✔ **What is the fund's *after-tax* performance?** Be sure to pay close attention to *after-tax* returns when looking at historical performance because these are a more accurate measure of the fund's performance — and how much money you get to keep after you pay Uncle Sam. Many funds will advertise in big, bold charts their performance before taxes, but these can be misleading because a significant portion of these returns end up in the government's coffers after taxes are taken out

✔ **What are the fund's fees and expenses?** Fees and expenses are always going to cut into how much money you can get out of the fund. Look for funds that have lower expenses and fees. This information is available in the prospectus.

✔ **What is the minimum capital an investor must commit?** A number of mutual funds require a minimum amount of money you have to invest in order to participate, ranging anywhere from $500 to $10,000 or more. The minimum requirement may also vary according to the type of investor. Someone investing for an IRA may have to put up less money up front than someone investing through a brokerage account. Finally, many funds also require *minimum incremental amounts* after the initial investment amount. So you could invest $1000 upfront but then be required to increase your investment by at least $100 each subsequent time you want to invest in the fund.

✔ **Are there different classes of shares?** Most mutual funds offer more than one class of shares to investors. The different classes are based on a number of factors, including sales charges, deferred sales charges, redemption fees, and investor availability. Make sure to examine each class of shares closely to determine which one is best for you.

✔ **What are the tax implications of investing in this fund?** Talk to your accountant in order to determine the tax consequences of any investment you make.

Like almost everything else in finance, investing in mutual funds requires mastery of specific terminology. Here are some of these technical terms to help you talk the talk:

✔ **Expense ratio:** The expense ratio is the percentage of the fund's total assets earmarked for general operational expenses. This is the amount used to run the fund and generally lowers total fund returns.

✔ **Sales Load:** Some mutual funds sell their shares through brokerage houses and other financial intermediaries. A *sales load* is the commission the mutual fund pays to brokers that sell their shares to the general public. The sales load is paid by the investor. Some funds don't have sales load, in which case they're called *no-load funds*.

✔ **Sales charge:** A sales charge, sometimes referred to as a *deferred sales charge,* is a fee paid by the mutual fund investor when she sells her mutual fund shares. This is also known as a *back-end charge* because you pay a fee after you want to sell your shares.

✔ **Net Asset Value (NAV):** A fund's Net Asset Value (NAV) is its total assets minus total liabilities. Mutual funds calculate NAV on a per share basis at the end of each trading day by dividing the difference between total assets and liabilities by the number of shares outstanding. A mutual fund's NAV is similar to a publicly traded company's stock price on a per share basis.

Taking a look at what's out there

You can choose from two main commodity mutual funds: the PIMCO Commodity Real Return Strategy Fund and the Oppenheimer Real Asset Fund.

With over $12 Billion in assets under management, the *PIMCO Commodity Commodity Real Return Strategy Fund* (PCRAX) is the largest commodity-oriented fund in the market. Although the fund is actively managed, it seeks to broadly mirror the performance of the Dow Jones-AIG Commodity Index (see Chapter 7 for the goods on this index). As such, the fund invests directly in commodity-linked instruments such as futures contracts, forward contracts, and options on futures. (For more on these instruments, flip on over to Chapter 9.)

Because these contracts are naturally leveraged, the fund also invests in bonds and other fixed-income securities to act as a collateral to the commodity instruments. This fund offers three classes of shares — A, B, and C — and I encourage you to examine each class carefully in order to choose the best one for you. For example, if you invest in Class A shares, there is a minimum investment amount of $5000, a front load of 5.5 percent, and an expense ratio of 1.24 percent. However, when you invest in Class B shares, there is no front load, although there is a deferred sales charge of 5 percent and an expense ratio of 1.99 percent.

With a little under $2 Billion in assets, the *Oppenheimer Real Asset Fund* (QRAAX) is considerably smaller than the PIMCO fund. It tracks the performance of the Goldman Sachs Commodity Index, an index that tracks a broad basket of 24 commodities. (I encourage you to read Chapter 7 for more on commodity indexes.)

With $1000 as its minimum investment requirement, Oppenheimer requires a little less capital upfront than PIMCO's fund. It offers five classes of shares (A, B, C, N, and Y), Class A being the most popular among average individual investors. Class A shares have no deferred sales charge, although they have a front load of 5.75 percent and an expense ratio of 1.32 percent. So even though you need less initial capital to invest in the Oppenheimer fund, it is slightly more expensive than the PIMCO fund because of the front load charges and its expense ratio.

Although Oppenheimer and PIMCO offer the two most popular commodity funds, a number of other firms are starting to offer similar products to satisfy the growing demand from investors for funds that have wide exposure to the commodities markets. Two newcomers to the market are the *Merrill Lynch Real Investment* (MDCDX) and the *Credit Suisse Commodity Return Strategy Fund* (CRSCX). As more investors seek exposure to commodities, expect more funds of this nature to crop up in the future. This is good news because you have more funds to choose from!

To find out more about commodity mutual funds, a very useful tool is the Morningstar Web site (www.morningstar.com). This is an all-around excellent resource for investors and includes lots of information related to commodity mutual funds, such as the latest news, updates, load charges, expense ratios, and other key data. It also uses a helpful five star ratings system to rate mutual funds.

Examining Exchange Traded Funds

Driven by a growing demand for commodities by the investor community, many financial institutions are now offering the commodities *Exchange Traded Fund,* or ETF. This new breed of fund allows you to buy into a fund that offers the diversification inherent in a mutual fund, with the added benefit of being able to trade that fund like a regular stock, giving you the powerful combination of diversification and liquidity.

Unlike a regular mutual fund, where the Net Asset Value is generally calculated at the end of the trading day, the ETF allows you to trade throughout the day. Furthermore, you can go both long and short the ETF, something you can't do with regular mutual funds. (For more on going long and short, turn a few pages to Chapter 9.)

The first commodity ETF in the United States was launched by Deutsche Bank in February 2006. The *Deutsche Bank Commodity Index Tracking Fund* (AMEX: DBC) is listed on the American Stock and Options Exchange (AMEX) and tracks the Deutsche Bank Liquid Commodity Index (DBLCI). The DBLCI in turn tracks a basket of six liquid commodities: light sweet crude oil (35%), heating oil (20%), gold (10%), aluminum (12.5%), corn (11.25%), and wheat (11.25%).

The DBC ETF is structured as a Commodity Pool Operator (CPO), and the fund invests directly in commodity futures contracts. (Check out the section, "Jumping into a commodity pool.") In order to capture additional yields, the energy contracts are rolled monthly, while the rest of the contracts are rolled on an annual basis. (Chapter 9 gives you more on rolling futures contracts.) The fund also invests in fixed income products, including the 3-month Treasury bill. This provides an additional yield for you as an investor. With an expense ratio of 1.5 percent, it is a reasonably priced investment.

One of the downsides of investing in ETFs is that they can be fairly volatile because they track derivative instruments that trade in the futures markets. A downside of the DBC specifically is that it tracks a basket of only six commodities. However, more commodity ETFs are in the pipeline that will offer even greater diversification benefits. While writing this book, a number of ETFs that track individual commodities have launched.

Here is a list of some of these recent commodity ETFs:

- ✔ **United States Oil Fund (AMEX: USO):** The *Unites States Oil Fund* (USO) is an ETF that seeks to mirror the performance of the *West Texas Intermediate* (WTI) crude oil futures contract on the New York Mercantile Exchange (NYMEX). Although the ETF doesn't reflect the movement of the WTI contract tick by tick, it does a good job of broadly mirroring its performance. It's a good way to get exposure to crude oil without going through the futures markets.

- ✔ **streetTRACKS Gold Shares (AMEX: GLD):** This ETF seeks to mirror the performance of the price of gold on a daily basis. The fund actually holds physical gold in vaults located in secure locations to provide investors with the ability to get exposure to physical gold without actually hold gold bullion.

- ✔ **iShares Silver Trust (AMEX: SLV):** This is the first ever ETF to track the performance of the price of physical silver. Like the gold ETF, the silver ETF holds actual physical silver in vaults. This is a safe way to invest in the silver markets without going through the futures or physical markets.

Mastering MLPs

If you're interested in investing in companies that are involved in the production, transformation, and distribution of commodities, one of the best ways to do so is by investing in a *Master Limited Partnership* (MLP). MLPs are a great investment because of their tax advantage and high cash payouts.

The ABCs of MLPs

MLPs are public entities that trade on public exchanges. Just like a company issues stock on an exchange, an MLP issues shares that trade on an exchange. You can get involved in an MLP by simply purchasing its shares on an exchange. This is why an MLP is also called a *Publicly Traded Partnership* (PTP).

The shares that an MLP issues are called *units,* and investors who own these units are known as *unit holders.*

Although a majority of MLPs trade on the New York Stock Exchange (NYSE), a few MLPs also trade on the Nasdaq National Market (NASDAQ) as well as on the American Stock and Options Exchange (AMEX). Make sure to browse through the section "The nuts and bolts of MLP investing" where I list a few MLPs and the exchange they trade on.

When you invest in an MLP, you are essentially investing in a public partnership. This partnership is run by a *General Partner* for his benefit and, more importantly, fort that of the *Limited Partners* (which you become when you buy MLP units). See the following sections "General Partner" and "Limited Partner."

The taxman only rings once

One of the reasons I like MLPs so much is that, unlike regular corporations, they're only taxed once. Many publicly traded companies are subject to double taxation: They're taxed at the corporate level as well as at the shareholder (individual) level. Not so with MLPs.

Because of congressional legislation, any MLP that derives 90 percent or more of its income from activities related to the production, distribution, and transformation of commodities qualifies for this tax-exempt status.

The income that an MLP uses to qualify for tax advantages is known as *qualifying income.* If an MLP is able to prove its qualifying income, it can "pass through" its income tax-free to its shareholders, who are then responsible for paying whatever taxes are appropriate for them. This is why MLPs are sometimes referred to as "pass through entities."

Curious to see how this tax advantage plays out in the real world? Suppose you are in a 35 percent tax bracket. You invest $1 in an MLP and $1 in a corporation. The corporation would need to generate $2.20 of income to distribute $1 of after-tax profits to you. The MLP, thanks to its favorable tax treatment, would only have to generate $1.54 of income to give you back $1 of after-tax profits!

MLP structure: The method behind the madness

Kinder Morgan is one of the largest energy transportation and distribution companies in the United States. The Kinder Morgan family of companies includes three separate entities, including its successful MLP, Kinder Morgan Energy Partners, L.P. (NYSE: KMP). Kinder Morgan's MLP is managed by a General Partner called Kinder Morgan Management, LLC (NYSE: KMR), which was established to manage the MLP. The Kinder Morgan GP is in turn owned by an even larger entity: Kinder Morgan, Inc. (NYSE: KMI). So the Kinder Morgan MLP (KMP) is run by the Kinder Morgan General Partner (KMR), which is owned by Kinder Morgan, Inc. (KMI). If you're scratching you're head trying to figure out this structure, don't worry! Because of regulatory, legal, and corporate reasons, the structures of many MLPs can get pretty convoluted. Another reason for reading this book before you get started!

This tax status gives MLPs a competitive advantage over other publicly-traded entities when they compete for assets. An MLP simply does not have to generate as much cash flow as a corporation in order to distribute similar levels of after-tax income to shareholders — and this has two possible implications. First the MLP can, if it wants, afford to overpay for an asset and still generate healthy cash flows for its investors. Alternatively, it can purchase an asset at a similar price from a competing corporation but generate more cash flow to investors because of its favorable tax treatment.

MLPs are required to distribute all available cash back to unit holders on a quarterly basis. When you own an MLP, you receive a K1 tax form, which is similar to the 1099 Tax Form you would receive from a corporation.

Be sure to inform your accountant of your MLP investments in advance because most K1 Forms aren't mailed out to shareholders until February. This only gives you a few weeks to account for the MLP income in your taxes.

General partner

The *General Partner's* (GP) main responsibility is running the MLP. The GP isn't always an individual. In fact, a majority of GPs are actually other corporate entities set up for the specific purpose of running the MLP. These entities are sometimes set up in the form of corporations or Limited Liability Companies (LLCs) and are often owned by an even larger corporation.

Besides managing the MLP, the GP generally has a financial stake in the MLP itself (usually 2 percent) and is eligible to receive *Incentive Distribution Rights* (IDRs) based on performance. IDRs are a percentage of the total payout the GP gets to keep after hitting specific targets. Because the raison d'être of the MLP is to distribute cash back to its unit holders, most MLPs include incentives for the GP if and when it distributes certain levels of cash back to the LPs.

The distribution rights that an MLP grants the General Partners are disclosed in the MLP's *Partnership Agreement* with the GP. Before investing in an MLP, make sure you comb through the Partnership Agreement carefully to understand the incentive rights granted to the GP. This is important because IDRs have a direct impact on how much money you get to keep at the end of the day. The most important piece of information you should look for in the Partnership Agreement is the MLP's IDR structure.

In order to understand the MLP structure, you need to fully appreciate the degree of autonomy that the GP has in running the MLP. Here are a few things to keep in mind:

- Limited Partners have limited voting rights.
- LPs have no say in day-to-day operations, which are carried out by the General Partner.
- The GP often has no fiduciary duty to the LPs.
- An MLP is not required to hold annual meetings for unit holders.

Essentially, when you invest in an MLP, you are turning over the keys of the kingdom over to the GP. The GP exercises a high degree of control over how the MLP is run, how much cash is distributed back to the unit holders, and the general governance matters relating to the MLP. So it's a good idea to thoroughly investigate the General Partner's track record and historical performance. At the end of the day, there is little you can do if you disagree with what the GP is doing except sell your units. In this way an MLP is very different than a corporation, where as a shareholder you can attend annual meetings, issue proxy statements, and generally exercise a larger degree of control. That said, most GPs do a good job of running MLPs because it's in their best financial interest to do so.

Limited partner

Although the General Partner is responsible for managing the MLP, the Limited Partners bring in the capital that the MLP manages. In order to become a Limited Partner in an MLP, all you have to do is purchase units of that MLP on an exchange. (For more on how to do this, read the section "Getting started.") Once you purchase the MLP units, you are officially a Limited Partner in that MLP.

As a Limited Partner, you have virtually no say in how the partnership is managed, but you will get to participate in the MLP's cash flow distribution, which is probably the most important reason you want to own MLP units in the first place.

When you purchase MLP units, you can make money from two sources: quarterly cash flow distributions and appreciation of the unit price. Because units are publicly traded, they may appreciate in value as the Partnership expands and grows over time. In addition, because the MLP is obligated to distribute all available cash back to its unit holders on a quarterly basis, your units generate you quarterly income as well.

As a matter of fact, the MLP *yields* (the amount of cash distributed back to shareholders) are among the highest of any asset class, with an average yield of 6 percent. Some MLPs actually have yields as high as 10 percent! MLP yields are similar to stock dividends, except they are slightly more advantageous thanks to the favorable tax treatment they enjoy. (More on that in the following section.)

The biggest drawback of being an LP is that you don't get to make any decisions about where the Partnership is heading. You essentially transfer power over to the GP who makes all operational decisions. However, because certain incentives built into the MLP agreement, it is in the GP's own self-interest to make sure that the MLP generates as much cash flow as possible.

Cash flow is king

The reason MLPs exist in the first place is to distribute all available cash back to the MLP unit holders, which has to be done on a quarterly basis. The amount of cash distributed to each investor is determined by a number of factors:

✓ How many units the investors hold

✓ The Incentive Distribution Rights (IDRs) created for the GP

✓ The difference between distributable and discretionary cash flow

The GP is responsible for distributing cash back to the LPs proportionally to their holdings. In other words, an investor who owns 1000 units will get twice as much cash as an investor who owns 500 units in the same MLP. (But remember, this doesn't mean that the investor with the greater number of units gets to keep all of that cash — she still has to pay taxes on this income based on her tax profile.)

In order to promote the GP's efforts to increase cash flow for shareholders, many MLPs include incentives for the GP. Generally speaking, the more cash flow the GP generates back to shareholders, the more cash she gets to keep.

Although IDRs are different for each MLP, they are always based on a *tier system*. A typical IDR incentive structure for GPs increases the distribution rate to unit holders, as shown in the following table:

Distribution Tier	Dollar Distribution	LP Payout	GP Participation
Tier 1	$0.50	98%	2%
Tier 2	$1.00	85%	15%
Tier 3	$1.50	75%	25%
Tier 4	$2.00	50%	50%

Using this tier distribution system, if the GP generates $1.00 of cash flow per unit (Tier 2), the LP would get $0.85 and the GP $0.15 of that dollar. However, if the GP is able to generate $2.00 of cash flow per unit (Tier 4), he would get to keep 50 percent of that amount, or $1.00; the LP would get a smaller percentage amount (50 percent down from 85 percent) but would get a higher cash payout ($1.00) than other tiers. The GP is thus encouraged to generate as much cash flow back because he gets a higher cut of the profits. This is the incentive behind this elegant and sophisticated tiered distribution system.

The distribution of cash flow is known as *splits* because the LPs split their share of cash flow with the GP. Tier 4, where the GP participates on equal footing with the LPs, is known as a *high split*.

It is therefore in the best interest of the GP to maximize the cash flow to the investor. This is important because the GP has a lot of discretion over how much of the available cash is actually redistributed to shareholders and how much will be used for operations related to the MLP — the difference between *distributable cash flow* and *discretionary cash flow*.

Distributable cash flow

As its name implies, *distributable cash flow* describes the amount of cash that is available to redistribute to shareholders. Generally speaking, most MLPs calculate distributable cash flow using the following formula:

MLP Distributable Cash Flow =

Income + (Depreciation and Amortization) – Capital Expenditures

This is the cash available to all members of the MLP, including both the GP and the LP. To calculate how much cash is distributed back to the LPs only, use the following formula:

LP Distributable Cash Flow =

Income + (Depreciation and Amortization) – Capital Expenditures – GP Distribution

This takes into account the cash flow participation of the GP and is a more accurate indicator of how much cash will flow back to the regular investors — the LPs.

Discretionary cash flow

The GP has a lot of discretion over how much cash flow is distributed to shareholders. Although he could theoretically distribute all available cash flow back to shareholders, it's unlikely he would do so because the GP has to have cash to operate the MLP. He may need to have some cash handy to finance growth projects, acquisitions, or other investments. This cash is known as *discretionary cash flow* and — like the name implies — the GP can use it at his discretion. While distributable cash flow is a measure of how much cash could theoretically be distributed back, *actual* cash flow is calculated by factoring in discretionary cash flow. This simple equation gives you a more accurate way to calculate how much money you'll end up with in the end:

Actual Cash Flow = Distributable Cash Flow – Discretionary Cash Flow

This is the difference between how much can be paid and how much is actually paid.

The nuts and bolts of MLP investing

So how do you actually go about investing in an MLP? It's quite simple, really. Because MLPs are publicly traded, you can purchase any of them on the exchange on which it's traded by calling your broker to purchase MLP units or by buying them through an online trading account, if you have one. Either way, buying MLP units is as simple as buying stocks.

In Table 6-1, I list some MLPs along with the exchange they're traded on.

Table 6-1	Exchange Traded MLPs	
MLP Name	*Investments*	*Exchange*
Kinder Morgan (KMP)	Energy transportation, storage and distribution	NYSE
Enterprise Products (EPD)	Oil and gas pipelines, storage and drilling platforms	NYSE
Enbridge Energy (EEP)	Energy pipelines	NYSE
Alliance Resources (ARLP)	Coal production and marketing	NASDAQ

Although a majority of MLPs in the United States trade on the NYSE, a few trade on the NASDAQ as well as the AMEX.

For a complete list of MLPs, check out the Web site www.ptpcoalition.org. Although this is a lobbying group for the industry, the site includes a complete listing of all available MLPs. I also recommend checking whether your brokerage firm has published any research on MLPs you're interested in.

About 50 MLPs are publicly traded in the United States; out of these, 40 are involved in the energy industry, with a focus on storage terminals, pipelines/transportation, refining, and distribution. Remember, MLPs invest in these assets because 90 percent of their income must be from infrastructure related to the production and distribution of commodities for them to be exempt from double taxation. In addition, many MLPs invest in pipelines and other energy infrastructure because these offer steady cash flow streams, which can then be distributed back to shareholders.

Before you invest in an MLP, ask your broker the following questions:

- ✔ What's the historical payout?
- ✔ How much is cash flow?
- ✔ What is the GP's IDR?
- ✔ What are the operational activities?
- ✔ How much assets are under management?

Heads Up! Risk and MLPs

Investing in MLPs comes with a number of risks. Here's a quick list of some of those risks — so that you don't come upon any surprises when you get your K1 tax form in February:

- ✔ **Management risk:** Because as a Limited Partner you have no say in the way the business is run, you're essentially handing over control to the General Partner to manage the MLP as he or she sees fit. If you are not satisfied with the GP's performance, there's really not much you can do about it except to withdraw your money from the MLP.

- ✔ **Environmental risk:** Many MLPs operate sophisticated infrastructures such as pipelines and drilling rigs, which are often vulnerable to natural disasters such as hurricanes and earthquakes. Any of these could have a negative impact on your bottom line.

> ✔ **Terrorism risk:** MLPs' assets often include sensitive infrastructures that may be vulnerable to a terrorist attack.

> ✔ **Liquidity risk:** Because the MLP market is still fairly small compared to other assets such as stocks and bonds, you may face liquidity issues should you wish to dispose of your units. Until liquidity increases in the MLP market, you risk not finding a buyer for your units.

These are a few of the risks associated with MLPs, which is still a growing market. However, because of the beneficial structure and scope of operations of these entities, I believe they have a place in any diversified portfolio.

Relying on a Commodity Trading Advisor

If you're interested in investing in commodities through the futures markets or on a commodity exchange, getting the help of a trained professional to guide you down this path is always a good idea. One option is to hire the services of a *Commodity Trading Advisor,* or CTA. The CTA is like a traditional stockbroker who specializes in the futures markets, and she can help you open a futures account, trade futures contracts, and develop an investment strategy based on your personal financial profile.

CTAs have to pass a rigorous financial, trading, and portfolio management exam called the Series 3. Administered by the National Association of Securities Dealers (NASD), this exam tests the candidate's knowledge of the commodities markets inside and out. By virtue of passing this exam and working at a commodities firm, most CTAs have a good fundamental understanding of the futures markets. CTAs are also licensed by the Commodity Futures Trading Commission (CFTC) and registered with the National Futures Association (NFA).

Here are a few resources I've used and have found helpful in finding the right CTAs:

> ✔ www.autumngold.com
> ✔ www.barclaygrp.com
> ✔ www.iasg.com

Each CTA has his own investment approach and trading philosophy. Before you select a CTA, find out about their investment style to see whether it squares with your investment goals. You also have to decide how much of a role you want the CTA to play in your investment life. Do you want someone to actively manage your funds or simply want someone who will provide you with advice?

In order to answer these questions, you must first decide how involved you want to be in running your portfolio. If you're a hands-on kind of investor with free time to invest, you could consider investing on your own but keeping a CTA close by to answer any questions you may have.

If, on the other hand, you don't have a lot of time or in-depth knowledge of commodities and would prefer the CTA to manage your funds for you, then ask yourself a few questions to determine which CTA is right for you.

Here are some points you may want to consider when looking for a CTA:

- **Track Record:** Web sites like `Autumngold.com` and `IASG.com` rank CTAs by their historical track record. I recommend you take a look at the longest historical track record, which is the annualized return since the CTA began trading. However, it can also be useful to look at one, three, or six months returns as well as one, three, and five year annualized returns.

- **Disciplinary Actions:** The National Futures Association (NFA) maintains a comprehensive database of all registered CTAs, including a record of any disciplinary action the CTA may have faced. Make sure that the CTA you're going to be doing business with has a clean record. The NFA database that tracks CTAs is called *Background Affiliation Status Information Center* (BASIC), and you can access it through the NFA Web site at `www.nfa.futures.org/basicnet`. An additional resource is the National Association of Securities Dealers (NASD), which also maintains a comprehensive database of CTAs and other securities professionals. You can order a report on a CTA from the NASD by going to `www.nasdbrokercheck.com`.

- **Management Fee:** A majority of CTAs, like most money managers, charge you a flat management fee. The industry average is 2 percent although some CTAs, depending on their track record — may charge you higher management fees. These fees generally go towards operational expenses: paying employees, taking care of rent, mailing and printing marketing material, running a trading platform, maintaining a 1-800 number, and so on.

- **Performance Fee:** Although a large portion of the management fee goes towards running the CTA's business, the performance fee provides an incentive for the CTA to generate the highest returns possible. This is the CTA's bread and butter. Again, performance fees differ from CTA to CTA, although I've found that 20 percent seems to be a benchmark for most CTAs. Some CTAs with good track records may have higher performance fees in place, in which case you want to compare historical and actual returns among different CTAs to find the one with the highest distribution back to investors. However, if the CTA doesn't reach certain levels, then she does not get any performance fee. In other words, the CTA will only be rewarded for good performance. If she doesn't hit her numbers, then she won't get to participate in the profits.

✔ **Miscellaneous Fees:** Watch out for these fees because they can add up really quickly — just like the miscellaneous fees you get on your cell phone bill. Ever opened up your phone bill and found that miscellaneous fees have increased your bill by 10 or 15 percent or higher? Your CTA may charge you for such items such as handling express mail deliveries, check and wiring fees, night desk charges (a fee you pay if the CTA trades your account after trading hours), and maintenance fees. For example, if you don't maintain a minimum amount in your account — such as $500 — you will be charged a fee!

✔ **Margin Requirements:** If you decide to open a *margin account* (as opposed to a cash account), you are able to borrow money from your CTA to purchase securities. Buying on margin provides you with a lot of leverage (both on the upside but also on the downside), so knowing the details of the margin requirement is absolutely critical. (For more on using margin, take a look at Chapter 3.)

✔ **Minimum Investment Requirement:** Many CTAs require that you invest a minimum amount of money with them. This can be as low as $1000 and as high as $200,000. I recommend that if you're going to invest with a CTA, you invest no more than 5 to 10 percent of your investing capital with them. This will help you diversify your holding to include managed futures, but this won't come back to haunt you should the CTA perform badly. (For more on how to construct a balanced, diversified portfolio, flip to Chapter 5.)

Jumping into a Commodity Pool

Another way you can get access to the commodities futures markets is by joining a *commodity pool.* As its name suggests, it is a pool of funds that trades in the commodities futures markets. The commodity pool is managed and operated by a designated *Commodity Pool Operator* (CPO) who is licensed with the NFA and registered with the CFTC. All investors share in the profits (and losses) of the commodity pool based on how much capital they've contributed to the pool.

Investing in a commodity pool has two main advantages over opening an individual trading account with a CTA. First, because you're joining a pool with a number of different investors, your purchasing power increases significantly. You get a lot more leverage and diversification if you're trading a $1 Million account as opposed to a $10,000 account.

The second benefit, which may not seem obvious at first, is that commodity pools tend to be structured as limited partnerships. This means that, as an investor with a stake in the pool, the most you can lose is the principal you invested in the first place. Losing your entire principal may seem like a bad deal, but for the futures markets this is pretty good!

Let me explain. With an individual account, you are able purchase securities on margin. That means you can borrow funds in order to buy futures contracts. What happens if the position you entered into with the borrowed funds does the opposite of what you expected it to? Now not only have you lost your principal, but you also have to pay back your broker, who lent you the money to open the position. This means that you lose your principal and you still owe money, which is known as a *margin call*.

Now because commodity pools are registered as limited partnerships, even if the fund uses leverage to buy securities and the fund gets a margin call, you are not responsible for that margin call. Hence, the (only) capital you risk is your principal! Of course, you want to perform due diligence on the CPO to make sure that the likelihood that the pool will go bust is as small as possible!

A good place to start looking for commodity pools is the Web site www. commodities-investor.com.

Chapter 7

Track and Trade: Investing through Commodity Indexes

*I*ndexes are useful tools in the world of investing. If the act of investing were similar to driving a car, the index would be the equivalent of the speedometer — it tells you how fast the car (or the market) is going. Indexes exist for all sorts of assets: You have indexes that track the top 30 blue-chip companies in the United States (Dow Jones Industrial Average) and the 500 largest companies (S&P 500), just to name a couple.

If you want to measure the performance of commodities, you also have at your disposal indexes whose function is to track baskets of commodities. These commodity indexes can be useful for two reasons. First, you can use them as market indicators, which allows you to gauge where the commodity markets are trading as a whole. Second, because most indexes are tradable instruments (through Exchange Traded Funds and other investment vehicles), you can profit by investing directly in the index.

In this chapter, I give you the goods on commodity indexes and show you how to profit by using these powerful tools.

Checking Out Commodity Indexes

A commodity index tracks the price of a futures contract of an underlying physical commodity on a designated exchange. When you invest through one of the commodity indexes I present in this chapter, you are actually investing in the futures markets. (For more on futures contracts please read Chapter 9.)

Indexes are known as passive, long-only investments because no one is actively trading the index, and the index only tracks the long performance of a commodity. It doesn't track commodities that are *short* (a sophisticated strategy meant to profit when prices go down). For more on long and short positions, refer to Chapter 9.

Is it "indexes" or "indices"? I use the plural form "indexes" because that's the more traditional way to refer to an index in the plural. You may also run into "indices" as a plural form for index. Dow Jones, which has its own commodity index, spells the plural form of index as "indexes." On the other hand, Standard & Poor's, which also has a commodity index, spells the plural form as "indices." At the end of the day, "indexes" and "indices" refer to the same thing!

What's the use of an index?

Using commodity indexes is a good way to determine where the commodity markets are heading. Just like stock indexes allow you to identify broad market movements (which allows you to implement and update your investment strategy accordingly), commodity indexes provide you with a way to measure the broad movements of the commodities markets.

In essence, a commodity index gives you a snapshot of the current state of the commodities market. This means you can use an index in one of three ways:

- **Benchmark:** You can use a commodity index to compare the performance of commodities as an asset class with the performance of other asset classes, such as stocks and bonds.

- **Indicator:** You can use the commodity index as an indicator of economic activity, possible inflationary pressures, and as a measure of the state of global economic production.

- **Investment vehicle:** Because a commodity index tracks the performance of specific futures contracts, you can replicate the performance of the index by trading the contracts it tracks. You can invest both directly (buying the contracts) and indirectly (mutual funds) in a commodity index, which I discuss in depth in the following section.

So how do I make money using an index?

You have a number of methods at your disposal to invest through a commodity index. There are five widely followed commodity indexes to choose from (which I cover in the section "Cataloguing the Indexes"), and each one can be tracked and traded in different ways.

Here are a few ways you can invest through a commodity index:

- ✔ **Owning the futures contracts:** One of the most direct ways of tracking the performance of an index is to own the contracts the index tracks. In order to do this, you must have a *futures account*. (Please refer to Chapter 6 to find out how to open a futures account.)

- ✔ **Investing with a third party manager:** A number of money managers use commodity indexes as the basis of their investment strategy. Some of these vehicles include mutual funds, commodity pools, and commodity trading advisors. (For more on selecting the right manager, make sure you read Chapter 6.)

- ✔ **Owning futures contracts of the index:** A few commodity indexes have futures contracts that track their performance. When you buy the futures contract of the index, it's similar to buying all the commodity futures contracts the index trades!

- ✔ **Exchange Traded Funds:** ETFs, as they're known on Wall Street, are a fairly new breed of investments that track the performance of a fund through the convenience of trading a stock. This is a popular alternative for folks who don't want to trade futures. (Make sure to explore the benefits and drawbacks of ETFs in Chapter 6.)

I've listed only a few ways you can get exposure to commodity indexes. As commodities become more popular with the investing community, expect to see more ways to get access to indexes. To keep track of all the new developments in index investing, make sure to keep checking my Web site at www.commodities-investor.com.

From Head to Toes: Anatomy of a Commodity Index

As an investor interested in making money through index investing, you have five commodity indexes at your disposal. Although the composition and structure of every index is different, their aim is the same — to track a basket of commodities. Before you get into the specific commodity indexes, here are some things you should look out for when you're shopping for an index:

✔ **Components:** Each index follows a specific methodology to determine which commodities are part of the index. Some indexes such as the GSCI (see the following section) include commodities based on their global *production value;* others such as the DBLCI include commodities based on their *liquidity* and *representational value* of a component class: For example, picking gold to represent metals and oil as a representative of the energy market.

✔ **Weightings:** Some indexes follow a *production-weighted methodology,* where weights are assigned to each commodity based on its proportional production in the world. Other indexes choose *component weightings* based on the liquidity of the commodity's futures contract. In addition, some weightings are fixed over a predetermined period of time, while others fluctuate to reflect changes in actual production values.

✔ **Rolling methodology:** Because the index's purpose is to track the performance of commodities and not take actual delivery of the commodity, the futures contracts that the index tracks must be *rolled* over from the *current month contract* to the *front month contract* (the upcoming trading month). Because this rolling process provides a *roll yield* (a yield that results from the price differential between the current and front months), you should examine each index's policy on rolling. You can find this information in the index brochure.

✔ **Rebalancing features:** Every index reviews its components and their weightings on a regular basis in order to maintain an index that reflects actual values in the global commodities markets. While some indexes rebalance annually, others rebalance more frequently. Before you invest in an index, find out when it is rebalanced and what methodology it uses to rebalance.

Although each index is constructed differently, all indexes have to follow certain criteria to determine whether a commodity will be included in the index:

✔ **Tradability:** The commodities have to be traded on a designated exchange and have a futures contract assigned to them. Steel, for example, while a crucial commodity, is not represented by an index because there are no futures contracts for steel.

✔ **Deliverability:** The contracts that go into the index must be for an underlying commodity that has the potential to be delivered. This eliminates the inclusion of futures contracts that represent financial instruments such as economic indicators, interest rates, and other "financials."

✔ **Liquidity:** The market for the underlying commodity has to be liquid enough to allow investors to move in and out of their positions without facing liquidity crunches, such as not being able to find a buyer or seller.

Cataloguing the Indexes

In the following sections, I go through each of the five major commodity indexes you can invest in. Each one is unique, so you'll be sure to find one that best suits your needs.

Goldman Sachs Commodity Index

The *Goldman Sachs Commodity Index* (GSCI) is one of the most closely watched indexes in the market. Launched in 1992 by the investment bank of the same name, it tracks the performance of 24 commodity futures contracts. The GSCI is the most heavily tracked index. As of 2006, investors poured $50 Billion to track the GSCI.

The GSCI is a production-weighted index because it assigns different weights to different commodities proportional to their current global production quantity, a method known as *global production weighting*. As such, crude oil is assigned more weight than cocoa in the index because this reflects actual world production figures — there's a lot more crude oil produced in the world than cocoa.

In order to calculate the contract production weight of each commodity (the percentage a commodity assigned to the index), the GSCI takes the average of that commodity's global production over the previous five years. The main advantage of using a five-year average as opposed to a one-year average is that the former takes into account any statistical aberrations related to the production of the specific commodity. For example, if a natural disaster affected the production of a particular commodity during one year, the five-year average would reflect that change but still maintain a heavy weighting on that commodity because that event was an aberration.

In Figure 7-1, I list the main component classes that the GSCI tracks.

Notice that the bulk of the GSCI is tied to energy contracts because global commodity production is dominated by energy products.

The GSCI is currently overweight energy, but this does not mean that this won't change in the future. If energy production decreases on a global scale, the index will reflect this change. The index reviews its weightings on an annual basis, reassigning weights to the index in January, so this weighting is likely to change year after year.

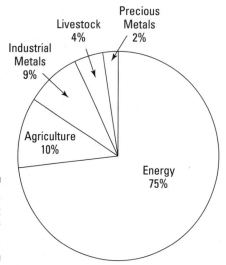

GSCI

Figure 7-1:
Component
classes of
the GSCI.

Table 7-1 lists the actual commodity futures contracts that make up the GSCI along with their correspondent weighting in the index. I also list the exchange on which they trade in case you want to purchase these contracts.

Table 7-1	GSCI Components	
Commodity	*Exchange*	*Weight*
Chicago Wheat	CBOT	2.47%
Kansas Wheat	KBOT	0.90%
Corn	CBOT	2.46%
Soybeans	CBOT	1.77%
Coffee	CSC	0.80%
Sugar	CSC	1.30%
Cocoa	CSC	0.23%
Cotton	NYC	0.99%
Lean Hogs	CME	2.00%

Commodity	Exchange	Weight
Live Cattle	CME	2.88%
Feeder Cattle	CME	0.78%
Heating Oil	NYMEX	8.16%
Gas-oil	ICE	4.41%
Unleaded Gas	NYMEX	7.84%
WTI Crude Oil	NYMEX	30.05%
Brent Crude Oil	ICE	13.81%
Natural Gas	NYMEX	10.30%
Aluminum	LME	2.88%
Copper	LME	2.37%
Lead	LME	0.29%
Nickel	LME	0.82%
Zinc	LME	0.54%
Gold	COMEX	1.73%
Silver	COMEX	0.20%

Because futures contracts have an expiration date, they must be rolled on a regular basis. Contracts such as the crude oil futures are rolled on a monthly basis because they expire every month. However, some contracts only have contract expiration dates during certain months of the year. (I discuss monthly contract tradability in Chapter 9.) These contracts, such as the contracts for cotton or gold, are rolled according to the available monthly contract trade.

The GSCI has a futures contract that tracks the index's performance. You can buy this contract on the Chicago Mercantile Exchange (CME). If you have a futures trading account (you can find out how to open one in Chapter 6), you can simply buy this contract to get direct access to the GSCI. The ticker symbol for the GSCI on the CME is GI.

Another way to access the GSCI is to invest in a managed fund that tracks its performance. One such fund is the Oppenheimer Real Asset Fund (which I discuss in Chapter 6). The Oppenheimer fund mirrors the performance of the GSCI. However, as a general rule, managed funds don't identically replicate the performance of an index because you have to take into consideration external factors such as loads, management fees, and other expenses related to the management of the fund.

Reuters/Jefferies Commodity Research Bureau Index

Created in 1957 as the Commodity Research Bureau's official commodity tracking index, this index is the oldest commodity index in the world. The original index received its most recent makeover in 2005 when it was renamed the *Reuters/Jefferies Commodity Research Bureau Index* (CRB) — quite a mouthful, isn't it!

The CRB index is widely followed by institutional investors and economists; out of all the indexes, it is perhaps the most widely used as an economic benchmark, although the GSCI and the DJ/AIGCI (introduced in the next section) are also widely used as references.

The CRB index has performed well since 2002. Table 7-2 lists the total annual returns of the CRB index.

Table 7-2	Annual Returns of the CRB Index, 2002 to 2005
Year	*Total return*
2002	23%
2003	8.9%
2004	11.2%
2005	16.9%

The CRB index tracks all the major commodity component classes, which you can see in Figure 7-2.

**Reuters/Jefferies CRB Index
Component Classes**

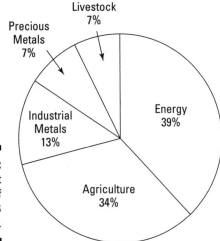

Livestock
7%

Precious
Metals
7%

Industrial
Metals
13%

Energy
39%

Agriculture
34%

Figure 7-2:
Component
classes of
the CRB
index.

The CRB Index currently tracks a basket of 19 commodities, which are selected based on their liquidity and production value. This index is quite unique because it is the only index that uses a *tiered methodology* of distributing weights to commodities. This hybrid approach gives a production value weight to energy products while assigning fixed weights to other commodities. The components and their weightings are reviewed on an annual basis. I list the index tiers along with the commodities the index tracks in Table 7-3.

Table 7-3	CRB Index Tiers and Components		
Tiers	*Commodity*	*Weight*	*Exchange*
Tier I	WTI Crude Oil	23%	NYMEX
	Heating Oil	5%	NYMEX
	Unleaded Gas	5%	NYMEX
Tier II	Natural Gas	6%	NYMEX
	Corn	6%	CBOT
	Soybeans	6%	CBOT

(continued)

Table 7-3 *(continued)*

Tiers	Commodity	Weight	Exchange
	Live Cattle	6%	CME
	Gold	6%	COMEX
	Aluminum	6%	LME
	Copper	6%	COMEX
Tier III	Sugar	5%	NYBOT
	Cotton	5%	NYBOT
	Cocoa	5%	NYBOT
	Coffee	5%	NYBOT
Tier IV	Nickel	1%	LME
	Wheat	1%	CBOT
	Lean Hogs	1%	CME
	Orange Juice	1%	NYBOT
	Silver	1%	COMEX

Dow Jones-AIG Commodity Index

With approximately $25 Billion tracking it (2006 figures), the *Dow Jones-AIG Commodity Index* (DJ-AIGCI) is one of the most widely followed indexes in the market. The DJ-AIGCI places a premium on liquidity but also chooses commodities based on their production value.

The DJ-AIGCI is one of the few indexes that places a *floor* and *ceiling* on individual commodities and component classes. For example, no component class (such as energy or metals) is allowed to account for more than 33 percent of the index weighting. Another rule is that no single commodity may make up less than 2 percent of the index's total weighting. The DJ-AIGCI follows these rules in order to ensure that all commodities are well represented while at the same time making sure that no commodity or component class dominates the index.

I list in Figure 7-3 the component classes of the DJ-AIGCI.

DJ-AIGCI Component Classes

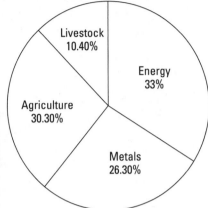

Figure 7-3:
Component classes of the DJ-AIGCI.

The component weightings are rebalanced on an annual basis. Currently the index tracks a group of 19 publicly traded commodities, which I list in Table 7-4.

Table 7-4	DJ-AIGCI Components
Commodity	*Weight*
Natural Gas	12.32%
WTI Crude Oil	12.78%
Unleaded Gas	4.05%
Heating Oil	3.84%
Live Cattle	6.09%
Lean Hogs	4.35%
Wheat	4.77%
Corn	5.87%
Soybeans	7.76%
Soybean Oil	2.76%
Aluminum	6.90%

(continued)

Table 7-4 *(continued)*

Commodity	Weight
Copper	5.88%
Zinc	2.70%
Nickel	2.66%
Gold	6.22%
Silver	2.00%
Sugar	2.96%
Cotton	3.16%
Coffee	2.93%

One way to access the commodities listed in the DJ-AIGCI is by investing in a mutual fund that tracks it. You're in luck because one of the largest commodity mutual funds, the *PIMCO Commodity Real Return Fund*, uses the DJ-AIGCI as its benchmark. Therefore you get a very high correlation between the performance of the index with that of the fund. Make sure to take a look at Chapter 6 where I present the PIMCO fund.

Another way to access the DJ-AIGCI is through the Chicago Board of Trade (CBOT). The CBOT offers a futures contract that tracks the performance of the DJ-AIGCI. This is very similar to the GSCI contract on the CME. The ticker symbol for the DJ-AIGCI on the CBOT is AI.

Rogers International Commodities Index

With a grand total of 35 listed commodities, the *Rogers International Commodities Index* (RICI) tracks the most commodities among the different indexes. The RICI is the brainchild of famed commodities investor Jim Rogers, who launched the index in order to achieve the widest exposure to commodities.

The RICI, like the other commodity indexes, includes traditional commodities such as crude oil, natural gas, and silver. However, it also includes some of the most exotic commodities you can think of, such as silk and adzuki beans! If you're looking for the broadest exposure to commodities, the RICI is probably your best bet.

The RICI was launched in 1998 and has performed extremely well. Between 1998 and 2006 its total return was 265.58 percent.

The RICI is a production-weighted index, assigning weightings to component classes based on their actual global production value and rebalancing the index every December. I list the main component classes of the RICI in Figure 7-4.

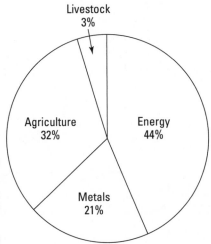

RICI Component Classes

Figure 7-4:
Component
classes of
the RICI.

I list the RICI components and their index weighting in Table 7-5.

Table 7-5	RICI Components
Commodity	*Weight*
Crude Oil	35%
Wheat	7%
Corn	4.75%
Aluminum	4%
Copper	4%
Cotton	4%
Heating Oil	3.75%

(continued)

Table 7-5 *(continued)*

Commodity	Weight
Unleaded Gas	3.75%
Natural Gas	3%
Soybeans	3%
Gold	3%
Live Cattle	2%
Coffee	2%
Zinc	2%
Silver	2%
Lead	2%
Soybean Oil	2%
Sugar	2%
Platinum	1.80%
Live Hogs	1%
Cocoa	1%
Nickel	1%
Tin	1%
Rubber	1%
Lumber	1%
Soybean Meal	0.75%
Canola	0.67%
Orange Juice	0.66%
Rice	0.50%
Adzuki Beans	0.50%
Oats	0.50%
Palladium	0.30%
Barley	0.27%
Silk	0.05%

If you want to invest in the RICI, you can do so through the *RICI TRAKRS* offered by the Chicago Mercantile Exchange (CME). *TRAKRS* (pronounced trackers) are similar to futures contracts offered by the CME. To trade the RICI TRAKRS on the CME, use the ticker symbol RCI.

Deutsche Bank Liquid Commodity Index

Launched in 2003 by Deutsche Bank, the *Deutsche Bank Liquid Commodity Index* (DBLCI) is the new kid on the index block and has the most distinct approach to tracking commodity futures contracts among all the commodity indexes. The DBLCI tracks just six commodity contracts: two in energy, two in metals, and two in agricultural products. Figure 7-5 shows the weighting of each of these component classes.

DBLCI Component Classes

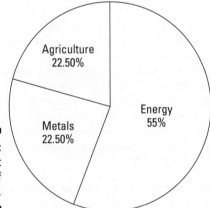

Figure 7-5: Component classes of the DBLCI.

The weighting of the DBLCI is done at the end of the year and it seeks to reflect global production values. Hence, like the other production-weighted indexes (such as the GSCI), it's also overweight energy because this reflects the current production values in the world.

Table 7-6 lists the commodities that make up the component classes of the DBLCI.

Table 7-6	DBLCI Components	
Commodity	*Exchange*	*Weight*
WTI Crude Oil	NYMEX	35%
Heating Oil	NYMEX	20%
Aluminum	LME	12.5%
Corn	CBOT	11.25%
Wheat	CBOT	11.25%
Gold	COMEX	10%

With so few underlying commodities, you may be asking yourself whether the DBLCI offers a broad and diverse enough exposure to the commodities markets. One of the advantages of the DBLCI is that it chooses only the most *liquid* and *representative* commodities in their respective component classes.

For example, the WTI Crude Oil contract is indicative of where the energy complex is moving. So instead of including unleaded gas, propane, natural gas, and other energy contracts, the DBLCI relies on WTI as a benchmark to achieve representation in the energy market as a whole. This is a unique approach in the world of commodity indexes that has its merits because the index is able to track the commodities markets by only monitoring the performance of a small number of commodities. This "less is more" approach is also helpful for individual investors who prefer to track indexes by buying the index contracts: Instead of buying 19 contracts, you only have to buy six contracts to mirror the index's performance.

The energy contracts of the DBLCI are rolled on a monthly basis, while the metal and agricultural contracts are rolled on an annual basis.

The DBLCI is the first commodity index to have its performance tracked by an Exchange Traded Fund (ETF). You can buy the ETF that will provide you with exposure to the DBLCI on the American Stock and Options Exchange (AMEX). This fund, whose ticker symbol is DBC, is also managed by Deutsche Bank. I discuss this ETF in depth in Chapter 6.

Which Index Should You Use?

With so many indexes to choose from, how do you decide which one to follow? Generally speaking, the Goldman Sachs Commodity Index (GSCI) is the most tracked index in the market — the one that has the most funds following, or tracking, its performance. As of 2006, over $55 Billion in assets track its performance, and this number is growing monthly. It is pretty popular with institutional and, increasingly, individual investors. It is perhaps the easiest one to follow because you can track it by investing through the Oppenheimer Real Asset Fund as well as through the GSCI futures contracts on the Chicago Mercantile Exchange (CME).

Although the GSCI is the most widely tracked index, the most closely *watched* index (there is a difference) is the Reuters/Jefferies CRB Index. The CRB Index is used as a global benchmark for what the commodities markets are doing. As such it is the equivalent of the Dow Jones Industrial Average in the commodity world. When investors want to gauge where the commodity markets are heading, they usually turn to the CRB Index. In addition, when analysts or journalists discuss the performance of the commodities markets, they usually make reference to the CRB Index.

For investors who don't trade futures or don't feel comfortable investing in an index through a mutual fund, you can always choose to invest in an index through ETFs, which offer the convenience of trading complex financial instruments with the ease of trading stocks. Currently, the DBLCI is the only index tracked by an ETF, the DBC. Buying the DBC is as simple as logging into your brokerage account or calling your broker and placing an order for the number of DBC units you want to purchase. An ETF is in the works to track the GSCI, and I expect to see more ETFs that track these commodity indexes as more investors seek to get access to this area of the market.

Chapter 8

Understanding How Commodities Exchanges Work

*T*he first commodity exchanges appeared in the United States during the 1800s, and their role was to match buyers and sellers interested in acquiring and selling commodities. The first traded commodities included wheat, butter, milk, cheese, and other agricultural products. Commodity exchanges soon evolved from simple places of commerce to highly regulated marketplaces where prices were established for all sorts of commodities.

The first image that usually comes to mind when you think of a commodity exchange is a group of brokers standing in a large circle, wearing bright-colored jackets, and shouting at each other while making funny gestures. If you've ever visited or seen television footage of a commodity exchange, you've probably wondered what all the fuss was about. Why are these guys yelling? What are they saying? Can anyone actually hear anything down there anyway?

Behind all this apparent chaos is a very rational, efficient, and orderly process that is responsible for setting global benchmark prices for the world's most important commodities. The prices established in the exchanges have a direct impact on our lives, from the price we pay to fill our gas tanks to how much we pay to heat our homes.

In this chapter, I give you a tour of a typical commodity exchange, explain to you the role that exchanges play in global capital markets, and introduce you to some of the players who are part of this fascinating world. I also examine some of the products traded on the exchanges and show you how you can get involved in the buying and selling of exchange-traded commodities.

Why Do We Have Commodities Exchanges, Anyway?

Whether you are an individual seeking to hedge commodity prices for the future or an investor interested in capturing price discrepancies and fluctuations in the global commodity markets, the commodity exchange will help you achieve your goals.

Commodity exchanges provide investors and traders with the opportunity to invest in commodities by trading futures contracts, options on futures, and other derivative products. (See Chapter 9 for more on these products.) By their very nature, these products are extremely sophisticated financial instruments used by only the savviest investors and the most experienced traders.

Although independent traders, like you and me, can and do trade the futures markets, the majority of players in the futures markets are large commercial entities who use the futures markets for price hedging purposes. For example, Hershey Foods Corporation is an active participant in cocoa futures because it wants to hedge against the price risk of cocoa, a primary input for making its chocolates. If you decide to trade cocoa futures contracts (covered in Chapter 19), you should remember that you're up against some large and experienced market players.

At the end of the day, the commodity futures exchanges are your gateway to the futures markets; in fact, they *are* the commodity futures markets. However, because of the fierce competition in these markets and because of the complexity of exchange traded products, you should only trade directly in the commodity futures markets if you have an iron clad grasp of the technical aspects of the markets and have a rock solid understanding of the market fundamentals. If you don't have either, I would recommend staying out of these markets because you could be subjecting yourself to disastrous losses. That said, you can hire a trained professional with experience trading commodity futures to do the trading for you, which I cover in the following sections and also in depth in Chapter 6.

Commodity futures exchanges serve a very important role in establishing global benchmark prices for crucial commodities such as crude oil, gold, copper, orange juice, and coffee. The exchanges are crucial for both producers and consumers of commodities. Producers, who use commodities as inputs to create finished goods, want to shelter themselves from the daily fluctuations of global commodity prices. Producers may use the commodity exchange to lock in prices for these raw materials for fixed periods of time using futures contracts (more on these in Chapter 9). This process is known as *hedging*. Similarly, traders may use the commodity exchange to profit from these fluctuations. This is sometimes known as *speculation*.

Whether you are an individual seeking to hedge commodity prices for the future or an investor interested in capturing price discrepancies and fluctuations in the global commodity markets, the commodity exchange will help you achieve your goals. There are a number of commodity exchanges operating worldwide, which specialize in all sorts of commodities. In the following sections, I identify the major commodity exchanges and list the commodities traded in them.

Identifying the Major Commodity Exchanges

A number of commodity exchanges operate worldwide and specialize in all sorts of commodities. Although you have some overlap among some of the commodities the exchanges offer — for example gold contracts are traded on both the *New York Mercantile Exchange* (NYMEX) and the *Chicago Board of Trade* (CBOT) — most exchanges offer unique contracts. As such, every exchange specializes in certain commodities. For instance, the NYMEX focuses on providing investors with products to trade energy and metals; it has contracts for crude oil, propane, and heating oil as well as gold, silver, and palladium.

The *New York Board of Trade* (NYBOT), on the other hand, focuses primarily on tropical or "soft" commodities such as coffee, cocoa, sugar, and frozen concentrated orange juice (covered in Chapter 19). The *Chicago Mercantile Exchange* (CME) offers a wide range of products but specializes in livestock, offering contracts for live cattle, feeder cattle, lean hogs, and frozen pork bellies.

Most commodities in the United States are only traded on one exchange. The feeder cattle contract is only traded on the CME, and frozen concentrated orange juice is only traded on the NYBOT. However, certain commodities are traded on more than one exchange. For example, the WTI crude oil contract is traded on both the NYMEX and the *Intercontinental Exchange* (ICE). In this case, you want to trade the most liquid market. You can find out where the most liquid market for a commodity is by consulting the *Commodity Futures Trading Commission* (CFTC), which keeps information on all the exchanges and their products. I discuss the CFTC and other market regulatory organizations in this section as well.

The main commodity exchanges in the United States are located in New York and Chicago, with a few other exchanges in other parts of the country. In Table 8-1, I list the major commodity exchanges in the United States along with the commodities traded in each one.

Table 8-1	The Major U.S. Commodity Exchanges	
Exchange Name	*Web site*	*Commodities Traded*
Chicago Board of Trade (CBOT)	www.cbot.com	Corn, Ethanol, Gold, Oats, Rice, Silver, Soybeans, Wheat
Chicago Mercantile Exchange (CME)	www.cme.com	Butter, Milk, Feeder Cattle, Frozen Pork Bellies, Lean Hogs, Live Cattle, Lumber
Intercontinental Exchange* (ICE)	www.theice.com	Crude Oil, Electricity, Natural Gas
Kansas City Board of Trade (KCBT)	www.kcbt.com	Wheat, Natural Gas
Minneapolis Grain Exchange (MGE)	www.mgex.com	Corn, Soybeans, Wheat
New York Board of Trade (NYBOT)	www.nybot.com	Cocoa, Coffee, Cotton, Ethanol, Frozen Concentrated Orange Juice, Sugar
New York Mercantile Exchange(NYMEX)	www.nymex.com	Aluminum, Copper, Crude Oil, Electricity, Gasoline, Gold, Heating Oil, Natural Gas, Palladium, Platinum, Propane, Silver

* The Intercontinental Exchange is one of the only exchanges without a physical trading floor — all orders are routed and matched electronically. It is in fact one of the only all-electronic exchanges.

Note: *This is only a small sampling of the commodities that these exchanges offer. The CME, for example, offers over 100 futures products that track everything from milk and feeder cattle to non-farm payrolls and currencies. I recommend visiting the exchange websites for a comprehensive listing of their product offerings.*

Fighting back fraud

The first contracts began trading on U.S. commodity exchanges in the middle of the 19th century. In the early part of the 20th century, the U.S. government decided that these exchanges should be regulated in order to prevent market fraud and abuse. So in 1936, Congress passed the Commodity Exchange Act (CEA), providing federal oversight and regulation of all commodity exchanges operating in the United States. In 2000, Congress passed the Commodity Futures Modernization Act (CFMA) to overhaul the CEA and adapt it to the modern financial marketplace.

It's a crude world: Reading between the lines

Have you ever picked up the newspaper and read that crude oil prices reached a new high? Have you ever asked yourself how these prices are determined? Well, they're determined on an exchange. The global benchmark for crude oil prices is a type of crude traded on the NYMEX, and it's called West Texas Intermediate (WTI). WTI comes from where its name suggests — West Texas. WTI is a light, sweet crude oil, and it's a benchmark because light, sweet crude is preferred by refiners to heavy, sour crude since they can get a lot more products out of it. (I take an in-depth look at the different types of crude oil in Chapter 12.)

Because the WTI is traded on the NYMEX as a futures contract, the price you read in the newspaper usually refers to the front month delivery of the contract. (For more on futures delivery dates please turn to Chapter 9.) So when you read that oil is now at $62 a barrel, this refers to WTI crude oil traded on the NYMEX for next month's delivery! This is very different than the current *spot market* price — the price you would pay if you were to purchase a barrel of oil right away, or on the *spot.* Additionally, the North Sea Brent — another light, sweet crude — which trades in London on the International Petroleum Exchange (which is now part of the Intercontinental Exchange), is used as a secondary global benchmark.

The technical name for a commodity exchange is *Designated Contract Market* (DCM). DCM is a designation handed by the Commodity Futures Trading Commission (CFTC) to exchanges that offer commodity products to the public. (More on the CFTC in the following section.)

If an exchange does not have the designation DCM, stay away from it!

Commodity exchanges are responsible for setting global benchmark prices for some of the world's most important commodities. As a result, the amount of liquidity they generate is enormous. For example, more than $1.5 Trillion worth of contracts are traded in the commodity exchanges mentioned previously — each day!

Although the bulk of commodity trading is done in the United States — the largest consumer market of commodities — there are commodity exchanges located in other countries. If you're in the United States, you may want to consider investing in overseas exchanges for liquidity purposes. For example, aluminum futures contracts are offered on both the American NYMEX as well as the British *London Metal Exchange* (LME). However, the aluminum contract in the LME is more liquid, so you could get a better price by buying aluminum contracts in London as opposed to New York. In Table 8-2, I list some of these international commodity exchanges.

Table 8-2	International Commodity Exchanges	
Exchange Name	*Country*	*Commodities Traded*
European Energy Exchange	Germany	Electricity
London Metal Exchange	United Kingdom	Aluminum, Copper, Lead, Nickel, Tin, Zinc
Natural Gas Exchange	Canada	Natural Gas
Tokyo Commodity Exchange	Japan	Aluminum, Crude Oil, Gasoline, Gold, Kerosene, Palladium, Platinum, Rubber, Silver

Commodity exchanges are under strict oversight in order to protect all market participants and to ensure transparency in the exchanges. Here are the main regulatory organizations that have oversight of commodity exchanges in the United States.

✔ **Commodity Futures Trading Commission (CFTC):** The CFTC is a federal regulatory agency created by Congress in 1974. Its main purpose is to regulate the commodity markets and to protect all market participants from fraud, manipulation, and abusive practices. Any exchange that conducts business with the public must be registered with the CFTC. You can visit their Web site at www.cftc.gov.

✔ **National Futures Association (NFA):** The NFA is the industry's self-regulatory body. It conducts audits, launches investigations to root out corrupt practices in the industry, and enforces the rules relating to the trading of commodities on the various exchanges. It also regulates every single firm or individual who conducts business with the you as an investor — including floor traders and brokers, futures commission merchants, commodity trading advisors, commodity pool operators, and introducing brokers.

You can check out the work of the NFA, as well as research individual commodities professionals, at the NFA Web site: www.nfa.futures.org.

Ready, Set, Invest: Opening an Account and Placing Orders

When you decide you're ready to start trading exchange-traded products, you have to choose the most suitable way for you to do so. Unless you're a member of an exchange or have a seat on the exchange floor, you have to open a trading account with a commodity broker who's licensed to conduct business on behalf of clients at the exchange.

The technical term for a commodity broker is a *Futures Commission Merchant* (FCM). The FCM is licensed to solicit and execute commodity orders and accept payments for this service.

Before choosing a commodity broker who will handle your account, you have to perform a thorough and comprehensive analysis of their trading platform. You want to get as much information as possible about the firm and its activities. A few things you should consider are firm history, firm clients, licensing information, trading platform, regulatory data, and employee information. Chapter 6 gives you a detailed analysis of the criteria you want to use to select a broker, so check it out.

Choosing the right account

After you select a commodity brokerage firm you're comfortable with, it's time to open an account and start trading! You can choose from a number of different brokerage accounts. Most firms will offer you at least two types of accounts, depending on the level of control you want to exercise over the account.

If you feel confident about your trading abilities, then a *self-directed account* where you call the shots is the most suitable account for you. On the other hand, if you don't feel comfortable calling the shots, then having a professional make the trading decisions for you through a *managed account* is your best bet. In this section, I go through the pros and cons of self-directed and managed accounts so you can determine which one is best for you.

Self-directed account

If you feel comfortable with exchange-traded products and are ready to take direct control of your account, then consider opening a self-directed account, also known as a *non-discretionary individual account.* This means that you take matters into your own hands and make all the trading decisions. If you have a good understanding of market fundamentals and want to get direct access to commodity exchange products, then a self-directed account is for you.

Before you open a self-directed account, talk to a few commodity brokers because each firm offers different account features. This is similar to buying a car. You want to test drive as many cars as possible to get the biggest bang for your buck. Same thing when you're opening a commodities trading account.

Specifically, ask about any minimum capital requirements the firm has. Some commodity brokers require that you invest a minimum amount of $10,000 or more. You also want to become familiar with account maintenance fees and with the commission scale the firm uses. Knowing this information upfront will save you a lot of heartache down the road. After you gather all the relevant information and open your account, you're finally ready to start trading and placing orders!

Managed account

In a managed account, you're essentially transferring the responsibility of making all buying and selling decisions over to a trained professional.

Open a managed account if:

- ✔ You don't follow the markets on a regular (i.e. daily) basis but are interested in getting exposure to commodities.
- ✔ You follow the markets regularly but are unsure about which trading strategy will maximize your returns.
- ✔ You don't have the time to manage a personal account.
- ✔ You feel comfortable knowing that someone else is making trading decisions for you.

If these statements apply to you, then you're ready to open a managed account. So how do you get started? First, you should determine your investment goals, time horizon, and risk tolerance. (For help determining your investment strategy, flip on over to Chapter 6.) Then you need to find out about any minimum capital requirements, commissions, or management fees you may face. (I cover these in depth in Chapter 6 also.) After you have this information, you can proceed to choose a Commodity Trading Advisor (CTA) to manage the account.

If you have mutual funds, the CTA is similar to a fund manager. The FCM, on the other hand, is more like a stock brokerage house. The FCM provides you with a trading platform, while the CTA actually manages your accounts for you.

A CTA is a securities professional who is licensed by the National Association of Securities Dealers (NASD) and the National Futures Association (NFA) to offer advice on commodities and to accept compensation for investment and management services. Before you select a CTA, I recommend you perform a rigorous background check on him. Because a CTA is required to register with the NFA to transact with the public, you can find out a lot about a CTA by simply visiting the NFA Web site (`www.nfa.futures.org`). (And check out Chapter 6 for more info on selecting CTAs and other money managers.)

Here are a few things to find out about your CTA:

- ✔ How many years of market experience does he have?
- ✔ What is his long-term performance record?
- ✔ What is his trading strategy and does it square with your investment goals?
- ✔ Does he have any complaints filed against him? (This information is publicly available through the NFA.)

> ✔ Many CTAs manage more than one account. Try and find out how many accounts he is currently managing. If the number seems too high then maybe your account won't be a high priority for him.
>
> ✔ Does he have a criminal record? If so, then find out the details of any arrests or convictions he has. This information is also available through the NFA.

After you perform due diligence on your CTA and feel comfortable with him, you're ready to turn over trading privileges to him. How do you do that? You actually have to sign a _power of attorney_ document. After that document is signed, your CTA will have full trading discretion and complete control over the buying and selling of commodities in your account. That means he makes all the decisions, and you have to live with the good (and sometimes bad) decisions he makes. If you trade stocks, this account is similar to having a discretionary individual stock account where your stockbroker makes trading decisions for you. The main benefit of the managed account is that you get a trained professional managing your investments. The drawback is you can't blame anyone but yourself if you incur any losses.

A CTA is allowed by law to manage more than one account and have more than one client. However, a CTA must keep all managed accounts separate. That means there is no commingling of funds allowed and no transferring of profits or losses between accounts. A managed account is very different from a _commodity pool,_ where your funds are "pooled" with those of other investors. In a commodity pool, the manager, who is known as a _Commodity Pool Operator_ (CPO), pools all the funds, and all profits or losses are shared by all investors. Make sure that when you choose a managed account you get a CTA who will manage your account based on your personal risk profile. (I cover CPOs and examine the differences between the CPO and the CTA more closely in Chapter 6.)

Placing orders

Your trading account is your link to the commodity exchange. The broker's trading platform gives you access to the exchange's main products such as futures contracts, options on futures, and other derivative products. Because the products traded on commodity exchanges are fairly sophisticated financial instruments, you need to specify a number of parameters in order to purchase the product you want.

Contract parameters

The lifeblood of the exchange is the contract. As an investor, you can choose from a number of different contracts — from plain vanilla futures contracts to exotic swaps and spreads. (I discuss these products in depth in Chapter 9.) Whether you're buying a forward contract or engaging in a swap, there are specific entry order procedures you need to follow.

Here is a list of the parameters you need to indicate to place an order at the exchange:

- ✔ **Action:** Indicate whether you are buying or selling.

- ✔ **Quantity:** Specify the number of contracts you're interested in either buying or selling.

- ✔ **Time:** By definition, commodity futures contracts represent an underlying commodity traded at a specific price for delivery at a specific point in the future. Futures contracts have delivery months, and you must specify the delivery month. Additionally, you should also specify the year because many contracts represent delivery points for periods of up to five years (or more).

- ✔ **Commodity:** This is the underlying commodity that the contract represents. It could be crude oil, gold, or soybeans. Sometimes, it's also helpful to indicate on which exchange you want to place your order. (This is fairly significant because more and more of the same commodities are being offered on different exchanges. For example, the benchmark WTI crude oil — which used to be traded only on the NYMEX — is now available both on the NYMEX floor as well as on the ICE electronic exchange.)

- ✔ **Price:** This could be the most important piece of the contract: the price at which you're willing to buy or sell the contract. Unless you're placing a market order (which is executed at current market prices), you should indicate the price you want your order to be filled.

- ✔ **Type of Order:** There are a lot of different types of orders, from plain vanilla market orders to more exotic ones such as *Fill or Kill* (FOK). See Table 8-3 for a list of the different types of orders. This is an important piece of the order since this is where you indicate how you want to buy or sell the contract.

- ✔ **Day or Open Order:** Market orders relate to price, while day or open orders relate to how long you want your order to remain open. In a *day order,* your order expires if it isn't filled by the end of the trading day. An *open order,* however, will remain open unless you cancel the order, the order is filled, or the contract expires.

Defining different types of orders

One of the most important pieces of information you need to indicate is the order type. This indicates how you want your order to be placed and executed. Table 8-3 lists the major types of orders along with a brief description of each one.

Table 8-3	Defining Different Types of Orders
Order Type	*What It Means*
Fill or Kill (FOK)	Use this order if you want your order to be filled right away at a specific price. If a matching offer is not found within three attempts, your order will be cancelled, or "killed."
Limit (LMT)	A limit order is placed when you want your order to be filled only at a specified price or better. If you're on the buy-side of a transaction, you want your limit buy order placed at or below the market price. Conversely, if you're on the sell-side, you want your limit sell order at or above market price.
Market (MKT)	A market order is perhaps the simplest type of order. When you choose a market order, you're saying you want your order filled at the current market price.
Market if Touched (MIT)	A market if touched order sounds intimidating, but it's not. When you place an MIT, you specify the price at which you want to buy or sell a commodity. When that price is reached (or "touched"), your order is automatically filled at the current market price. A buy MIT order is placed below the market, while a sell MIT order is placed above the market. In other words, you buy low and sell high.
Market on Close (MOC)	When you place a market on close order, you're not selecting a specific price but a specific time to execute your order. Your order will be executed at whatever price that particular commodity happens to close at the end of the trading session.
Stop (STP)	A stop order is a lot like a market if touched order because your order is placed when trading occurs at or through a specified price. However, unlike an MIT order, a buy stop order is placed above the market, and a sell stop order is placed below market levels.
Stop Close Only (SCO)	If you choose a stop close only order, your stop order will be executed only at the closing of trading and only if the closing trading range is at or through your designated stop price.
Stop Limit (STL)	A stop limit order combines both a stop order and a limit order. Once the stop price is reached, the order will become a limit order and the transaction will be executed only if the specified price at which you want the order to go through has been reached.

In order to put theory into practice, here are a couple sample orders:

- ✔ **Buy ten June 2006 COMEX Gold at $550 Limit Day Order.** This means you're buying ten contracts for gold on the COMEX (the metals complex of the NYMEX) with delivery date of June 2006. You are willing to pay $550 per troy ounce per contract, or better. (A troy ounce is the measurement unit for gold at the COMEX.) Because this is a day order, if your order isn't filled by the end of the trading day, it will expire.

- ✔ **Sell 100 September 2007 NYMEX Crude at Market Open Order.** Through this order, you're selling 100 contracts of crude oil on the NYMEX with delivery date of September 2007. You are willing to sell them at the current market price. Because this is an open order, your order will remain open for multiple trading sessions until it is filled.

Say that "Mary" is an investor who has recently opened a self-directed account with Infinity Brokers, a commodity brokerage firm. She keeps track of the markets and is comfortable placing orders that will take advantage of current market fundamentals. Mary picks up her newspaper one morning and reads that there is political turmoil in Nigeria, one of the world's top oil exporters. Rebels have seized a major pipeline, and Nigeria's oil exports will be cut by 15 percent. This will have a significant impact on global oil prices, which are already sensitive to any supply disruptions.

Anticipating higher oil prices due to this latest development, Mary picks up the phone and calls her broker (sometimes known as an *account executive*), and instructs him to buy a contract for 1000 Barrels of oil at current market prices on the NYMEX for next month delivery. The account executive takes down her order and informs her that he'll notify her as soon as her order is executed.

What happens between the time the orders are placed and then executed? In the following section, I give you a behind-the-scenes look at what actually goes on at the exchange that enables your orders to go through. I introduce you to some of the players who are responsible for seeing through the orders from start to finish.

Tracking your order from start to finish

When you pick up the phone or log into your online account and place an order, it's sometimes easy to forget that your order isn't placed in a vacuum. You place the order and wait for the confirmation number. Seems simple, right? Not quite. A number of people are involved in making sure your order is executed as smoothly and efficiently as possible, and your order goes through an extensive supply chain before it's executed. In this section, I shed some light on how your orders are executed and introduce you to some of the people who make this possible.

The clerk

The first point of contact at the exchange with the outside world is the clerk. The *clerk* isn't an employee of the exchange but is employed by the various commodity brokers who are licensed to conduct business at the exchange. The clerk works the phones and is responsible for taking down client orders. Once the clerk receives an order by phone (and now increasingly through e-mail as well), he fills out an order ticket, which he then passes on to the floor broker.

The floor broker

The *floor broker* (FB) is the one in the large ring shouting and making funny gestures. The FB is responsible for actually executing the order. The FB is in the front lines of every transaction that goes through the exchange during the open outcry sessions. Once the FB receives the order ticket from the clerk, it's his responsibility to find a matching offer and to fill the order. The FB shouts and makes gestures (which are actually derived from American Sign Language) to interact with other brokers and traders in the ring. Once he finds a broker or trader who is willing to fill his order, he writes down on the order ticket the time the agreement was entered into.

The floor trader

The *floor trader* (FT) is different than a floor broker because the FB is licensed to buy and sell commodities on behalf of clients. The trader may only trade on behalf of his personal account. The FT, sometimes known as a "local," provides much-needed liquidity to the exchange. An FT may be the person who will sell or buy a contract from the FB.

When both buyer and seller at the exchange agree on price and other contractual terms, both must write down that the transaction went through on their tickets. However, only the *seller* is responsible for notifying the exchange that the transaction went through. How does he do that? He fills out an order ticket with the price, quality, and quantity of the contract along with the time the transaction took place. He must then physically throw the ticket order to the card clocker.

The card clocker

The *card clocker* sits in the middle of the ring, where he's literally at the center of the action. The responsibility of the clocker is to time stamp every ticket order and record the time of each transaction that takes place on the exchange floor. He is an employee of the exchange and processes about 1000 tickets every minute! Because brokers and traders are throwing order tickets at them, they must wear eye goggles to protect themselves.

The floor runner

The *floor runner* is also employed by the exchange, and her responsibility is to gather all time-stamped ticket orders from the card clocker and hand them to the data-entry folks at the exchange. She is called a floor runner because she has to literally run between the card clocker and data-entry to deliver the ticket orders. Data-entry is responsible for recording the exact time and nature of the contract for the exchange's internal compliance records.

The price reporter

The *price reporter* is a major link between what goes on inside the trading rings and the outside world. The price reporter is responsible for noting the price and time of every transaction that takes place inside the ring. The price reporter notes this information down on a hand-held computer which is directly linked to the exchange's floor board. The price the reporter notes flashes directly and instantaneously on the board, where it is then disseminated to the outside public via various news and wire services.

The price you read in a crawling news ticker is the price that's recorded by the price reporter during trading hours, and it represents the settlement price of the latest transaction for a given contract. However, unless you subscribe to a wire service that provides you with "real-time access" to the prices on the exchange, the price you read is usually delayed by 15 to 20 minutes. This is because news providers such as Bloomberg, Dow Jones, and Reuters pay a premium to get access to exchange prices in real-time.

If you want real-time exchange quotes, you have to subscribe to one of these business news services. This is why if you ever visit an exchange, cameras, cellphones, and other recording devices are strictly prohibited. The news providers and the exchanges don't want you to get access to the latest information, fearing that you might disseminate it to the outside world for free!

The ring supervisor

Every exchange has a floor with more than one ring in it. A ring, sometimes known as a *pit,* is where specific commodity contracts are bought and sold during the open outcry sessions. For example, the floor of the NYMEX has a natural gas ring, a crude oil ring, and a heating oil ring. The brokers and traders in each ring may buy and sell only the specific commodity that is traded in that ring. Every ring has a supervisor who is responsible for overseeing trading activity and maintaining orderly conduct in the ring. (I know it's a little hard to imagine order in a trading pit but that's their job!) The ring supervisor is similar to the umpire in a tennis game — she oversees the game to make sure that all the rules are followed and intervenes whenever they are not.

Keeping up at the exchange

Working at the commodity exchange is not for the faint-hearted! Many people are attracted by the energy (pun intended) and fast pace of the exchanges, but you should remember that this is a high-pressure environment where the competition is ruthless. Brokers are paid by how many transactions they successfully complete, so the pressure to close as many deals as possible is intense. If you ever consider a career working on the exchange floor, you should always keep this in mind.

These are only some of the people involved in making the exchanges run as smoothly and efficiently as possible. As an investor with a brokerage account, all you see after you place your order is a confirmation number, and most investors fail to recognize the complexity behind placing orders at the commodity exchanges. Understanding the mechanism behind the order placement procedure will go a long way to making you a better investor. The more information you have on the mechanics of the exchange, the better off you are placing your trades with confidence.

It's also important to note that the *open outcry system* (where brokers stand in a trading pit filling and executing orders manually) has faced increased competition from electronic trading platforms, where orders are matched electronically. As a matter of fact, out of the major exchanges in the United States, only the NYMEX, COMEX, and NYBOT still rely heavily on the open outcry system to conduct business. Most exchanges now use a combination of electronic and open outcry, and many believe that the open outcry system is in jeopardy of being retired altogether. For example, in 2005 the open outcry at the Chicago Mercantile Exchange only accounted for 30 percent of the exchange's total volume — 70 percent of orders were placed electronically.

Owning a Piece of an Exchange

Savvy investors always keep their pulse on the markets and seek to develop investment strategies that take advantage of the market fundamentals. One of the biggest trends in the global investment game in the beginning of the 21st century is the increasing popularity of commodities in investor portfolios. Driven by high commodity prices, many investors are looking for ways to profit in this sector — after all, that's why you're reading this book! (For an in-depth analysis of this trend, please turn to Chapter 5.)

Commodity exchanges are becoming popular vehicles through which investors access the commodity markets. Because of their unique position, commodity exchanges stand to gain tremendously from this interest from the investing public. Interested in cashing in on this trend without trading a single contract on a single commodity exchange?

Sometimes, with all the commotion associated with the trading floors on commodity exchanges, it's easy to forget that an exchange is a business like any other business. Exchanges have employees, board members, revenues, earnings, expenses, and so on. These are not charitable organizations; a commodity exchange is a for-profit enterprise. While a car manufacturer sells cars to customers, commodity exchanges sell commodity contracts to customers. That's their bread and butter — their business is to sell financial instruments to the investing public. As any company, they charge a fee for this service.

For most of their existence, exchanges have been privately held companies whose business side remained under close wraps. However, because of the increasing popularity of commodities and the rise of the electronic trading platform, a large number of commodity exchanges are now going public. That is, they're becoming public companies with shareholders and outside investors. Most of the commodity exchanges are now traded on stock exchanges just like Microsoft, Ford, or Wal-Mart!

In 2003, the Chicago Mercantile Exchange (the nation's largest commodity exchange in terms of volume) went public. Its shares are now traded on the New York Stock Exchange under the ticker symbol CME. CME went public at a price of $43 a share. By March 2006, the stock price of CME reached an astonishing $435 a share! That's more than a 1000 percent increase in a period of three years. (See Figure 8-1.) Encouraged by these results, a number of other commodity exchanges went public soon after, and more are following suit. You can cash in on this trend by becoming a shareholder in one of these exchanges, since commodity exchanges are increasingly becoming hot investments in their own right.

Figure 8-1:
CME
Historical
Chart.

Before you go and purchase equity (stock) in one of the commodity exchanges, make sure you perform a thorough analysis of the stock and the company fundamentals. A stock will never go up in a straight arrow — it always retreats before making new highs. Sometimes, it doesn't make new highs at all.

I recommend you follow a stock on paper — that is, follow its movements without actually owning the stock — for a period of at least two weeks. That way you can get a feel for how the stock moves with the rest of the market. This will allow you to pinpoint the right entry and exit points.

Table 8-4 lists some of the commodity exchanges that recently have gone public.

Table 8-4	Exchanges Gone Public			
Exchange Name	*Ticker*	*Listed in*	*IPO Date*	*IPO Price*
Chicago Mercantile Exchange	CME	NYSE	Dec 2002	$43.60
Chicago Board of Trade	BOT	NYSE	Oct 2005	$96.00
Intercontinental Exchange	ICE	NYSE	Nov 2005	$39.00

If you're interested in profiting from the popularity of commodity exchanges, a unique way to do so is to purchase equity in these exchanges directly. The benefit is that you get to capitalize on the growing commodity trend without actually having to buy commodity exchange–traded products!

Chapter 9

Back to the Future: Getting a Grip on Futures and Options

*S*ome investors think that "futures and options" and "commodities" are basically the same thing, but this is not the case. *Commodities* are a class of assets that includes energy, metals, agricultural products, and similar items. *Futures* and *options* are investment vehicles through which you can invest in commodities. Think of it this way: If commodities were a place, futures and options would be the vehicle you use to get there. In addition to commodities, futures and options also allow you to invest in a variety of other asset classes such as stocks, indexes, currencies, bonds, and even interest rates.

In Wall Street lingo, futures and options are known as *derivatives* because they *derive* their value from an underlying financial instrument such as a stock, bond, or commodity. However, futures and options are different financial instruments with singular structures and uses — but I'm getting ahead of myself.

Futures and options conjure up a lot apprehension and puzzlement among investors. A majority of investors have never used them and those who have often come back with stories about losing their life savings trading them. While their negative aspects are slightly exaggerated, trading futures and options is not for everyone.

Futures and options, by their very nature, are complex financial instruments. It's not like investing in a mutual fund, where you mail your check and wait for quarterly statements and dividends. If you invest in futures and options contracts, you need to monitor your positions on a daily basis, often even on an hourly basis. You have to keep track of the expiration date, the premium paid, the strike price, margin requirements, and a number of other shifting variables. (I discuss these in the section "Contract specs: Keeping track of all the moving pieces.")

That said, understanding futures and options can be very beneficial to you as an investor because they are powerful tools. They provide you with leverage and risk management opportunities that your average financial instruments don't offer. If you can harness the power of these instruments, you can dramatically increase your leverage — and performance — in the markets.

My aim in this chapter is not to make you an expert in trading these sophisticated financial instruments, but to introduce you to these vehicles so that you have a working knowledge of what they are. If you then choose to use them in your trading strategy, you will at least have a good understanding of how to best utilize them. Or if you decide to hire a professional money manager to invest in the futures markets for you, you'll know the lingo and key concepts so you can ask them the right questions. I include a comprehensive list of money managers who specialize in helping investors invest in the futures markets on my Web site www.commodities-investor.com. I also discuss how to go about choosing a money manager in Chapter 6.

The futures markets are only one way for you to get involved in commodities and, because they can be fairly volatile, it's important you have a solid understanding before you jump in.

Although a number of books deal specifically with futures and options, I recommend checking out John Hull's *Options, Futures and Other Derivatives* (Prentice Hall) for its thoroughness. Another book I recommend is *Derivatives Demystified* by Andrew Chisholm (Wiley).

The Future Looks Bright: How to Trade Futures Contracts

The futures market is divided into two segments: one that's regulated and another one that's unregulated. Trading in the regulated portion of the futures market is done through designated commodity futures exchanges such as the New York Board of Trade (NYBOT) and the Chicago Mercantile Exchange (CME), which I cover in Chapter 8. Trading in the unregulated portion of the futures market is done by individual parties outside the purview of the exchanges. This is known as the *Over-The-Counter market.*

The futures market is the opposite of the cash market, often known as the *spot market,* because transactions take place right away, or on the spot.

A *futures contract* is a highly standardized financial instrument whereby two parties enter into an agreement to exchange an underlying security (such as soybeans, palladium, or ethanol) at a mutually agreed-upon price at a specific time in the future — which is why it's called a futures contract.

Futures contracts, by definition, trade on designated commodity futures exchanges, such as the London Metal Exchange (LME) or the Chicago Board of Trade (CBOT). The exchanges provide liquidity and transparency to all market participants. However, the structure of the futures market is such that only about 20 percent of market activity takes place in the exchange arena. The overwhelming majority of transactions in the futures markets take place in the *Over-The-Counter market* (OTC). The OTC market is not regulated or monitored by the exchanges, and it usually involves two market participants that establish the terms of their agreements through forward contracts. *Forwards* are similar to futures contracts except that they trade in the OTC market, and thus allow the parties to come up with flexible and individualized terms for their agreements. Generally speaking, the OTC market is not suitable for trading by individual investors who seek speculative opportunities because it consists primarily of large commercial users (such as oil companies and airlines) who use it solely for hedging purposes.

In this chapter, I focus on derivatives that trade on the commodity exchanges. I don't focus on the OTC market because it does not lend itself to trading by individual investors. So when I refer to the "futures market" in this chapter, I'm talking about the trading activity in the designated commodity futures exchanges.

Despite the fact that futures contracts are designed to accommodate delivery of physical commodities, such delivery rarely takes place because the primary purpose of the futures markets is to minimize risk and maximize profits. The futures market, unlike the cash or spot market, is not intended to serve as the primary exchange of physical commodities. Rather, it is a market where buyers and sellers transact with each other for hedging and speculative purposes.

Out of the billions of contracts traded on commodity futures exchanges each year, only about 2 percent of these contracts result in the actual physical delivery of a commodity.

In the land of futures contracts, both the buyer and the seller have the right *and* the obligation of fulfilling the contract's terms. This is different than in the realm of options, where the buyer has the right but *not* the obligation to exercise the option, but where the seller has the obligation but *not* the right to fulfill her contractual obligations. This can get a little confusing, I know! That's why I dig deeper into these issues in the section "Keeping Your Options Open".

The competition: Who trades futures?

Essentially two types of folks trade futures contracts. The first are commercial producers and consumers of commodities who use the futures markets to stabilize either their costs (in the case of consumers) or revenues (in the case of producers). The second group is made up of individual traders, investment banks, and other financial institutions who are interested in using the futures markets as a way of generating trading profits. Both groups take advantage of the futures markets' liquidity and leverage (which I discuss in the following sections) to implement their trading strategies.

If you ever get involved in the futures markets, it's important to know who you're up against. I examine the role of these hedgers and speculators in the following sections so you're ready to deal with the competition.

Scene one, take one: Getting over the hedge

Hedgers are the actual producers and consumers of commodities. Both producers and consumers enter the futures markets with the aim of reducing price volatility of the commodities that they buy or sell. Hedging provides these commercial enterprises the opportunity to reduce the risk associated with daily price fluctuations by establishing fixed prices of primary commodities for months, sometimes even years, in advance.

Hedgers can be on either side of a transaction in the futures market, either on the *buy-side* or the *sell-side*. Here are a few examples of entities that use the futures markets for hedging purposes:

- ✔ Farmers who want to establish steady prices for their products use futures contracts to sell their products to consumers at a fixed price for a fixed period of time, thus guaranteeing a fixed stream of revenues.

- ✔ Electric utility companies that supply power to residential customers can buy electricity on the futures markets to keep their costs fixed and protect their bottom line.

- ✔ Transportation companies whose business depends on the price of fuel get involved in the futures markets to maintain fixed costs of fuel over specific periods of time.

To get a better idea of hedging in action, take a look at a hedging strategy employed by the airline industry.

One of the biggest worries that keeps airline executives up at night is the unpredictable price of jet fuel, which can vary wildly from day to day on the spot market. Airlines don't like this kind of uncertainty because they want to keep their costs low and predictable (they already have enough to worry about with rising pension and health care costs, fears of terrorism, and other external factors). So how do they do that? By hedging the price of jet fuel through the futures market.

Southwest Airlines (NYSE: LUV) is one of the most active hedgers in the industry. At any one point, Southwest may have up to 80 percent of a given year's jet fuel consumption fixed at a specific price. Southwest will enter into agreements with producers through the futures markets, primarily through Over-The-Counter agreements, to purchase fuel at a fixed price for a specific period of time in the future.

The benefit for Southwest (and its passengers) is that they have fixed their costs and eliminated the volatility associated with the price fluctuation of the jet fuel they're consuming. This has a direct impact on their bottom line. The advantage for the producer is that they now have a customer who is willing to purchase their product for a fixed time at a fixed price, thus providing them with a steady stream of cash flow.

However, unless prices in the cash market remain steady, one of the two parties who enters into this sort of agreement may have been better off without the hedge. If prices for jet fuel increase, then the producer has to bear that cost because they still have to deliver jet fuel to the airline at the agreed-upon price, which is now below the market price. Similarly, if prices of jet fuel go down, the airline would have been better off purchasing jet fuel on the cash market. But because these are unknown variables, hedgers still see a benefit in entering into these agreements to eliminate this unpredictability.

The truth about speculators

For some reason, the term *speculator* carries some negative connotation, as if speculating was a sinful or immoral act. The fact of the matter is that speculators play an important and necessary role in the global financial system. In fact, whenever you buy a stock or a bond, you are speculating. When you think prices are going up, you buy. When they're going down, you sell. The process of figuring out where prices are heading and how to profit from this is the essence of speculation. So we're all speculators!

In the futures markets, speculators provide much needed liquidity that allows the many market players the opportunity to match their buy and sell orders. Speculators, often simply known as *traders,* buy and sell futures contracts, options, and other exchange-traded products through an electronic platform or a broker to profit from price fluctuations. A trader who thinks that the price of crude oil is going up will buy a crude oil futures contract to try to profit from his hunch. This adds liquidity to the markets, which is valuable because liquidity is a prerequisite for the smooth and efficient functioning of the futures markets.

When markets are liquid, you know that you will be able to find a buyer or a seller for your contracts. You also know that you are assured a reasonable price because liquidity provides you with a large pool of market participants who are going to compete for your contracts. Finally, liquidity means that when a number of participants are transacting in the marketplace, prices are not going to be subject to extremely wild and unpredictable price fluctuations. This doesn't mean that liquidity eliminates volatility, but it certainly helps reduce it.

At the end of the day, having a large number of market participants is positive, and speculators play an important role due to the liquidity they provide to the futures markets.

Contract specs: Keeping track of all the moving pieces

Trading futures contracts takes a lot of discipline, patience, and coordination — one of the biggest deterrents to participating in the futures markets is the number of moving pieces you have to constantly monitor. In this section, I go through the many pieces you have to keep track of should you decide to trade futures.

Because futures contracts can only be traded on designated and regulated exchanges, these contracts are highly standardized. *Standardization* simply means that these contracts are based on a uniform set of rules. For example, the New York Mercantile Exchange (NYMEX) crude oil contract is standardized because it represents a specific grade of crude (West Texas Intermediate) and a specific size (1000 Barrels). Therefore you can expect all NYMEX crude contracts to represent 1000 Barrels of West Texas Intermediate crude oil. In other words, the contract you purchase won't be for 1000 Barrels of *Nigerian Bonny Light,* another grade of crude oil.

The regulatory bodies that are responsible for overseeing and monitoring trading activities on commodity futures exchanges are the Commodity Futures Trading Commission (CFTC) and the National Futures Association (NFA). I discuss these at length in Chapter 8.

The buyer of a futures contract is known as the *holder;* when you buy a futures contract you are essentially "going long" the commodity. The seller of a futures contract is referred to as the *underwriter* or *writer.* If you sell a futures contract, you are holding a short position. Remember that "going long" simply means you're on the buy-side of a transaction; conversely, going short means you're on the sell-side. In other words, when you "go long," you expect prices to rise, and when you "go short" you anticipate prices to decrease.

Underlying asset

The *underlying asset* is the financial instrument that is represented by the futures contract. The underlying asset can be anything from crude oil and platinum to soybeans and propane. Because futures contracts are traded on designated exchanges, every exchange offers different types of assets you can trade. For a list of these assets, make sure to read Chapter 8.

Futures contracts can be used to trade all sorts of assets, and not just traditional commodities like oil and gold. Futures can be used to trade interest rates, indexes, currencies, equities, and a host of other assets. There are even futures contracts that allow you to trade weather!

Although most of the world's major commodities are traded on exchanges through futures contracts, one of the only major commodities that does not have a futures contract assigned to it is steel. A few of the major exchanges, such as the New York Mercantile Exchange (NYMEX) and the London Metal Exchange (LME), have considered offering steel futures, but a steel futures contract is still not available to investors.

Before you place your order, make sure you're very clear about the underlying commodity you want to trade. Make sure to specify on which exchange you want your order executed. This is important because you have contracts for the same commodities that trade on different exchanges. For example, aluminum futures contracts are traded on both the COMEX division of the NYMEX as well as on the London Metal Exchange (LME). When you're placing an order for an aluminum contract, it's important you specify where you want to buy the contract: either on the COMEX or on the LME.

Underlying quantity

The contract size, also known as the *trading unit,* is how much of the underlying asset the contract represents. In order to meet certain standards, all futures contracts have a predetermined and fixed size. For example, one futures contract for ethanol traded on the Chicago Board of Trade is the equivalent of one rail car of ethanol, which is approximately 29,000 Gallons.

The light sweet crude oil contract on the NYMEX represents 1000 US Barrels, which is the equivalent of 42,000 Gallons. On the Chicago Mercantile Exchange, a futures contract for frozen pork bellies represents 40,000 Pounds of pork.

Make sure you know exactly the amount of underlying commodity the contract represents before you purchase a futures contract.

Because more individual investors want to trade futures contracts, many exchanges are now offering contracts with smaller sizes, which means that the contracts cost less. The NYMEX, for instance, now offers the miNY™ Light Sweet Crude Oil contract, which represents 500 Barrels of oil and is half the price of its traditional crude oil contract.

Product grade

Imagine you placed an order for a Ford Mustang and instead got a Ford Taurus. You'd be pretty upset, right? I know I would! In order to avoid unpleasant surprises should delivery of a physical commodity actually take place, exchanges require that all contracts represent a standard product grade. For instance, gasoline futures traded on the NYMEX are based on contract specifications for New York Harbor Unleaded Gasoline. This is a uniform grade of gasoline widely used across the East Coast, which is transported to New York Harbor from refineries in the East Coast and the Gulf of Mexico. Thus, if delivery of a NYMEX gasoline futures contracts takes place, you can expect to receive NY Harbor Unleaded Gas.

If your sole purpose is to speculate and you're not intending on having gasoline or soybeans delivered, then knowing the product grade is not as important as if you were taking physical delivery of the commodity. However, it's always good to know what kind of product you're actually trading.

Price quote

While most futures contracts are priced in US Dollars, some contracts are priced in other currencies, such as the Pound Sterling or the Japanese Yen. The price quote really depends on which exchange you're buying or selling the futures contract from. Keep in mind that if you're trading futures in a foreign currency, you're potentially exposing yourself to currency exchange risks.

Price limits

Price limits help you determine the value of the contract. Every contract has a minimum and maximum price increment, also known as *tick size*. Contracts move in ticks, which is the amount by which the futures contract increases or decreases with every transaction. Most stocks, for example, move in cents. In futures, most contracts move in larger dollar amounts, reflecting the size of the contract. In other words one tick represents different values for different contracts.

For example, the *minimum tick size* of the ethanol futures contract on the Chicago Board of Trade (CBOT) is $29 per contract. This means every contract will move in increments of $29. On the other hand, the *maximum tick size* for ethanol on the CBOT is $4350, meaning that if the tick size is greater than $4350, trading will be halted. Exchanges step in when contracts are experiencing extreme volatility in order to calm the markets.

Minimum and maximum tick sizes are established by the exchanges and are based on the settlement price during the previous day's trading session.

Determining the value of the tick allows you to quantify the price swings of the contract on any given trading session.

Trading months

Although you can trade futures contracts practically around the clock, certain commodities are only available for delivery during certain months.

For instance, frozen pork bellies on the Chicago Mercantile Exchange (CME) are listed for the months of February, March, May, July, and August. This means that you can trade a July contract at any given point, but you cannot trade a June contract — a contract that's deliverable in June — because that contract does not exist. On the other hand, crude oil on the NYMEX is available for all 12 months of the year.

Check the contract listing before you trade so you know for which delivery months you can trade the contracts.

The *front month* is simply the upcoming delivery month. For example, June is the front month during the May trading session.

In the world of futures, trading and delivery months have specific abbreviations attributed to each month. I list these abbreviations in Table 9-1:

Table 9-1		Monthly Abbreviation Codes	
Month	*Code*	*Month*	*Code*
January	F	July	N
February	G	August	Q
March	H	September	U
April	J	October	V
May	K	November	X
June	M	December	Z

Traders use these abbreviations to quickly identify the months they're interested in trading. If you're placing an order with a futures broker (which I discuss in Chapter 6), knowing these abbreviations is helpful.

Delivery location

In case of actual delivery, exchanges designate areas where the physical exchange of commodities actually takes place. For instance, delivery of the NYMEX's WTI crude oil contract takes place in Cushing, Oklahoma, which is a major transportation hub for crude oil in the United States.

Last trading day

All futures contracts must expire at some point. The *last trading day* is the absolute latest time you have to trade that particular contract. Trading days change from exchange to exchange and from contract to contract. Make sure to check out the contract specifications at the different exchanges for information on the last trading day.

Trading hours

Before the days of electronic trading, contracts were traded through the open outcry system during specific time periods. Now, with the advent of electronic trading you have more time to trade the contracts.

Knowing at what times to place your trades has a direct impact on your bottom line because the number of market participants varies throughout the day. Ideally, you'd like to execute your orders when there are the most buyers and sellers because this increases your chances of getting the best price for your contracts.

Check the exchange Web sites (which I list in Chapter 8) for information on trading hours.

For a Few Dollars Less: Trading Futures on Margin

One of the unique characteristics of futures contracts is the ability to trade with margin. If you've ever traded stocks, you know that *margin* is the amount of borrowed money you use to pay for stock. Margin in the futures markets is slightly different than stock market margin.

In the futures markets, *margin* refers to the minimum amount of capital that must be available in your account for you to trade futures contracts. Think of margin as collateral that allows you to participate in the futures markets. The amount of capital that has to be in your account before you place a trade is known as *initial margin*. Because profits and losses on your open positions are calculated every day in the futures markets, you also have to maintain an adequate amount of capital on a daily basis. This is known as *maintenance margin*.

- **Initial margin:** The minimum amount of capital you need in your account to trade futures contracts.

- **Maintenance margin:** The subsequent amount of capital you must contribute to your account in order to maintain the minimum margin requirements.

Margin requirements are established for every type of contract by the exchange on which those contracts are traded. However, the futures broker you use to place your order may have different margin requirements. Make sure you find out what those requirements are before you start trading.

In the stock market, capital gains and losses are calculated after you close out your position. In the futures market, capital gains and losses are calculated at the end of the trading day and credited to or debited from your account. If you experience a loss in your positions on any given day, you will receive a *margin call,* which means that you have to replenish your account to meet the minimum margin requirements if you want to keep trading.

Trading on margin provides you with a lot of leverage because you only need to put up relatively small amounts of capital as collateral in order to invest in significant dollar amounts of a commodity. For example, if you want to trade the soybean futures contracts on the CBOT, the initial margin requirement is $1100. With this small amount you can control a CBOT soybeans futures contract that has a value of approximately $28,400 (5000 Bushels at $5.68 per bushel)! This translates to a minimum margin requirement of less than 4 percent!

Margin is a double-edged sword because both profits and losses are amplified to large degrees. If you're on the right side of a trade, you're going to make a lot of money. However, you're also in a position to lose a lot (much more than your initial investment) should things not go your way. Knowing how to use margin properly is absolutely critical. I discuss in depth how to use leverage responsibly in Chapter 3.

Taking a Pulse: Figuring Out Where the Futures Market Is Heading

You need to be familiar with a couple of technical terms related to movements in the futures markets if you want to successfully trade futures contracts. Before I name them, I have to advise you that you may want to take a couple of aspirins before trying to pronounce them. Even by Wall Street standards, these terms are kind of out there. The first one is *contango* and the second is *backwardation.* (I warned you!)

Contango: It takes two to tango

Futures markets, by definition, are predicated on the future price of a commodity. Analyzing where the future price of a commodity is heading is what futures trading is all about. Because futures contracts are available for different months throughout the year, the price of the contracts changes from month to month. When the *front month* trades higher than the current month, this market condition is known as *contango*. The market is also in contango when the price of the front month is higher than the spot market, and also when late delivery months are higher than near delivery months. I include an example of the NYMEX Crude Oil contract in contango in Table 9-2.

Table 9-2	NYMEX Crude Oil in Contango
Month	*Settlement Price*
June 06	$74.05
July 06	$75.30
August 06	$75.85
September 06	$76.30
October 06	$76.58
November 06	$76.65

As the contract extends into the future, the price of the contract increases. Contango is thus a bullish indicator, showing that the market sentiment is that the price of the futures contract is going to increase steadily into the future.

Backwardation: One step forward, two steps back

Backwardation is the opposite of contango. When a market is experiencing backwardation, the contracts for future months are decreasing in value relative to the current and most recent months. This means that the spot price is greater than the front month, which is greater than future delivery months. Table 9-3 shows the NYMEX Copper contract in backwardation.

Table 9-3	NYMEX Copper in Backwardation
Month	*Settlement Price*
July 06	$3.08
August 06	$3.07
September 06	$3.04

The Metallgesellschaft debacle

Trading futures contracts is certainly not for the faint hearted. Even the pros can run into lots of trouble in the futures markets. A case in point is what happened in the 1990s to a company called Metallgesellschaft. Metallgesellschaft (I'll call it MG for short so you won't have to go through the trouble of pronouncing it!) was a German company partly owned by a conglomerate led by Deutsche Bank, which specialized in metals trading. In 1993, MG lost a staggering $2.2 Billion trading futures contracts.

In the early 1990s, MG set up an energy division to trade futures contracts in the United States. Its motive was to profit by betting on the price fluctuations of crude oil. MG's strategy was based on taking advantage of the price differential between crude oil on the spot markets and futures markets. Specifically, MG sold long-term futures contracts to various parties and hedged its long-term risk by buying short-term contracts and rolling them on a monthly basis. This strategy works beautifully — but only when the long-term prices are lower than the short-term prices. In other words, this is a good strategy when the markets are in backwardation.

However, in 1993, long-term crude oil prices started increasing, and MG was caught short with these contracts. When the markets moved to contango (prices for future months were higher than the current month), MG found itself unable to hedge the long-term contracts and was forced to meet the obligations on those long-term contracts. Because it held such large open positions, MG eventually lost a mind-numbing $2.2 Billion! The parent company pulled the plug, and MG was forced into liquidation.

The moral of this story is that futures trading can be volatile and risky, even for seasoned professionals. Fortunately for investors like you and me who are interested in commodities, the futures market is only one way through which to invest in this asset class. If you are interested in accessing the futures markets, I recommend you use the help of a Commodity Trading Advisor (CTA) or a Commodity Pool Operator (CPO). If you want to explore other ways to invest in commodities (such as through mutual funds or exchange traded funds), I recommend reading Chapter 6.

A market in backwardation is a bearish sign because the expectation among traders is that prices over the long term are going to decrease.

Keeping Your Options Open: Trading with Options

Before I start this section on options, I want to stress the fact that there is a big difference between futures and options. Often times, folks tend to think of futures and options as being one and the same — that's understandable since whenever you hear "futures," "options" is never too far behind! However, as I explain in the following sections, futures and options are different financial instruments with singular structures and uses. Realizing this difference right off the bat will help you understand these financial instruments better.

While futures give the *holder* (buyer) and *underwriter* (seller) both the right *and* the obligation to fulfill the contract's obligations, options give the holder the right (or option) — but not the obligation — to exercise the contract. The underwriter of the option, on the other hand, is required to fulfill the contract's obligations if the holder chooses to exercise the contract.

When you're buying an option, you're essentially paying for the right to buy or sell an underlying security at a specific point in time at an agreed-upon price. The price you pay for the right to exercise that option is known as the *premium*.

The technically correct way of thinking about options is "options on futures contracts;" in other words, the options contracts give you the option to buy futures contracts for commodities such as wheat and zinc. This is different than stock options, which give you the option to purchase stocks. In this section, I examine options on futures contracts because that's the focus of this chapter. If you want an overview of stock options, I recommend *Stock Options For Dummies* (Wiley).

Cutting to the chase: Options in action!

Understanding options can be challenging because they're in fact derivatives used to trade other derivatives (futures contracts). So here's an example that applies the concept of options to a real world situation.

You walk into a car dealership and you see the car of your dreams: It's shiny, it looks beautiful, and you know you'll look great in it! Unfortunately it costs $100,000, and you can't spend that amount of money on a car right now. However, you're due for a large bonus at work — or you just made a killing trading commodities, have your pick! — and you'll be able to pay for it in two weeks. So you approach the car dealer and ask him to hold the car for you for two weeks, at which point you can make full payment on it.

The dealer agrees but insists that he will have to charge you $5000 for the option to buy the car in two weeks for the set price of $100,000. You agree to the terms and give him a non-refundable deposit of $5000 (known as the *premium* in options speak), which gives you the right, but not the obligation, to come back in two weeks and purchase the car of your dreams. The dealer, on the other hand, is obligated to sell you the car should you choose to exercise your option to do so. In this situation, you are the *holder* of the option, while the dealer is its *underwriter*.

Consider two different scenarios that unfold during the two-week period. The first one is that a few days after you purchase the option to buy the vehicle, the car manufacturer announces that it will stop making vehicles of this kind — the car is now a limited series edition and becomes a collector's car. Congratulations! The value of the car has now doubled overnight! Because you and the dealer entered into an options agreement, the dealer is obligated to sell you the car at $100,000 even though the car now costs $200,000 — should you choose to exercise your rights as the option holder. You come back to see the dealer, and you buy the car at the agreed upon price of $100,000. You can now either drive your new car or you can turn and sell it at current market price for a cool $95,000 profit ($200,000 – $100,000 – $5000 = $95,000)!

The second scenario isn't as rosy as the first. A few days after you sign the options agreement, the car manufacturer announces that there is a defect with the car's CD player. The car works fine so the manufacturer doesn't need to recall it, but the built-in CD player is defective and not usable. Because of this development, the value of the car drops to $80,000 (drivers like listening to their CDs after all). As the holder of the option you are not obligated to purchase the car. Remember, you have the right — but not the obligation — to follow through on the contractual agreements of the contract. If you choose not to purchase the car, you will have incurred the $5000 loss of the premium you paid for the option.

That, in a nutshell, is what trading options is all about. You can now take this concept and apply it to profit in the capital markets in general, and the commodities market in particular. If you expect, for example, the price of the June copper futures contract on the COMEX/NYMEX to increase, you can buy an option on the COMEX/NYMEX that gives you the right to purchase the June copper futures contract for a specific price. You pay a *premium* for this option and, if you don't exercise your option before the expiration date, the only thing you lose is the premium.

Trader talk

When talking about options, there are certain terms you have to know:

- **Premium:** The price you actually pay for the option. If you don't exercise your option, then the only money you lose is the premium you paid for the contract in the first place.

- **Expiration date:** The date at which the option expires. After the expiration date, the contract is no longer valid.

- **Strike price:** The predetermined price at which the underlying asset is purchased or sold.

- **At-the-money:** When the strike price is equal to the market price, the option is known as being at-the-money.

- ✔ **In-the-money:** In a call option, when the asset's market price is above the strike price, it is in-the-money. In the land of puts, an option is in-the-money when the market price is below the strike price.

- ✔ **Out-of-the-money:** When the market price is below the strike price in a call option, that option is a money-loser: It's out-of-the-money. When the market price is greater than the strike price in a put option, it's out-of-the-money.

- ✔ **Open interest:** The total number of options or futures contracts that are still open on any given trading session. This is an important measure of market interest.

Options have character

Every option has different characteristics, depending on how you want to exercise the option and what action you want to conduct once it is exercised. Put simply, you can use options that allow you to either buy or sell an underlying security. You can further specify at which point you want to exercise the options agreement. This section lays out these characteristics for you.

Call options: Calling all investors

If you expect rising prices, you can buy a *call option* that gives you the right — but not the obligation — to *purchase* a specific amount of a security at a specific price at specific point in the future.

When you buy a call option, you're being bullish and are expecting prices to increase — call options are similar to having a long position. When you *sell* a call option, you expect prices to fall. If the prices fall and never reach the strike price, then you get to keep the premium. If prices increase and the holder exercises her option, you're obligated to sell her the underlying asset at the agreed-upon price.

Putting everything on the line: Using put options

A *put option* is the exact opposite of a call option because it gives you the right, but not the obligation, to *sell* a security at some point in the future for a predetermined price. When you think the price of a security is going down, you want to use a put option to try and take advantage of this price movement.

Buying a put option is one way of shorting a security. If prices do decrease, you can then purchase the security at the agreed-upon (lower) price and then turn back and sell it on the open market and pocket the difference. If, on the other hand, prices increase, then you can choose to let the option expire. In this case you will only lose the premium you paid for the option.

When you *sell* a put option, you believe that prices are going to increase. If you're correct and prices increase, then the holder won't exercise the option, which means you get to collect the premium. So when you sell a put option, you're actually being bullish.

Here are the possible combinations of buying and selling put and call options, accompanied by their corresponding market sentiment:

- ✔ Buying a call: Bullish
- ✔ Selling a call: Bearish
- ✔ Buying a put: Bearish
- ✔ Selling a put: Bullish

Buy American: Looking at American options

When you buy an American option, you have the right to exercise that option at any time during the life of the option — from the start of the option until the expiration date. Most options traded in the United States are American options. You get a lot more flexibility out of them because you have the freedom to exercise them at any point.

The European alternative

The European option allows you to exercise the option only at expiration. This is a fairly rigid kind of option. The only possible advantage of a European option over an American option is that you may be able to pay a smaller premium for this option. However, because of its rigidity, I highly recommend you use American options in your trading strategies.

Chapter 10

Technically Speaking: Using Technical Analysis

I gotta start out this chapter by saying that technical analysis — like investing in general — is not an exact science. I've been on Wall Street long enough to know that there is a raging debate about the role of technical analysis in the financial markets. Although a number of investors and traders claim to have made fortunes using technical analysis, another large group of investors believes it's nothing more than voodoo. So just what is technical analysis?

Put simply, *technical analysis* is used to examine a security's past price patterns in order to forecast its future price movements. Technical analysis is based on the study of the interaction between supply and demand and its effect on a security's price. It assumes that there is a constant battle between buyer and sellers (between bulls and bears), and it seeks to profit from this battle by predicting the winner. This analysis is thus based partly on market psychology and partly on market forces.

So when should you actually use technical analysis? Technical analysis can be applied at various stages of the investing cycle. Some of the most frequent users of technical analysis are active day traders who want to profit by making short-term bets on the direction of a security. So, if you're an active trader, then technical analysis can be a very useful tool for you. If you're investing for the long term, technical analysis can still provide useful insight that other types of analyses don't provide.

In order to examine the interaction between buyers and sellers — and between supply and demand — technical analysis relies on a number of technical indicators. In this chapter, I examine the most widely used indicators so that you have a solid set of tools in your technical analysis toolkit. If you want more information on other technical indicators, I recommend you check out *Technical Analysis For Dummies* (Wiley).

As a general rule, don't rely on just one indicator to make buying or selling decisions. Rather, use each of the indicators I discuss in the chapter in conjunction with other key metrics to drive a rational and balanced investment approach. Relying on one metric is not very wise — you want to take into consideration as many factors as possible to make an informed trading decision.

Looking at Charts: A Picture Is Worth More Than a Thousand Words

The foundation of technical analysis is a chart that shows a security's price movements over a certain period of time; the primary charts are the line chart, the bar chart, and the candlestick chart.

All graph charts include an X and Y axis. Price is always plotted on the Y axis and time — which could be days, weeks, months, years, or even minutes — is plotted on the X axis.

You can choose different timeframes for the chart — one day, one week, one month, three months, six months, one year, three years, five years, and so on —depending on a number of factors, such as your investment time frame, holding period, and risk tolerance (which I cover in Chapter 3).

I recommend you look at a chart from the point the security you're analyzing started trading. This will give you a complete and comprehensive view of the performance of that security, helping you develop both a long-term as well as a short-term strategy. If you're using a chart viewing service (such as the ones I present below), you would get this information by clicking on *Historical Performance*.

Here are a few Web sites that offer good chart viewing services:

- ✔ `Finance.yahoo.com`: This is an all-around excellent financial Web site that includes charts for everything from equities to commodity Exchange Traded Funds (ETFs).

- ✔ `Futures.tradingcharts.com`: This Web site includes advanced graph functions for the world's major commodities, from soybeans to platinum.

✔ **Barchart.com:** This site has a comprehensive list of all commodities and futures contracts that trade on the major exchanges. A subscription is required to access advanced chart services, although their non-member section is quite useful as well.

Line it up: Checking out line charts

A *line chart* is the most commonly used type of chart. It plots the closing price of a security by taking one price point and connecting it with other price points over a specific time period. The line chart is formed once all these price points are connected to each other. See Figure 10-1 for an example of a line chart.

The advantage of using a line chart is that you get a quick overview of the commodity's previous closing prices over a specific period of time. However, the line chart leaves out crucial pieces of information — such as the opening price or the day's highs and lows — which can be useful to you as you're conducting your technical analysis.

Going for bar charts

I like using *bar charts* because they contain a lot of practical information to help you make better informed trading decisions. In a bar chart, every trading session is represented by a vertical line — sometimes known as a *tick*. The tick contains four critical pieces of information about a security's price during a particular trading session: the opening price, the day's high, the day's low, and the closing price. Because it includes all this information, the bar chart provides a more complete picture of a security's price movements than the line chart. In Figure 10-2, I show you how these pieces of information are depicted on a bar chart tick.

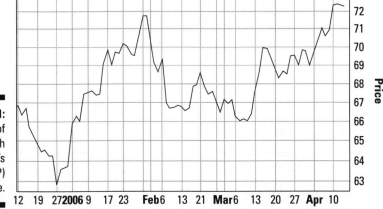

Figure 10-1:
Line chart of British Petroleum's (NYSE: BP) stock price.

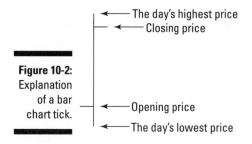

Figure 10-2:
Explanation
of a bar
chart tick.

 Take a look again at Figure 10-2. How do you know which horizontal tick represents the closing price and which one the opening price? The convention used in bar charts is that all *closing prices* are noted by a horizontal tick on the right side of the vertical line, and all *opening prices* are represented by the horizontal tick on the left. Figure 10-3 gives you an actual example of a bar chart.

 Not all bar charts include these four pieces of information. Some charts include the day's high, the day's low, and the closing price, but not the opening price. In these types of graphs, the closing price is depicted as a horizontal tick that crosses both the right and left sides of the vertical line.

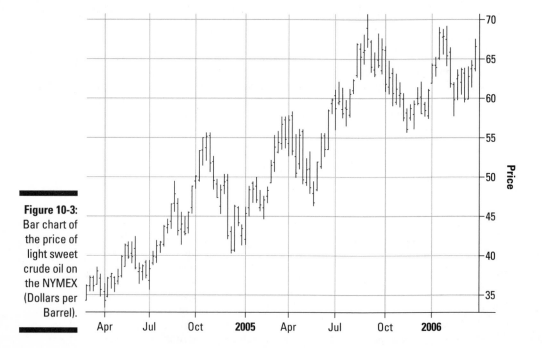

Figure 10-3:
Bar chart of
the price of
light sweet
crude oil on
the NYMEX
(Dollars per
Barrel).

Lighting up the chart with candlesticks

Like bar charts, *candlestick charts* include information on the four crucial pieces of a security's performance during a trading session: opening price, daily high, daily low, and closing price. Figure 10-4 demonstrates a candlestick tick.

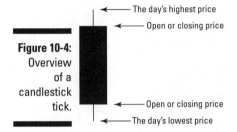

The day's highest price

Open or closing price

Open or closing price

The day's lowest price

Figure 10-4: Overview of a candlestick tick.

In addition, candlesticks use a color-coordinated system to identify whether the trading session for a commodity ended higher or lower. Essentially, when a commodity closes lower than its opening price, called a *downtick,* it will be a dark color. Conversely, when the commodity closes higher than when it opened, called an *uptick,* it will be a light color (see Figure 10-5).

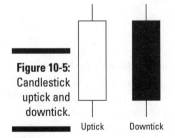

Figure 10-5: Candlestick uptick and downtick.

Uptick   Downtick

Most charts include traditional black and white colors, although some use more exotic colors such as red (downtick) and green (uptick).

This system allows you to quickly determine the commodity's performance during a particular trading session. Out of all the charts, candlesticks provide you with the most detailed information about a security, which is why I prefer using them over bar charts and line charts. That said, if you're looking for a quick overview of performance, I recommend using the line chart. If you're looking for something that combines the detail of the candlestick chart and the big picture approach of the line chart, then the bar chart is your best bet. Take a look at Figure 10-6 for an actual example of a candlestick chart.

Figure 10-6: Candlestick chart of the Deutsche Bank Commodities Tracking Index Fund (DBC).

Identifying Patterns: The Trend Is Your Friend

The basic premise of technical analysis is the constant interaction between buyers and sellers of a particular financial instrument, which is really just the interplay between the forces of supply and demand. Put simply, everything else constant, when there is increased demand for a security, the price of that security goes up. Conversely, when there is more supply of a security than demand, prices will go down. This information then helps you determine the future price direction of a commodity.

Support and *resistance* are two important technical indicators that seek to gauge the relationship between buyers and sellers. In this section, I show you how to identify support and resistance lines and what to do with them.

Identifying support and resistance

When demand for a commodity is strong enough, prices begin to remain at or above a particular level, which is known as *support*. Support is nothing more than a line that supports preexisting price levels. Technically, support is where demand is strong enough — or at least stronger than supply — that it prevents any further price declines. Figure 10-7 is an example of a support line in action.

Figure 10-7:
Support line
of Plains
Exploration
Co. (NYSE:
PXP), an oil
and gas
exploration
company.

On the other end of the spectrum is resistance. *Resistance* is the exact opposite (or mirror) of support in that it is the level where supply (number of sellers) is so strong that it prevents any further price increases. Figure 10-8 is an
example of resistance, where prices are not able to go past a certain point.

Figure 10-8:
Resistance
line of
ExxonMobil
Corp.
(NYSE:
XOM).

So how do you actually establish support and resistance? It's quite simple:
Use the commodity's previous highs to establish resistance and use its previous lows to establish its support line. For resistance, take the average of the

previous highs, as seen on the chart, and draw a straight line through that average. For support, you take the average of the previous lows on the chart and draw a straight line through that.

Again, support and resistance lines are not set in stone and are likely to fluctuate as prices increase or decrease. These lines are meant to give you a ballpark estimate of a commodity's trading range.

What is the difference between technical and fundamental analysis?

If you want to witness a good argument, put a fundamental analyst and a technical analyst in the same room — but I recommend you take a couple of steps back because the argument may get a little heated! Just as there's a constant battle between bulls and bears in the financial markets, it seems that fundamental analysts and technicians are constantly at odds with each other. Perhaps it's because each side approaches investing in radically different ways.

Fundamental analysis is a method of investing that places a premium on the fundamentals of a financial instrument. For example if a fundamental analyst is analyzing a company's stock, she will take a look at the company's balance sheet, income statement, and statement of cash flows. She will analyze the underlying health of a company, focusing on data on assets and liabilities and on income and expenses. As such, fundamental analysis focuses on the "basics" of a company or security. (I examine some of these key fundamental metrics for energy companies in Chapter 14 and for mining companies in Chapter 18.)

Technical analysis, on the other hand, does not concern itself too much with the underlying security's health. Technical analysis studies the interaction between sellers and buyers of a security and attempts to predict future price patterns based on a study of this interaction.

Technicians rely on graphs, charts, and other trading information to forecast the price of a security. They tend to only concern themselves with what's going on in the actual marketplace.

So which is the better approach? As a general rule, investors who have a long investment horizon use fundamental analysis to identify a company or commodity that's in good health. They choose the healthiest company and park their money there, not worrying about day-to-day fluctuations. The assumption is that a security with good fundamentals will tend to outperform a security whose fundamentals are shaky over the long term (Warren Buffett's investment strategy is based on this philosophy). Most short-term investors (traders) seek to profit in the marketplace by placing short-term bets on a security's price movements. These traders rely on technical analysis because it gives them a good idea of where a security is heading in the short term.

In a nutshell, if you're investing for the long term, then fundamental analysis may provide you with better results. If, on the other hand, your investing timeframe is short, then technical analysis may give you better results. That being said, I recommend you use a combination of both fundamental and technical analysis when you're investing because each one provides information that the other one does not.

Trend lines: Ride the trend till the end

Support and resistance lines are used to identify and establish price trend lines. One of the major assumptions of technical analysis is that prices tend to move in established patterns; in other words they follow a trend. Trend lines are in fact based on Isaac Newton's First Law of Motion, which states that an object in uniform motion tends to remain in uniform motion, unless it is acted upon by outside forces. This is what technical analysis is all about: identifying the trend and then riding that trend till the end, either when it stops or reverses.

You want to be familiar with the two types of trend lines that exist in the world of technical analysis: uptrends and downtrends.

Uptrends

An *uptrend line* has a positive slope and is nothing more than an upward sloping support line. Support is established because there are more buyers than sellers and this drives up the price of the commodity. Figure 10-9 shows an example of an uptrend line in action.

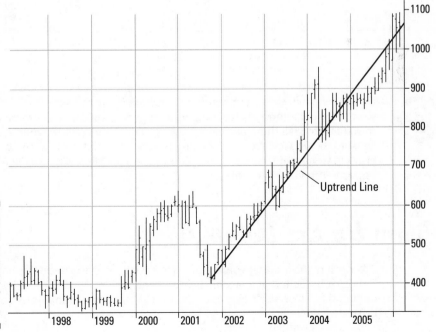

Figure 10-9:
Uptrend line of Platinum on the NYMEX (Dollars per Troy Ounce).

Downtrends

A *downtrend line* has a negative slope and is the equivalent of a downwardly sloped resistance line. When a commodity is trending downward, there are more sellers than buyers, and this is what puts downward pressure on the price. Figure 10-10 shows a good example of a downtrend line in action.

Figure 10-10: Downtrend line for Frontline (NYSE: FRO), an oil tanker stock.

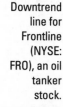

Once you identify a trend, I would not recommend trading against that trend because a confirmed trend tends to continue along the same path. In other words, if a commodity is trending upward, you probably want to be on the buy-side because there are more buyers than sellers (that's what is actually causing the upward trend). The only time you should trade against a pre-existing trend is if that trend breaks down or establishes a new trend in the opposite direction (known as a trend reversal).

Pump Up the Volume!

After price, the trading volume of a security is perhaps the most important indicator in technical analysis. If you ever consider buying or selling a commodity — or any other security for that matter — looking at volume is critical.

What does volume indicate, anyway? *Volume* is the best measure of interest by the investing community in a commodity or other security. When investors are interested in an asset — whether on the buy side or the sell side — you are going to see large spikes in volume, which is an indication of large amounts of trading activity. When investors aren't interested in a commodity, volume will be fairly dry.

An increase in trading volume accompanying a price spike is a sign of *accumulation* — that investors are busy accumulating, or acquiring, the commodity. This is a very good, bullish sign if you're long the commodity or considering going long the commodity. (Turn to Chapter 9 for more on going long.) This means that the trend has been identified and, more importantly, it has been confirmed. In Figure 10-11, I give you an example of a price increase accompanied by a spike in volume.

Besides being a measure of supply and demand, volume can confirm whether a commodity is experiencing a reliable run-up in price or whether it is going through a false breakout. A price increase that's not accompanied by a spike in volume is not such a good sign because the price is increasing without heavy accumulation. This signals that the price run-up could falter — that this may be a false breakout. Volume, therefore, provides confirmation of the trend.

If the price of the commodity is going down on heavy volume (when volume is high), get out! This means that the commodity is experiencing heavy *distribution,* or selling. Of course, if you're short the commodity, then by all means hold on to your position. (For more on going long and short, make sure you check out Chapter 9.)

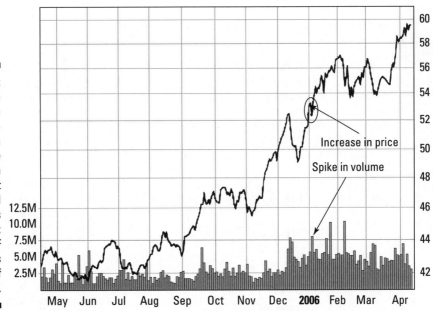

Figure 10-11:
A spike in volume accompanies a price increase in Street Tracks Gold Trust Shares (NYSE: GLD), an ETF that tracks the price of gold.

Moving Averages: Anything But Average

The *Moving Average* (MA) is a widely used technical indicator that charts the average of a security's price over a specific period of time. You can use two types of Moving Averages: the *Simple Moving Average* (SMA) and the *Enhanced Moving Average* (EMA).

Keeping it simple with the SMA

The SMA, like its name implies, takes a straightforward, equally weighted approach to the concept of moving averages. The SMA takes the average of a security's price over a specific period of time and places an equal weighting on all the averages. In other words, the price of the commodity during each of the trading sessions has the same statistical significance.

For example, if you take a 50-day SMA of a security, the performance of that security on Day 3 has the same weight as its performance on Day 44.

Calculating the moving average is not very difficult. Simply add the closing prices of the commodity over X number of days and then divide the total by X. For instance, to calculate the 200-day SMA, add the closing prices of the commodity over the past 200 trading sessions and divide it by 200.

While you can create an SMA for any period of time, the most widely used SMAs are the 50-day SMA and the 200-day SMA.

The SMA is a fluid metric that is in constant flux because it takes into account the commodity's closing price over a fixed number of trading sessions. Figure 10-12 shows an SMA overlay to illustrate this point.

Taking it up a notch with the EMA

One of the biggest drawbacks of the SMA is that it places the same weight on a commodity's most recent prices as it does on older prices. This creates a lag in the SMA's sensitivity to recent price changes, making it a less accurate portratyal of current trends. As a result, many investors use an improved (or at least a more accurate) version of the SMA: the *Enhanced Moving Average* or EMA (sometimes also known as the *Exponential Moving Average*).

The EMA is an extension of the SMA and emphasizes a commodity's more recent prices over older ones. This emphasis allows for a better price reaction sensitivity, which means that the EMA reacts more quickly and accurately to recent price movements. This, in turn, is a more accurate predictor of where the commodity's price is heading. Notice in Figure 10-13 that the EMA for

Newmont Mining (NYSE: NEM) is much more sensitive to price movements than the SMA in Figure 10-13, particularly towards the most recent trading sessions.

Figure 10-12: 50-day SMA of Newmont Mining (NYSE: NEM), one of the world's largest mining companies.

Figure 10-13: 50-day EMA for Newmont Mining.

Both the SMA and EMA are good indicators of established price trends. But which is better? I recommend using the SMA if your investment time horizon is long term because the SMA is a more accurate projection of long-term price patterns and doesn't fluctuate as much with recent price moves. On the other hand, if you're investing for the short term, then you want to be able to react as quickly as possible to recent and sudden price fluctuations, in which case the EMA is a better indicator.

Both the SMA and EMA are good indicators when the commodity is following a confirmed trend — either an upward trend or a downward trend. But don't rely too heavily on the moving averages when the security is not following a confirmed trend line because MAs are *lagging* indicators whose strength is in identifying confirmed patterns, not in predicting sudden price reversals or breakdowns.

It's All Relative: Using the RSI

The *Relative Strength Index*, also known as the RSI, is a useful tool you can use to measure the *price momentum* or *velocity* of a commodity. The RSI measures the rate of change of a commodity's price by comparing the average price change of a commodity's price increases with the average price change of that commodity's price decreases.

The technical designation of the RSI is *momentum oscillator* because it tries to gauge the *momentum,* or how fast a commodity is changing, over a certain period. The RSI quantifies the magnitude between a commodity's upward and downward price movements by using the following formula:

$$RSI = 100 - 100/(1 + RS)$$

Where

RS = Average gain of the days the commodity closes upward divided by

Average gain of the days the commodity closes downward

The number of days taken into consideration is up to you, although most RSI indicators take into account a period of 14 trading sessions.

The RSI is measured by a number between 0 and 100. The higher the RSI, the more the commodity is said to be *overbought*. In other words, it is overvalued, and a decrease in price may be around the corner. Although there isn't a specific number that indicates with absolute certainty whether a commodity is overvalued, 70 is generally used as the cutoff.

Similarly, an RSI figure of 30 or below indicates that a commodity is *oversold,* or undervalued. A low RSI number is a bullish indicator and may signal price increases in the near future. Take a close look at how the RSI moves — or oscillates — with the price of the security in Figure 10-14.

As a general rule, a high RSI is a sell signal while a low RSI is a buy signal.

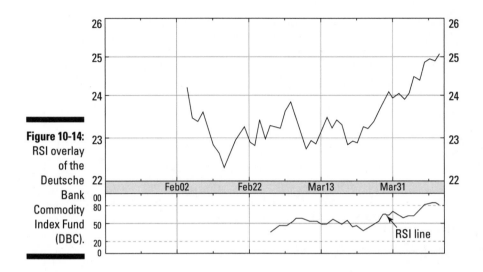

Figure 10-14: RSI overlay of the Deutsche Bank Commodity Index Fund (DBC).

Breaking into Bollinger Bands

Bollinger Bands, developed by the analyst John Bollinger, is a technical indicator that uses a system of fluctuating bands that encompass the security to determine its volatility.

The Bollinger Bands system uses three bands. The *primary,* or middle, band — the basis of the Bollinger Bands system — is a straightforward Simple Moving Average (SMA) The second, upper band is plotted as the SMA plus two standard deviation units. The third, lower band is the SMA minus two standard deviation units.

In statistics, *standard deviation* is often used as a measure of volatility. Standard deviation is calculated using a mathematical formula that essentially measures how spread out certain points are from a given arithmetic mean. This is sometimes known as *statistical dispersion* and is applied in technical analysis to determine volatility.

Because Bollinger Bands move in tandem with the SMA, they continually shadow the price of the security on a relative basis. When prices become more volatile, the Bollinger Bands tend to expand. Similarly, when prices become more stable, the Bollinger Bands adjust themselves by contracting.

When prices approach the upper band, this indicates that the commodity is *overbought.* The commodity is *overvalued* and will likely face downward price pressures in future trading sessions. In other words, prices approaching the upper band is a bearish sign.

On the other hand, when the price flirts with the lower band, this indicates that the commodity is *oversold* and *undervalued*. When the price approaches the lower band, this is generally viewed as a bullish signal. Take a look at Figure 10-15 to see how Bollinger Bands move in tandem with a security.

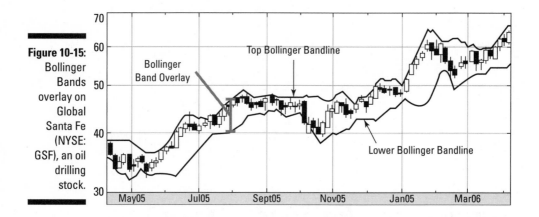

Figure 10-15:
Bollinger Bands overlay on Global Santa Fe (NYSE: GSF), an oil drilling stock.

Bollinger Bands are best used in conjunction with other technical metrics. When I'm using technical analysis, the first things I look at are the support and resistance lines and the moving averages, and I use this information to identify trend lines and the likely direction of the commodity. If I need additional confirmation of a trend, I will then use secondary technical indicators such as the Relative Strength Index (RSI) and Bollinger Bands. In other words, use Bollinger Bands after you've looked at the other primary technical metrics for confirmation purposes.

Part III
The Power House: How to Make Money in Energy

The 5th Wave   By Rich Tennant

©RICHTENNANT

SALAD BARS

"It's this trend that leads us to believe we should supplement our oil commodities with investments in some of the earth's rich vinegar and crouton reserves."

In this part . . .

Energy is the largest commodities asset class and pre-sents some solid investment opportunities. I help you find out the ins and outs of the energy markets and show you ways to profit in this sector, from trading crude oil futures contracts to investing in diversified electric utilities.

Chapter 11

It's a Crude, Crude World! Investing in Crude Oil

• •

In This Chapter

▶ Taking a look at key metrics

▶ Getting a grip on the market fundamentals

▶ Profiting from the high price of crude

• •

Crude oil is undoubtedly the king of commodities, in terms of both its production value and its importance to the global economy. Crude oil is the most traded nonfinancial commodity in the world today, and it supplies 40 percent of the world's total energy needs — more than any other single commodity. In fact, more barrels of crude oil are traded on a daily basis (85 Million Barrels, 2006 figures) than any other commodity. Crude oil's importance also stems from the fact that it is the base product for a number of indispensable goods. Gasoline, jet fuel, plastics, and a number of other necessary products are derived from it.

The importance of crude oil to the global economy was illustrated during the Arab Oil Embargo of 1973. During that year, the Arab members of the Organization of Petroleum Exporting Countries (OPEC) placed an embargo on crude oil shipments to Western countries. Within a matter of weeks, the price of crude oil skyrocketed by 400 percent, and a number of industrialized nations were thrown into recessions, experiencing high inflation and high unemployment for a number of years thereafter. The oil price shocks of the 1970s and their debilitating effects on the global economy underscored crude oil's indispensability.

Oil is truly the lifeblood of the global economy. Without it, the modern world would come to a screeching halt. Drivers wouldn't be able to drive their cars, ships would have no fuel to transport goods around the world, and airplanes would be grounded indefinitely.

Because of its preeminent role in the global economy, crude oil makes for a great investment. In this chapter, I show you how to make money investing in what is arguably the world's greatest natural resource. However, the oil industry is a multidimensional, complex business with many players with often conflicting interests. So proceeding with a bit of caution and making sure to understand the market fundamentals is essential for success.

In the following sections, I give you an overview of the global oil industry and the many links in the oil supply chain. I analyze consumption and production figures, introduce you to the major players (both countries and companies), and show you the best ways to execute a sound investment strategy.

Crude Realities

Having a good understanding of the global consumption and production patterns is important if you're considering investing in the oil industry. Knowing how much oil is produced in the world, by which countries, and to which consumers it is shipped allows you to develop an investment strategy that benefits from the oil market fundamentals.

I'm sometimes amazed at some of the misconceptions regarding the oil industry. For example, I was once speaking with students about energy independence and I was shocked when a majority of them claimed that the United States got over 50 percent of its oil from the Persian Gulf and Saudi Arabia in particular; in fact, nothing could be further from the truth.

The United States is the third largest producer of crude oil in the world. Take a look at Table 11-2, and you'll quickly see that the United States produces over 7 Million Barrels a day (this includes oil products), behind only Saudi Arabia and Russia. In fact, the United States didn't become a net importer of oil until 1993; up until that point the United States produced over 50 percent of the oil it consumed domestically.

Currently (2006 figures) the United States imports about 65 percent of its oil. If energy (oil) independence is measured by the percentage of oil a country imports, then the United States is more energy independent than both Germany (which imports 80 percent of its oil) and Japan (which imports more than 90 percent).

The biggest oil exporter to the United States isn't a Middle Eastern country but our friendly northern neighbor. That's right: Canada is the largest exporter of crude oil to the United States in the world! Persian Gulf oil makes up about 20 percent of imported oil.

Mad Max is mad about oil

Remember the 1980s movie *Mad Max,* which launched Mel Gibson's career? The movie, which was released only a few years after the Arab Oil Embargo of 1973, is actually a depiction of a world without oil. If you recall, the movie portrays a society that is plunged into civil disorder, chaos, and unrest as a result of a fuel shortage. The citizens resort to violence and mayhem in order to steal any fuel they can get their hands on.

This high-octane drama demonstrates the extent to which societies were affected by the oil shocks of the 1970s and underscores the importance of oil as an essential element of modern life.

My point here is that there's a lot of misinformation out there about this topic, and you need to be armed with the correct figures to be a successful investor. In the following sections, I show you which metrics are closely monitored by all the market participants (traders, major oil companies, and producing/consuming countries) — such as global reserve estimates, daily production rates, daily consumption rates, daily export figures, and daily import figures. I present you with the most up-to-date information regarding oil production and consumption patterns. Because these patterns are likely to change in the future because of supply and demand, I also show you where you can go to get the latest information on the oil markets. This will make you a better investor.

No need for a reservation: Examining global reserve estimates

As an investor, knowing which countries have large crude oil deposits is an important part of your investment strategy. As demand for crude oil increases, countries that have large deposits of this natural resource stand to benefit tremendously. One way to benefit from this trend is to invest in indigenous countries and companies with large reserves of crude oil (I go through this strategy in detail in the last section of this chapter).

The *Oil & Gas Journal* estimates that global proven crude oil reserves are 1,292 Billion Barrels (1.29 Trillion Barrels). In Table 11-1, I list the countries with the largest proven crude oil reserves. These figures may change as new oilfields are discovered and as new technologies allow for the extraction of additional oil from existing fields.

Table 11-1	Largest Oil Reserves by Country, 2006 Figures	
Rank	**Country**	**Proven Reserves (Billion Barrels)**
1	Saudi Arabia	261
2	Iran	125
3	Iraq	115
4	Kuwait	101
5	United Arab Emirates	98
6	Venezuela	77
7	Russia	60
8	Libya	39
9	Nigeria	35
10	United States	21

Source: Oil & Gas Journal.

Although Canada is not on this list, it has proven reserves of 4.7 Billion Barrels of *conventional* crude oil — crude that is easily recoverable and accounted for. In addition to conventional crude, Canada is rich in unconventional crude oil located in oil sands. Oil from oil sands is much more difficult to extract and, as a result, is generally not included toward the calculation of official and conventional reserve estimates. However, if Canada's oil sands were included, Canada would be catapulted to the number-two spot with a grand total of 178 Billion Barrels.

Another point to keep in mind is that having large deposits of crude doesn't mean that a country has exploited and developed all of its oilfields. For example, although Iraq has the third largest oil deposits in the world, it's not even in the top ten list of producing countries because of poor and underdeveloped infrastructure. There is a big difference between proven reserves and actual production. (See Table 11-2 in the following section.)

The calculation of proven, recoverable deposits of crude oil is not an exact science. For example, the *Oil & Gas Journal* figures are different from those of the Energy Information Administration (EIA), which in turn are different from those from the International Energy Agency (IEA). I recommend following a "big picture" approach to global reserve estimates and consulting all the major sources for these statistics. To keep up on updated figures and statistics on the oil industry, check out the following organizations:

✔ **Energy Information Administration (EIA):** www.eia.doe.gov

✔ **International Energy Agency (IEA):** www.iea.org

✔ **BP Statistical Review (BP):** www.bp.com

✔ *Oil & Gas Journal*: www.ogj.com

Staying busy and productive: Looking at production figures

Identifying the countries with large reserves is important, but it's only a starting point as you start investing in the oil markets. In order to determine which countries are exploiting these reserves adequately, I recommend looking at another important metric: actual production. Having large reserves is meaningless if a country isn't tapping those reserves to produce oil. In Table 11-2, I list the top ten producers of crude oil.

Table 11-2	Largest Producers of Crude Oil, 2006 Figures	
Rank	*Country*	*Daily Production (Million Barrels)*
1	Saudi Arabia	10.3
2	Russia	9.2
3	United States	7.2
4	Iran	4.1
5	Mexico	3.8
6	China	3.6
7	Norway	3.1
8	Canada	3.1
9	Venezuela	2.9
10	United Arab Emirates	2.7

A number of factors influence how much crude a country is able to pump out of the ground on a daily basis, such as geopolitical stability and the application of technologically advanced crude recovery techniques. Also, remember that daily production may vary across the year because of disruptions resulting from geopolitical events such as embargos, sanctions, and sabotage that put a stop to daily production or from other external factors like weather. Think of Hurricane Katrina and its devastating effect on U.S. oil supply in the summer of 2005.

You need to keep a close eye on global daily supply because any disruption in the production supply chain can have a strong impact on the current price of crude oil. Because there is a tight supply-and-demand equation, any disruption in supply can send prices for crude skyrocketing.

Traders in the commodity exchanges follow the daily crude oil production numbers closely. Benchmark crude oil contracts such as the *West Texas Intermediate* (WTI) traded on the New York Mercantile Exchange (NYMEX) and the North Sea Brent traded on the Intercontinental Exchange (ICE) in London are affected by supply numbers. As a result, any geopolitical event or natural disaster that may reduce production is closely watched by the market. (Check out Chapter 9 for more on the crude oil futures contracts.)

If you're an active oil trader with a futures account, then following these daily production numbers — which are available through the Energy Information Administration (EIA) Web site at www.eia.doe.gov — is crucial. The futures markets are particularly sensitive to these numbers, and any event that takes crude off the market can have a sudden impact on crude futures contracts. If, on the other hand, you're a long-term investor in the markets, monitoring this number is also important because production figures can have an effect on the general stock market performance as well. For example, if rebels seize a pipeline in Nigeria and 300,000 Barrels of Nigerian crude are taken off the market, this will result in higher crude prices, which will have an impact on U.S. stocks (they generally fall). Thus your stock portfolio holdings may be at risk because of daily crude oil production disruptions. Therefore monitoring this statistic regularly is important for both short-term traders as well as long-term investors.

It can be demanding: Checking out demand figures

The United States tops the list of oil consumers and has been the single largest consumer of crude oil for the last 25 years. While a lot of folks pay attention to the demand increase from China and India, most of the demand for crude oil (and the resulting price pressures) still comes from the United States. While supply is a closely watched metric by traders around the world, demand figures are equally important because they indicate a steady and sustained increase in crude demand for the mid- to long term. This is likely to maintain increased pressure on crude prices. I list the top ten consumers of crude oil in the world in Table 11-3.

Table 11-3	Largest Consumers of Crude Oil, 2006 Figures	
Rank	*Country*	*Daily Consumption (Million Barrels)*
1	United States	20.5
2	China	6.5
3	Japan	5.4
4	Germany	2.6
5	Russia	2.6
6	India	2.3
7	Canada	2.3
8	Brazil	2.2
9	South Korea	2.1
10	France	2.0

As of 2006, global consumption stood at approximately 85 Million Barrels per day. The United States and China are currently the biggest consumers of crude oil in the world, and this trend will continue throughout the 21st century, with global consumption expected to increase to 120 Million Barrels a day by 2025.

Figure 11-1 shows you the expected global consumption through 2025 as well as the expected growth from the two largest consumers — the United States and China.

Figure 11-1:
Expected daily global consumption of crude oil from 2000 to 2015.

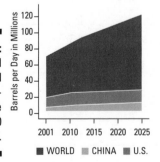

Always design an investment strategy that will profit from long-term trends. This steady increase in global demand for crude oil is a good reason to be bullish on oil prices.

Going in and out: Eyeing imports and exports

Another pair of numbers you need to keep close tabs on is export and import figures. Exports are different from production because a country can produce a lot of oil and consume most, if not all, of it — just like the United States. On the other end of the spectrum, a country can produce plenty of oil and export most of it. Identifying the top exporting countries is helpful because this allows you to zero in on the countries that are actually generating revenues from the sale of crude oil to other countries. Countries that are net exporters of crude stand to benefit tremendously from the oil boom and you can get in on the action by investing domestically in these countries, a strategy I outline in the final section of this chapter. In Table 11-4, I list the top oil-exporting countries in 2006.

Table 11-4	Top Ten Oil Exporters, 2006 Figures	
Rank	**Country**	**Daily Oil Exports (Million Barrels)**
1	Saudi Arabia	8.7
2	Russia	6.6
3	Norway	2.9
4	Iran	2.5
5	Venezuela	2.3
6	United Arab Emirates	2.3
7	Kuwait	2.2
8	Nigeria	2.1
9	Mexico	1.8
10	Algeria	1.6

What is OPEC and how does it affect the oil markets?

The *Organization of Petroleum Exporting Countries* (OPEC) is made up of countries that are involved in the production and export of crude oil products around the world. Currently OPEC has 11 member countries: Algeria, Indonesia, Iran, Iraq, Kuwait, Libya, Nigeria, Qatar, Saudi Arabia, the United Arab Emirates (UAE), and Venezuela. Because OPEC's members collectively hold about 65 percent of total crude oil reserves and produce 40 percent of the world's oil, they have considerable influence on the markets.

OPEC's members meet regularly at its headquarters in Vienna, Austria, in order to establish the course of action for its members. Because its members are key players in the global oil markets, any decision taken by OPEC can significantly affect the price of oil on a global scale. One mechanism through which OPEC achieves this influence is through the use of a quota system, where individual members must follow pre-established production quotas.

OPEC quotas are an important statistic to regularly keep your eye on because they dictate the level of oil production for some of the world's most important oil producers. But even more important than the self-imposed quotas is the actual oil production from each member country because that may differ from the quotas: Some countries, enticed by the high price of crude, are sometimes tempted to increase their production because this means more petrodollars in their coffers. This is ironic because the production quota is partly responsible for the increased prices, meaning prices decrease as production increases. You can keep track of regular developments from OPEC that may affect oil markets through the OPEC Web site at `www.opec.org`. Although OPEC's influence on the markets has diminished since the 1973 Arab Oil Embargo, it still wields considerable influence over the oil markets.

Although exports receive a lot of attention from traders, imports, which represent the other side of equation, are equally important. Countries that are main importers of crude oil are primarily advanced, industrialized societies like Germany and the United States. This means that these countries are rich enough that they can absorb crude oil price increases, but as a general rule, the importers face a lot of pressure during any price increases. This pressure is sometimes translated into lower stock market performances in the importing countries, which means you should be careful if you're exposed to the domestic stock markets of these oil importers. I list the top crude oil importing countries of 2006 in Table 11-5.

Table 11-5	Top Ten Oil Importers, 2006 Figures	
Rank	*Country*	*Daily Oil Imports (Million Barrels)*
1	United States	11.8
2	Japan	5.3
3	China	2.9
4	Germany	2.5
5	South Korea	2.1
6	France	2.0
7	Italy	1.7
8	Spain	1.6
9	India	1.5
10	Taiwan	1.0

Going Up the Crude Chain

Crude oil by itself isn't very useful; it derives its value from its derivative products. Only after it is processed and refined into consumable products such as gasoline, propane, and jet fuel does it become so valuable. In the following sections, I explain the contents of crude oil and go through some of the products that can be extracted from crude.

Crude oil was formed across millions of years from the remains of dead animals and other organisms whose bodies decayed in the Earth. Because of a number of geological factors such as sedimentation, these remains were eventually transformed into crude oil deposits. Therefore, crude oil is literally a *fossil fuel* — a fuel derived from fossils. As a matter of fact, the word *petroleum* comes from the Latin words *petra*, which means rock, and *oleum*, which means oil. So the word petroleum literally means oil from the rocks!

Take a look at some of the products an average barrel of crude oil yields in Figure 11-2.

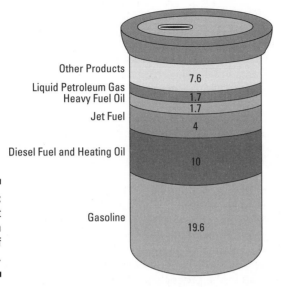

Figure 11-2:
Product
yields from
a barrel of
crude oil.

Other Products — 7.6
Liquid Petroleum Gas — 1.7
Heavy Fuel Oil — 1.7
Jet Fuel — 4
Diesel Fuel and Heating Oil — 10
Gasoline — 19.6

A barrel holds 42 Gallons of crude oil or crude oil equivalents. (That's about 159 Liters.) Barrel is abbreviated as *bbl*; barrels as *bbls*.

You want that light and sweet or heavy and sour?

Not all crudes are created equal. If you invest in crude oil, you need to realize right off the bat that crude oil comes in different qualities with different characteristics. You'd be surprised at how different that "black stuff" can be from region to region. Generally speaking crude oil is classified into two broad categories: light and sweet, and heavy and sour. There are other classifications, but these are the two major ones.

The two criteria most widely used to determine the quality of crude oil are density and sulfur content. *Density* usually refers to how much a crude oil will yield in terms of products, such as heating oil and jet fuel. For instance, a crude oil with lower density, known as a *light crude,* tends to yield higher levels of products. On the other hand, a crude oil with high density, commonly referred to as a *heavy crude,* will have lower product yields.

The density of a crude oil, also known as the *gravity,* is measured by a scale devised by the American Petroleum Institute (API). The higher the API number, expressed in degrees, the lower the density of the crude oil. Therefore, a crude oil with density of 43 degrees API will yield more desirable crude oil products than a crude oil with 35 degrees API. Heavy crude (which is found in Venezuela and Canada) has an API degree of 20 or below.

Sulfur content is another key determinant of crude oil quality. Sulfur is a corrosive material that decreases the purity of a crude oil. Therefore a crude oil with high sulfur content, which is known as *sour,* is much less desirable than a crude oil with low sulfur content, known as *sweet* crude.

How is this important to you as an investor? First, if you want to invest in the oil industry, you need to know what kind of oil you're going to get for your money. If you're going to invest in an oil company, you need to be able to determine which type of crude it is processing. You can find this information in the company's annual or quarterly reports. A company involved in the production of light, sweet crude will generate more revenue from this premium crude than one involved in the processing of heavy, sour crude. This doesn't mean you shouldn't invest in companies with exposure to heavy, sour crude; you just have to factor the type into your investment strategy.

In Table 11-6, I list some important crude oils and their characteristics.

Table 11-6	Crude Oil Grades	
Crude Oil	*Density (API)*	*Sulfur Content*
North West Shelf (Australia)	60.0	0.01
Arab Super Light (Saudi Arabia)	50.0	0.06
Bonny Light (Nigeria)	35.4	0.14
Duri (Indonesia)	21.5	0.14

As you can see, you can choose from a wide variety of crude oil products as investments. If you're interested in investing in a specific country, you need to find out what kind of crude oil it produces. Ideally you want a crude oil with low sulfur content and a high API number as a density benchmark.

What's the deal with peak oil?

Is the world really running out of oil? The concept of *peak oil* has generated much attention in recent years. A plethora of books have been written about whether the world is running out of oil, and proponents (and opponents) of this theory have hit the airwaves en masse. This is a serious topic, but unfortunately folks tend to get carried away and start spinning tales of global gloom and doom. It's important to remain level headed when talking about this issue. Basically, you have two schools of thought on the matter.

The first school argues that the world has already reached peak production and that demand is going to quickly suck out what's remaining of crude in the world. The other side argues that the world still has abundant crude oil supplies and that, through technological developments and other means, crude oil that wasn't previously extractable will be brought to market. Both arguments have some merit. First, crude oil is a finite resource and, by definition, is available only in limited quantities. However, people have been saying that the world is going to run out of oil since the first commercially viable oil well was discovered in Titusville, Pennsylvania, back in 1859. One hundred and fifty years later and the world still hasn't run out of oil. Does this mean that the world will never run out of oil? Of course not. But it does indicate that these calls have been made before and are likely to continue well into the future.

Many experts agree that completely running out of oil in the near future is an unlikely event. I prefer to put it this way: The world is not about to run out of oil — the world is about to run out of cheap, high-quality, and readily available oil.

The light, sweet crude oil that refiners prefer because of its high products yield (discussed in the section "You want that light and sweet or heavy and sour?" and in Chapter 13) is running low. However, the world still has plenty of crude that's of a heavier quality. Just look at Canada's oil sands. This heavy crude is not preferred because of its low quality, but there is plenty of it to go around for a long time. In addition, technological advances (such as horizontal drilling) are enabling previously unextractable oil to now be extracted. Therefore the oil fields are yielding more crude than ever before, both percentagewise and on an absolute basis.

What you should be concerned about at the end of the day as an investor are the fundamentals of the market. Whether the world is running out of oil is a hot debate that receives a lot of attention; but panic is not an investment strategy. If the world is truly running out of oil, you just need to look at the market fundamentals and develop an investment strategy that's going to take advantage of these fundamentals.

If history is a guide, humans can be extremely resourceful when it comes to sustaining themselves. If crude does run out, there will be other alternative sources of energy (which I look at in Chapter 13). Because energy is necessary to human life, you can be sure that alternatives will be developed. There is already a move towards investing in alternative energy sources, such as wind and solar energy, as well as other more abundant fossil fuels such as coal. This trend should continue in the coming years. As an investor, you need to go where the value is.

Make Big Bucks with Big Oil

The price of crude oil has skyrocketed during these first years of the 21st century; if these years are any indication for what's in store for oil, then you definitely want to develop a winning game plan to take advantage of this trend. Figure 11-3 shows the increasing price of crude oil from 1997 to 2006.

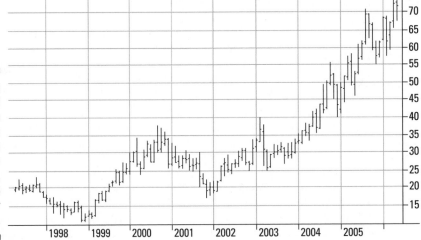

Figure 11-3:
Price of
West Texas
Intermediate
(WTI) crude
oil on the
NYMEX,
1997 to 2006
(Dollars per
Barrel).

I talk about how to invest directly in West Texas Intermediate crude oil and other oil futures contracts in Chapter 9.

A lot of people are making a lot of money from the high price of crude and gasoline. Why shouldn't you be one of them? In this section, I show you how to actually profit from the high prices at the pump!

Oil companies: Lubricated and firing on all cylinders

Oil companies get a lot of bad rap. Whatever you may think of them, they make for a great investment. Oil companies are responsible for bringing precious energy products to consumers, and for this service they are compensated — handsomely. Oil companies are for-profit companies that are run for the benefit of their shareholders. Instead of complaining about oil companies, why not become a shareholder of one (or more)!

In this section, I talk about the integrated oil companies, sometimes known as "big oil," "the majors," or "integrated oil companies." These are the oil companies that are involved in all the phases of the oil production process — from exploring for oil, to refining it, to transporting it to consumers. ExxonMobil, Chevron Texaco, and BP are all "big oil" companies.

Big oil companies aren't the only players in the oil business. A number of other companies are involved in specific aspects of the transformational process of crude oil. For example, you have companies like Valero that are primarily involved in refining and others such as General Maritime that own fleets of tankers that transport crude oil and products. I discuss how to invest in these companies — the refiners, transporters, and explorers — in Chapter 14.

Flying solo: Looking at individual oil companies

The major oil companies have been posting record profits. In 2005, ExxonMobil announced the largest annual corporate profit in history as it earned a staggering $36.1 Billion on revenues of $371 Billion! To put it in perspective, Saudi Arabia's 2005 GDP was $338 Billion. Exxon's 2005 profits were 20 percent higher than its 2004 profits, which were over 10 percent higher than the previous year's!

Another big oil company, ConocoPhillips, raked in $13.53 Billion in profits for 2005, up 66 percent from the previous year. Chevron Corp., meanwhile, posted $14.1 Billion in earnings for 2005. These mouthwatering announcements are a direct result of the increased global demand for crude oil and its products. As global demand continues and supplies remain limited, I expect big oil companies to keep generating record revenues and profits. This is an investment you cannot afford to miss. In Table 11-7, I list some of the companies that you could include in your portfolio.

Table 11-7	Major Integrated Oil Companies, 2005 Figures			
Oil Company	*Ticker*	*Market Cap*	*Revenues*	*Earnings*
ExxonMobil	XOM	$360 Billion	$371 Billion	$36 Billion
Total	TOT	$282 Billion	$165 Billion	$14 Billion
BP	BP	$230 Billion	$265 Billion	$20 Billion
Shell	RDS-B	$219 Billion	$310 Billion	$24 Billion
PetroChina	PTR	$175 Billion	$69 Billion	$16 Billion
Chevron	CVX	$127 Billion	$198 Billion	$15 Billion
ConocoPhillips	COP	$100 Billion	$171 Billion	$14 Billion
Eni	E	$42 Billion	$93 Billion	$9 Billion
Repsol	REP	$32 Billion	$57 Billion	$4 Billion

This is only a brief snapshot of some of the major integrated oil companies you can choose from to add to your portfolio. For a more comprehensive list, check out Yahoo! Finance's section on integrated oil companies at `http://biz.yahoo.com/ic/120.html`.

Market capitalization, sometimes abbreviated as *market cap,* is a measure of the size of a corporation. Market cap is calculated by multiplying the number of shares outstanding by the price per share.

Most of these traditional oil companies have now moved into other areas in the energy sphere. These companies not only process crude oil into different products, but they also have vast petrochemicals businesses as well as growing projects involving natural gas and, increasingly, alternative energy sources. (To reflect this shift, for example, BP has changed its name from *British Petroleum* to *Beyond Petroleum.*) The bottom line is that investing in these oil companies gives you exposure to other sorts of products in the energy industry as well.

Although market capitalization, revenues, and earnings are important metrics to look at before investing in these companies, you also need to perform a thorough due diligence that takes into consideration other important factors that determine a company's health. I introduce some of these key metrics to help you decide the most suitable energy companies for your portfolio in Chapter 14.

Oil company ETFs: Strength in numbers

If you can't decide which oil company you want to invest in, you have several other options at your disposal, which allow you to buy the market, so to speak. One option is to buy Exchange Traded Funds (ETFs) that track the performance of a group of integrated oil companies (I discuss ETFs in Chapter 6). Here are a few oil company ETFs to consider:

- **iShares S&P Global Energy Sector (AMEX: IXC):** This ETF mirrors the performance of the Standard & Poor's Global Energy Sector index. Buying this ETF gives you exposure to companies such as ExxonMobil, Chevron, ConocoPhillips, and Royal Dutch Shell. The ETF, launched at the end of 2001, has 35 percent aggregate returns for a 3-year period.

- **Energy Select Sector SPDR (AMEX: XLE):** The XLE ETF is the largest energy ETF in the market. It is part of the S&P's family of *Standard & Poor's Depository Receipts* (SPDR), commonly referred to as *spiders,* and tracks the performance of a basket of oil company stocks. Some of the stocks it tracks include the majors ExxonMobil and Chevron; however, it also tracks oil services companies such as Halliburton and Schlumberger (which I discuss in Chapter 14). You get a nice mix of integrated oil companies as well as other independent firms by investing in the XLE.

✔ **iShares Goldman Sachs Natural Resources Sector (AMEX: IGE):** The IGE ETF mirrors the performance of the Goldman Sachs Natural Resources Sector index, which tracks the performance of companies like ConocoPhillips, Chevron, and BP as well as refiners such as Valero and Suncor. (I talk about refiners in Chapter 14.) Although a majority of this ETF is invested in integrated oil companies, it also provides you with a way to play a broad spectrum of energy companies.

Get your passport ready: Investing overseas

Another great way to capitalize on oil profits is to invest in an emerging market fund that invests in countries that sit on large deposits of crude oil and that have the infrastructure in place to export crude oil.

Even though a country may have large deposits of crude oil, it isn't necessarily able to produce and export crude oil for a profit. Iraq is a good example. Even though it sits on the third largest reserves of crude oil in the world (see Table 11-1), Iraq isn't even one of the top ten exporters of crude because the infrastructure and security environment isn't secure enough.

John D. Rockefeller: Father of the modern oil industry

A majority of today's most important oil companies are offspring of the Standard Oil Company, which was started by John Rockefeller in the late 19th century. Perhaps no other company has had such an impact on an industry as much as Standard Oil on the oil industry. Standard Oil was one of the first truly global companies that was involved in all aspects of the oil supply chain, from extraction and production to transportation, distribution, and marketing. The company got so big that the Department of Justice ordered its breakup. The resulting companies are still today's dominant energy companies. Standard Oil of New Jersey became Exxon and Standard Oil of New York became Mobil — the two companies eventually merged and are now ExxonMobil; Standard of California became Chevron; and Standard of Ohio is now known as Marathon Oil. Even though the company was forced to break up, the influence of Rockefeller's Standard Oil company is still felt in the industry today.

Countries that export crude oil have seen their current account surpluses reach record highs. (*Current account* measures a country's balance of payments as they relate to trade.) These windfall profits are having a tremendous effect on the economies of such countries. The stock markets of some of these countries, particularly the Persian Gulf countries (known as the *Gulf Cooperation Council* — or GCC), have had stellar performances lately. Table 11-8 shows the performance of the Persian Gulf countries' stock markets awash in petrodollars.

Table 11-8	Stock Market Performance in the Persian Gulf
Stock Market	*Performance (2003–2005)*
Dubai (UAE)	123.33%
Qatar	113.26%
Saudi Arabia	107.02%
Abu Dhabi (UAE)	77.28%
Kuwait	69.51%
Oman	46.18%
Bahrain	21.86%

The current account surplus is an important measure of how much a country is benefiting from the current oil boom. Saudi Arabia's current account surplus, for example, reached a record-setting $150 Billion in 2005, thanks largely to its oil exports. OPEC countries (see the sidebar "What is OPEC and how does it affect the oil markets?") are expected to generate a whopping $500 Billion current account surplus in 2006 because of the high price of oil.

For the uninitiated, investing directly in emerging markets can be a risky proposition and requires a lot of research. Some countries have different regulatory rules than the United States, and you need to know what these are before you get involved in a foreign venture.

One way to play emerging markets while avoiding the direct risks that this may entail is by investing in emerging markets funds that are located in the United States. These funds hire professionals who are familiar with the business environment in target countries and are able to navigate these foreign investment seas. These funds allow you to take advantage of booms in foreign countries, while remaining within the safe regulatory and investing environment of the United States.

Dubai: An oasis in the desert

Dubai, in the oil-rich United Arab Emirates, is but one of many striking examples of the transformative power of crude oil on a local economy. What was once a small desert town has transformed itself into a global financial powerhouse and a major trading hub. Fueled by the boom in crude oil exports, both in the UAE and from other Persian Gulf countries, Dubai has thriving financial services, construction, media, and manufacturing sectors.

Dubai's GDP has grown at an annual rate of 12 percent a year since the late 1990s as the price of crude oil has skyrocketed. As the price of crude continues to go up, driven by increased demand and tight supply, expect to see countries that export this black gold thrive. One way to benefit from this is by investing in the indigenous economies of oil-exporting countries.

Here are a couple emerging markets funds that give you an indirect exposure to the booming oil-exporting countries:

- ✔ **Fidelity Emerging Markets** (FEMKX)
- ✔ **Evergreen Emerging Markets Growth I** (EMGYX)

For more information on how to choose the right mutual fund manager, please turn to Chapter 6.

If you're interested in finding out more about the global oil industry, I highly recommend you read Daniel Yergin's masterpiece on the subject, *The Prize: The Epic Quest for Oil, Money and Power.*

Chapter 12

Welcome to Gas Vegas, Baby! Trading Natural Gas

• •

In This Chapter

▶ Identifying the main uses of natural gas

▶ Figuring out how to pick up on market signals

▶ Taking a look at Liquefied Natural Gas (LNG)

▶ Investing in natural gas companies and futures

• •

*I*f crude oil is the king of commodities, natural gas is sometimes said to be the queen. While crude oil accounts for about 40 percent of total energy consumed in the United States (the biggest energy market in the world), approximately 25 percent of energy consumption comes from natural gas. Natural gas is therefore an important source of energy both in the United States and around the world and can offer tremendous money-making opportunities.

Like crude oil (see Chapter 11) and coal (see Chapter 13), natural gas is a *nonrenewable fossil fuel* found in large deposits under the Earth. As a matter of fact, natural gas is sometimes found not too far away from crude oil deposits. While crude oil is the liquid fossil fuel and coal the solid one, natural gas is the gaseous fossil fuel.

Many people are sometimes confused by the term *natural gas* because they think (incorrectly) that it refers to the *gas* (gasoline) they use to fill their tanks. Although natural gas is sometimes used as a transportation fuel, the gasoline you buy at the gas station and natural gas have nothing to do with each other. The gasoline your car consumes is a product of crude oil, while natural gas is an entirely different member of the fossil fuel family used primarily for heating, cooling, and cooking purposes.

Because of its importance as a source of energy, natural gas makes for a good investment. It's an important commodity with many applications. In this chapter, I present you with all the information you need to develop an investment strategy in the natural gas segment of energy.

Because it's important you get all the facts upfront about this commodity, I first provide you with all the hands-on information about natural gas' applicability — how is it used and how you can profit from these uses. Then I give you a snapshot of the global natural gas market — this provides you with a road map so you know who's producing it and who's consuming it. Identifying these patterns is a necessary part of developing a sound investment strategy. Finally, I show you how to actually start investing in and trading Nat Gas, as traders sometimes call it. Natural gas may not get the same kind of attention as crude oil, but it still makes for a great investment!

What's the Use? Looking at Natural Gas Applications

Natural gas, because it is one of the cleanest-burning fossil fuels, has become increasingly popular as an energy source. In the United States alone, natural gas accounts for nearly a quarter of total energy consumption, as seen in Figure 12-1.

Figure 12-1: Breakdown of the total energy consumed in the United States in 2000. Source: US Department of Energy.

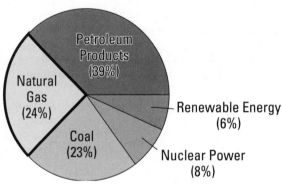

As you can see from Figure 12-1, natural gas is second only to petroleum when it comes to generating energy in the United States.

So who uses all this natural gas? The primary consumers of this commodity are the industrial sector, commercial interests, residential elements, transportation, and electricity generation. I list the consumption ratio of these sectors in Figure 12-2.

Figure 12-2:
Primary
consumers
of natural
gas in the
United
States.
Source: US
Department
of Energy

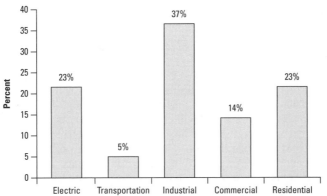

How do you measure natural gas?

Measuring natural gas can be confusing because there are multiple measurement methods. These measurements basically boil down to this: How much physical natural gas there is and how much energy does the natural gas generate.

While crude oil is measured in barrels (each barrel containing 42 Gallons of oil), natural gas is measured in cubic feet. Recall from chemistry class that a cubic foot is a measure of volume for a square prism with six sides each consisting of 1 foot in length. (The technical name for this shape is a *regular hexahedron*.) Or, you can simply think of it as the shape of a sugar cube! Because natural gas is in a gaseous state, it's easier to measure it in cubic feet. (Sometimes, natural gas is converted into liquid form, known as Liquefied Natural Gas (LNG), which I cover in the section "Liquefied Natural Gas: Getting Liquid without Getting Wet." LNG is also measured in cubic feet.

The abbreviation for cubic feet is *cf* (both letters are lower case). Therefore 10 cubic feet is abbreviated as 10 cf. In order to have practical applications, cubic feet must be able to measure large amounts of volume. Here are the abbreviations for measuring larger volume amounts of cubic feet:

✔ 100 cubic feet: 1 Ccf

✔ 1000 cubic feet: 1 Mcf

✔ 1 million cubic feet: 1 Mmcf

✔ 1 billion cubic feet: 1 Bcf

✔ 1 trillion cubic feet: 1 Tcf

Note that *cf* is always in lower case, while the first letter of the abbreviation is always capitalized. Many futures contracts based on natural gas are measured in cubic feet.

Natural gas may also be measured by the amount of energy it generates. This energy content is captured by a unit of measurement known as the *British Thermal Unit* or *Btu*. One Btu measures the amount of heat necessary to increase the temperature of one pound of water by one degree Fahrenheit. To put it in perspective, 1 cf is the equivalent of 1027 Btus. Btus, sometimes called *therms*, is the number that may appear in your gas bill to express the amount of natural gas your household consumed during a particular period of time.

For investment purposes, however, natural gas is generally quantified using cubic feet.

Calling all captains of industry: Industrial uses of natural gas

The industrial sector is the largest consumer of natural gas, accounting for almost 40 percent of total consumption. While industrial uses of natural gas have always played a major role in the sector, their significance has increased over the last several years and will continue to do so. As you can see in Figure 12-3, the industrial sector has always accounted for a large part of natural gas use and because this trend is going to continue, this is a good area to consider investing in. (Actually, demand for natural gas products as a whole is going to increase throughout the first quarter of the 21st century, for reasons I discuss in the next section. See Figure 12-8.)

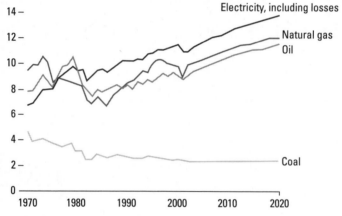

Figure 12-3: Industrial consumption of energy products, 1970 to 2020 (projected). Source: Energy Information Administration.

This increased demand should put upward price pressures on natural gas; one way to profit from this is by being long natural gas futures (for more on going long on futures, flip to the section "Natural selection: Trading Nat Gas futures").

As an investor, looking at long-term trends helps you develop an investment strategy that takes advantage of the market fundamentals.

So what specific parts of the industrial sector use natural gas? Natural gas is a truly versatile form of energy because it has many applications in industry. Here are a few industrial applications of natural gas products:

✔ Food processing

✔ Glass melting

✔ Metal smelting

✔ Waste incineration

✔ Fueling industrial boilers

✔ Feedstock for fertilizers

The chemical composition of natural gas consists primarily of *methane,* a hydrocarbon molecule. It also includes other hydrocarbons such as *butane, ethane,* and *propane* — all gases that have important industrial uses.

When the industrial sector is firing on all cylinders, so to speak, demand for natural gas will tend to increase. Keep an eye out for increased activity from the industrial sector because this is a bullish sign for natural gas. One indicator you can use to gauge the economic output from the industrial sector is the *Producer Price Index* (PPI). The PPI measures the average change in prices received by producers for their products, expressed as a percent change. The PPI, compiled by the Bureau of Labor Statistics (BLS), is a good measure of the health in the industrial sector. You can get the latest PPI reports at www.bls.gov/ppi.

If you can't stand the heat, get out of the kitchen! Natural gas in your home

Residential usage accounts for almost a quarter of total natural gas consumption (see Figure 12-2). A large portion of homes in the United States, as well as other countries, use natural gas for both their cooking and heating needs — the two largest applications of natural gas in the home.

About 70 percent of households in the United States have natural gas ovens in the kitchen. The use of natural gas for cooking purposes has steadily increased as technological developments have allowed for an efficient and safe use of natural gas. How does this affect you as an investor? As long as folks need to cook, you can bet that natural gas will be there to fill this important need. This essential usage assures that demand from the residential sector for natural gas will remain strong — a bullish sign for Nat Gas.

Over 50 percent of homes in the United States use natural gas for heating purposes. One way to benefit from this particular application is by identifying peak periods of natural gas consumption. Specifically, demand for natural gas for heating increases in the northern hemisphere during the winter seasons. Therefore one way to profit in the natural gas markets is by calibrating your strategy to this cyclical, weather-related trend. In other words, all things constant, natural gas prices should go up during the winters as folks seek to stay warm.

Although my aim in this book is to help you make money by *investing* in commodities such as natural gas, I'm going to take the liberty of showing you how to *save* money by using natural gas in your home. Natural gas is one of the cheapest energy forms as measured by dollars per unit of energy generated. Look at Figure 12-4, and you'll quickly realize that you get more energy from natural gas per dollar (as measured in *British Thermal Units* — the standard energy measurement unit), than from almost any other source.

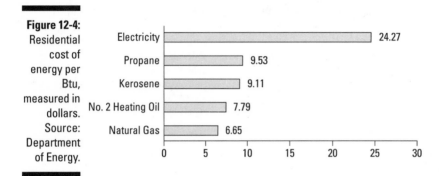

Figure 12-4: Residential cost of energy per Btu, measured in dollars. Source: Department of Energy.

Check to see how you supply heat to your home because using natural gas may save you some money during the winters — which you can then use to bulk up on your commodities investments!

Going commercial: Natural gas's commercial uses

About 40 percent of the energy consumed by commercial users, such as hospitals and schools, comes from natural gas, accounting for about 15 percent of total natural gas consumption. I list in Figure 12-5 the uses of natural gas by the commercial sector.

Because commercial users include establishments such as schools, hospitals, restaurants, movie theaters, malls, and office buildings, demand for natural gas from these key drivers of the economy will rise during times of increasing economic activity. This means that, all things equal, you should be bullish on natural gas during times of economic growth. (For more on how to gauge economic activity, please turn to Chapter 3.)

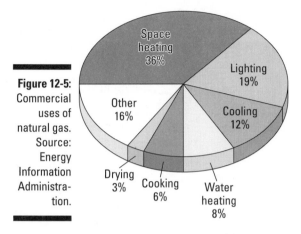

Figure 12-5:
Commercial
uses of
natural gas.
Source:
Energy
Information
Administra-
tion.

One place to look for important economic clues that affect demand for natural gas is the Energy Information Administration (EIA), a division of the U.S. Department of Energy (DOE). The EIA provides a wealth of information regarding consumption trends of key energy products, such as natural gas, from various economic sectors. For information on the commercial usage of natural gas please visit www.eia.doe.gov/oiaf/aeo/aeoref_tab.html.

Truly electrifying! Generating electricity with natural gas

Natural gas is quickly becoming a popular alternative to generate electricity, with just under 25 percent of natural gas usage going towards generating electricity. Actually, natural gas is used to produce approximately 10 percent of electricity generation in the United States. As you can see from Figure 12-6, that figure is going to increase dramatically in the coming years.

The long term trend is that more natural gas is going to be required to generate electricity. This increased demand from a critical sector will keep upward pressures on natural gas prices over the long term. Keep this in mind as you consider investing in this commodity.

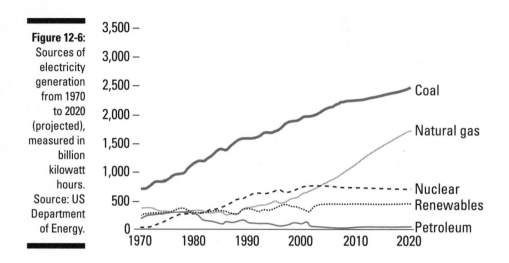

Figure 12-6:
Sources of
electricity
generation
from 1970
to 2020
(projected),
measured in
billion
kilowatt
hours.
Source: US
Department
of Energy.

Getting from here to there: Natural gas and transportation

It's not a widely known fact, but natural gas is used in a number of vehicles (approximately 3 million worldwide) as a source of fuel. These vehicles, known simply as *Natural Gas Vehicles* (NGV), run on a grade of natural gas called *Compressed Natural Gas* (CNG). While this usage accounts for only about 5 percent of total natural gas consumption, demand for NGV could increase as a viable (cheaper) alternative to gasoline (a crude oil derivative).

Keep a close eye on technological developments of natural gas in the transportation sector. If natural gas were to grab a slice of the transportation market, which now accounts for almost two-thirds of crude oil consumption, prices for natural gas could increase dramatically. One place you could check out for the latest on NGV is the *International Association of Natural Gas Vehicles*. Their Web site is: www.iangv.org.

Liquefied Natural Gas: Getting Liquid without Getting Wet

Liquefied Natural Gas, or LNG, is a recent development in the field. LNG is exactly what it says it is: natural gas in a liquid form. The reason for this development is quite simple: As demand for natural gas increases, you need to be able to transport this precious commodity across vast distances (for example, across continents and through oceans). That is difficult to do when it is in a gaseous state. Enter LNG: which is nothing but natural gas in a liquid state to make it easy to transport.

Transforming natural gas from its gaseous state into a liquid state is a very complex process. The Nat Gas must first be cooled to a temperature of –260°F in order to transform it to its liquid state. An additional advantage of LNG is that it takes up considerably less space — about 600 times less — which means you can transport a lot more of it farther and more economically. Once the Nat Gas is in a liquid state, it is usually transported in specially designed tankers to consumer markets. (I present some of the companies who transport energy products around the world in Chapter 14.) Before it's actually delivered to consumers, it goes through a regasification process.

In the United States, the majority of natural gas is transported through pipelines in a gaseous state. The natural gas pipeline system in the United States is one of the most extensive in the world — 300 million miles of pipeline — and it connects major Nat Gas producing regions (such as the Gulf of Mexico) to large Nat Gas consumers (such as the East Coast). While this remains the dominant method of transporting Nat Gas, LNG is quickly establishing itself as a viable source of Nat Gas, particularly as domestic production declines and imports increase. Some of the major operators of these pipelines that transport both Nat Gas and LNG are entities known as *Master Limited Partnerships* (MLPs). The good news is that you can profit from moving Nat Gas across the United States by investing in MLPs, which I cover in Chapter 6.

In 2005, the United States received only about 1 percent of its total natural gas (0.17 Tcf) through LNG. However, that number is expected to increase at a solid rate of 15.8 percent annually over the next 20 years, to reach 4.8 Tcf by 2025.

Investing in Natural Gas

The future for natural gas looks bright. The total natural gas consumption on a global scale in 2005 was approximately 100 Trillion cubic feet (100 Tcf). By 2025, that figure is estimated to increase by over 50 percent — at a rate of 2.3 percent annually — to a total of 156 Tcf, as you can see in Figure 12-7.

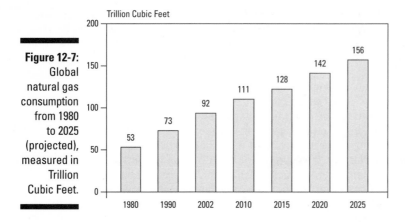

Figure 12-7:
Global
natural gas
consumption
from 1980
to 2025
(projected),
measured in
Trillion
Cubic Feet.

Knowing that demand for natural gas will remain steady until 2025 is an important piece of information for you as an investor. What's perhaps even more important is to figure out which countries and companies will be meeting this demand. Figuring out who's going to be supplying this natural gas will help you to devise an investment strategy to profit from this increased natural gas demand. Table 12-1 lists the countries with the largest reserves of natural gas in the world.

Table 12-1   Top Ten Natural Gas Reserves by Country, 2005 Figures

Rank	Country (Tcf)	Proven Reserves	Percent of World Total
1	Russia	1680	27.8%
2	Iran	940	15.6%
3	Qatar	910	15.1%
4	Saudi Arabia	235	3.9%
5	United Arab Emirates	212	3.5%
6	United States	189	3.1%
7	Nigeria	176	2.9%
8	Algeria	161	2.7%
9	Venezuela	151	2.5%
10	Iraq	110	1.8%

Global natural gas reserves are estimated at 6040 Tcf, which is the equivalent of approximately 6 Quadrillion cubic feet. (Quadrillion — not Zillion! — is the next figure above Trillion.) You can get exposure to this huge natural gas market in a couple ways: by trading futures contracts or by investing in companies that are involved in the production and development of natural gas fields in some of the countries listed in Table 12-1. I discuss the pros and cons of each investment method in the following sections.

Natural selection: Trading Nat Gas futures

The most direct method of investing in natural gas is by trading futures contracts on one of the designated commodities exchanges (see Chapter 8). The New York Mercantile Exchange (NYMEX), the preeminent exchange for energy products, provides you with the option of buying and selling natural gas futures and options.

In order to trade futures, you need to have a futures account with a designated broker, known as the Futures Commission Merchant (FCM). After you open a futures account, you can start trading these derivative products. For more on futures and options, turn to Chapter 9. To find out how to open a futures account, make sure to read Chapter 6.

The Nat Gas futures contract is the second most popular energy contract on the NYMEX, right behind crude oil. It is traded under the ticker symbol NG, and it trades in increments of 10,000 Mmbtu. You can trade it during all the calendar months, to periods up to 72 months after the current month. (I cover tradability in Chapter 9.)

The NYMEX offers a mini version of this contract for individual hedgers and speculators. Check out the Nat Gas section of the NYMEX Web site for more on this contract: `www.nymex.com/ng_pre_agree.aspx`.

Trading Nat Gas futures contracts and options is not for the faint hearted. Even by commodities standards, Nat Gas is a notoriously volatile commodity subject to wild price fluctuations. If you're not an aggressive investor willing to withstand the financial equivalent of a wild roller coaster ride, then Nat Gas futures may not be for you. To give you a picture of the prices, Figure 12-8 shows you a historical overview of the price action of the NYMEX Nat Gas contract.

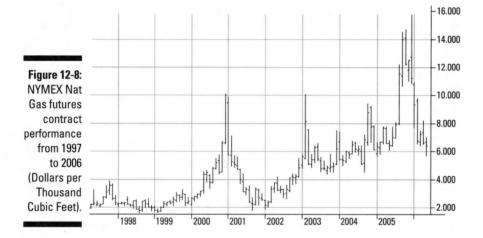

Figure 12-8:
NYMEX Nat Gas futures contract performance from 1997 to 2006 (Dollars per Thousand Cubic Feet).

Nat Gas companies: The natural choice

Investing in companies that process natural gas is a balance positive investment choice because it offers you exposure to this market through the expertise and experience of industry professionals, without the volatility of the futures market. Some natural gas companies are involved in the production of natural gas fields, while others are responsible for delivering natural gas directly to consumers.

I list companies that are *fully integrated* natural gas companies, which means they are involved in all the production, development, transportation, and distribution phases of natural gas. Investing in these companies provides you with a solid foothold in this industry. Here is your hit list:

- ✔ **Alliant Energy (NYSE: LNT):** Provides consumers with natural gas and electricity derived from natural gas throughout the United States. A good choice if you want exposure to the North American Nat Gas market.

- ✔ **Allegheny Energy (NYSE: AYE):** This S&P 500 company provides Nat Gas-based electricity to consumers in the eastern United States, primarily in Pennsylvania, Virginia, and Maryland. If you want regional exposure to Nat Gas production, then AYE is a good option.

- ✔ **Nicor Inc. (NYSE: GAS):** Nicor's operations are primarily centered in the Illinois area, where it provides Nat Gas to over 2 million consumers. This is another good regional investment.

For a complete listing of companies involved in natural gas production and distribution, look at the American Gas Association Web site: www.aga.org.

Chapter 13

Fuel for Thought: Looking at Alternative Energy Sources

....

....

*T*he world's demand for energy is in an upward trend and is likely to remain elevated for decades to come. Currently almost 90 percent of the world's total energy needs are met by fossil fuels: crude oil (39 percent), natural gas (24 percent), and coal (24 percent). For a number of reasons — environmental, political, geopolitical — there is a strong push to move away from fossil fuels as the main sources of energy and toward alternative energy sources such as nuclear, wind, and solar. As a result, these alternative sources may provide you with some solid money-making opportunities.

In this chapter, I go through the global energy scene and identify some of the major trends affecting it. I also introduce you to alternative energy sources and show you how to profit from this segment of the energy market. Specifically, I provide you with investment opportunities in the following areas: coal, nuclear power, and electricity, as well as solar and wind power.

Out with the Old and in with the New?

As the global population increases and as emerging countries industrialize (see Chapter 2), the demand for energy products will rise throughout the first quarter of the 21st century. The Energy Information Administration (EIA) anticipates that global demand for energy products will increase by over 70 percent between 2003 and 2030. You can take a look at this expected increase in Figure 13-1.

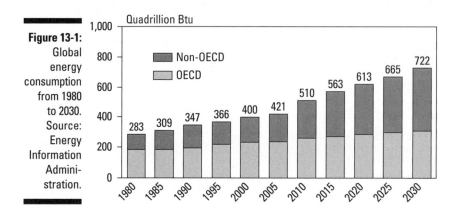

Figure 13-1: Global energy consumption from 1980 to 2030. Source: Energy Information Administration.

In 2003, fossil fuels (oil, natural gas, and coal) accounted for 87 percent of total energy consumption. Crude oil alone was responsible for almost 40 percent of global energy use. However, as the price of these traditional energy sources increases (driven by both strong demand and limited supply), the calls for new sources of energy are increasing as well. For example, in 2005 many members of Congress pushed for an alternative energy initiative to promote the use of solar, wind, and other renewable energy sources.

Despite numerous calls, however, the energy landscape is unlikely to change any time soon, which means that fossil fuels will remain the dominant source of global energy for years to come. This is not to say that the alternative energies won't generate a lot of attention — they will. But how much actual progress will be made is still up in the air. Keep this in mind as you're looking at investing in these alternatives.

For example, take a look at Figure 13-2. You can see that the energy picture until 2030 will remain fairly static on a percentage basis. That is to say that fossil fuels are going to remain the dominant fuel for the global economy, while alternatives will keep playing an important but less significant role.

Despite the dominance of fossil fuels, particularly crude oil, the alternative space is a dynamic area and a fertile ground for investment opportunities. I present you below with all the money-making opportunities in this sector.

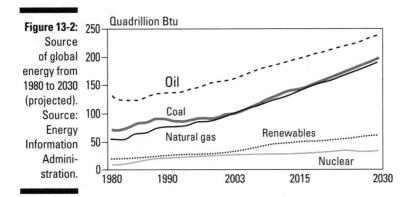

Figure 13-2:
Source
of global
energy from
1980 to 2030
(projected).
Source:
Energy
Information
Admini-
stration.

King Coal: Not as Scary as You Think

Before the beginning of the 20th century, coal was truly the king of commodities. Coal was the dominant source for energy during the tumultuous industrial revolution. People still often associate the industrial revolution with images of coal mines. The beginning of the end of coal as the dominant energy source can be traced to a fateful day in 1912 when the First Lord of the Admiralty in the British Navy ordered the conversion of all coal ships to oil. That move resulted in the rise of oil as the dominant global energy source at the expense of coal. That First Lord of the Admiralty was none other than Winston Churchill.

Although Churchill's decision to switch the British Navy from coal to oil effectively dethroned coal as the fossil fuel of choice, coal still enjoys an elevated position in global energy markets. For example, in 2004 (the latest year for which data is currently available) in the United States (the world's most important energy market), coal accounted for 26 percent of total fossil fuel consumption, 22.39 Quadrillion Btu (British thermal unit) out of a total 85.65 Quadrillion Btu of fossil fuel consumption. Therefore coal is still an important source of energy and can provide some good money-making opportunities. In this section, I show you how to make money in coal.

Coal hard facts

Coal is used primarily for electricity generation (steam coal) and steel manufacturing (metallurgical coal). Besides its practical uses in these two important areas, coal is an increasingly popular fossil fuel because of its large reserves. Specifically, companies in the United States have long touted the benefits of moving towards a more coal-based economy because the United States has the largest coal reserves in the world. I list in Table 13-1 the countries with the largest coal reserves.

Coal is measured in short tons. One *short ton* is the equivalent of 2000 lbs. In terms of energy, one short ton of *anthracite*, the coal of highest quality (see section "Paint it black"), contains approximately 25 Million Btu of energy.

Table 13-1	Coal Reserves by Country, 2005 Figures		
Rank	**Country**	**Reserves (Million Short tons)**	**Percent of World Total**
1	United States	246,643	27.13%
2	Russia	157,010	17.27%
3	China	114,500	12.60%
4	India	92,445	10.17%
5	Australia	78,500	8.64%
6	South Africa	48,750	5.36%
7	Ukraine	34,153	3.76%
8	Kazakhstan	31,279	3.44%
9	Poland	14,000	1.54%
10	Brazil	10,113	1.11%

Source: World Energy Council

If you're going to invest in companies that process coal, I recommend selecting a company with a heavy exposure in one of the countries listed in Table 13-1. Specifically, because the United States, Russia, and China collectively hold more than 55 percent of the world's total coal reserves, investing in a coal company with large operations in any of these countries will provide you with exposure to this important segment of the market. I introduce some of these coal companies in the section "It's a coal investment."

Just because a country has large deposits of a natural resource, however, doesn't mean that it exploits them to full capacity. As such, there is a significant gap between countries with large coal reserves and those that produce the most coal on an annual basis. To give you a better idea of this market characteristic, I list in Table 13-2 the top coal producing countries.

Table 13-2		Coal Production by Country, 2005 Figures	
Rank	*Country*	*Production (Million Short Tons)*	*Percent of World Total*
1	China	989.8	36.23%
2	United States	567.2	20.76%
3	Australia	199.4	7.30%
4	India	188.8	6.91%
5	South Africa	136.9	5.01%
6	Russia	127.6	4.67%
7	Indonesia	81.4	2.98%
8	Poland	69.8	2.55%
9	Germany	54.7	2.00%
10	Kazakhstan	44.4	1.63%

Demand for coal is expected to increase during the first quarter of the 21st century. In Figure 13-3, you can see that demand for coal is going to increase dramatically from now until 2025. Most of this growth will come from the emerging market economies, particularly the economies of China and India which will account for approximately 75 percent of the demand increase for coal. (China is currently the largest consumer of coal in the world, ahead of the United States, India, and Japan.)

Figure 13-3: Global coal consumption from 1970 to 2025 (projected). Source: Energy Information Administration.

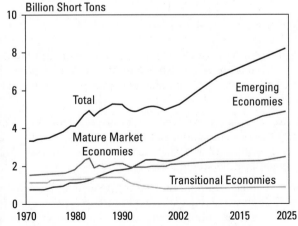

The coal markets have already started reacting to this increased demand for the product. From 2002 to 2005, as you can see in Figure 13-4, the price of coal in the spot market rose from approximately $25 per Short Ton in January 2002 to reach a high of more than $60 per Short Ton by January 2005.

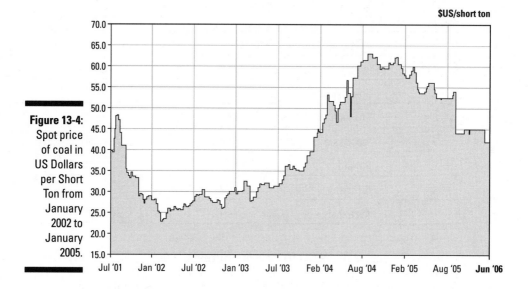

Figure 13-4:
Spot price of coal in US Dollars per Short Ton from January 2002 to January 2005.

Paint it black

You should know that, like other fossil fuels, coal comes in different qualities. Specifically, coal comes in four categories and is classified by its carbon, sulfur, and ash contents, as well as by the level of energy it releases.

Here are the four major categories of coal:

- **Lignite:** Lignite contains the least amount of carbon and the most sulfur and ash of all coal types and is therefore considered to be of the least value. Sometimes called brown coal, its primary use is in electricity generation.

- **Sub-bituminous:** This type of coal contains a little more carbon than lignite and is therefore considered to be of a higher quality. It also has lower levels of sulfur and ash than lignite. It is used mostly to heat water in electricity-generating steam turbines.

- **Bituminous:** Because bituminous coal burns well and creates a lot of energy, it is of high value. It's the most common type of coal found in the United States and is used both in electricity generation, as well as in the steel industry to create high quality steel.

✔ **Anthracite:** Anthracite is by far the most valuable type of coal because it contains the highest levels of carbon and the least amount of sulfur and ash; it also provides the most energy on a per unit basis. Because of its high value, anthracite is used for residential and commercial space heating.

Before you invest in companies involved in the coal business, find out which type of coal they produce. This information will help you develop a better understanding of the company's business and profit margins. You can find this type of information in a company's annual and quarterly reports.

It's a coal investment

You can get access to the coal markets by either trading coal futures directly or by investing in coal companies.

The big sandy: Coal futures contract

Like other members of the fossil fuel family, coal has an underlying futures contract that trades on a commodity exchange, in this case the New York Mercantile Exchange (NYMEX). This coal contract provides commercial users (such as coal producers, electric companies, and steel manufacturers) with the opportunity to hedge against market risk and offers speculators a chance to profit from this market risk. (For more on the NYMEX and other commodity exchanges, please turn to Chapter 8.)

The coal futures contract on the NYMEX tracks the price of the *Central Appalachian* type of coal. Central Appalachian coal, known as CAPP, is a high quality coal with low sulfur and ash contents. The CAPP futures contract, sometimes affectionately called "the big sandy" by traders because it is produced in the area between West Virginia and Kentucky where the Ohio River flows, is the premium benchmark for coal prices in the United States.

It trades under the ticker symbol QL and is tradable during all the calendar months of the current year, in addition to all calendar months in the subsequent three years. Additional information on this futures contract is available on the NYMEX Web site at www.nymex.com/coa_fut_descri.aspx.

While the coal futures contract does offer you exposure to coal, I should warn you that the market for this contract is fairly illiquid, meaning that the trading volume is low. Most of the traders involved in this market represent large commercial interests that transact with each other. While there are a few speculators trading the coal futures markets, they don't represent a significant portion of the market. This means that you may not be able to get involved directly in this market without large capital reserves to compete with the commercial interests.

I encourage you to read Chapter 9 for more on futures contract specifications.

Coal company

One of the best ways to invest in coal is by investing in a company that mines it. The following three companies are the best in my opinion:

- ✔ **Peabody Energy (NYSE: BTU):** Peabody Energy is the largest coal company with approximately 10 Billion Short Tons of coal reserves. The coal it produces is responsible for generating approximately 10 percent of the electricity in the United States. With 2005 revenues approaching $5 Billion, it is the largest coal company out there today. It is the ExxonMobil of coal companies. I like Peabody Energy because of its size and because it has mining operations in the United States but also in Australia and Venezuela, two important coal markets.

- ✔ **Consol Energy (NYSE: CNX):** With headquarters in Pittsburgh, Consol Energy has significant operations in the coal mines of Pennsylvania and neighboring coal-rich states of West Virginia and Kentucky. As of 2005, it controlled 4.5 Billion Short Tons of coal reserves, with operations in over 17 mines across the United States. CNX is well positioned to take advantage of the booming domestic coal market.

- ✔ **Arch Coal (NYSE: ACI):** Arch coal is smaller in size than its main competitors Peabody and Consol, but I like it because the coal it produces is of very high quality. It operates over 20 mines on the continental United States and controls over 3 Billion Short Tons of reserves. It has operations in the largest coal producing regions in the United States, including in the Appalachian, the Powder River Basin (between the Montana/Wyoming border), and the Western Bituminous region (between the Colorado/Utah border).

If you want to invest in coal companies with a more international exposure to markets in Russia, China, and other coal-rich countries, I recommend you consult the World Coal Institute. Their Web site is www.worldcoal.org.

Investing in Nuclear Power: Going Nuclear without Going Ballistic

When most people think of nuclear power, they tend to think of nuclear weapons and mushroom clouds. However, nuclear power also has an important civilian role. Civilian and commercial nuclear power is an integral part of the global energy supply chain and is a valuable energy source for residential, commercial, and industrial consumers worldwide. In fact, nuclear power generates over 20 percent of the electricity in the United States. In countries like France, nuclear power generates over 75 percent of electricity!

Splitting atoms

The primary use of civilian nuclear power is in generating electricity. Electricity is generated by heating water to very high temperatures to create steam that powers the turbines in a steam turbine. In a nuclear power plant, the water is heated through a process known as nuclear fission, where atoms are split apart to release large amounts of energy. (This is the opposite of nuclear fusion where atoms are fused together.)

Nuclear power currently accounts for about 5 percent of total global energy consumption (see Figure 13-2), and it is expected to remain at these stable levels until 2030. But if the price of fossil fuels (oil, natural gas, and coal) dramatically enough to start affecting demand (creating what is called *demand destruction*), nuclear may play an important role in picking up the slack.

One way you can profit from increased interest in nuclear power is by investing in uranium, the most widely used fuel in nuclear power plants. You may be surprised to find out that there has been a bull market in uranium from 2000 to 2006, and this shows no sign of slowing. However, you're not likely to hear about this opportunity from your local financial media because uranium is a pretty obscure investment area. But sometimes as an investor, you need to be able to think creatively and look at opportunities that other investors haven't considered. Investing in uranium to benefit from the increased demand in nuclear power is not a well-known or well-advertised investment play, but it is lucrative nevertheless. Take a look in Figure 13-5 at the spot price of uranium from 1994 to 2005.

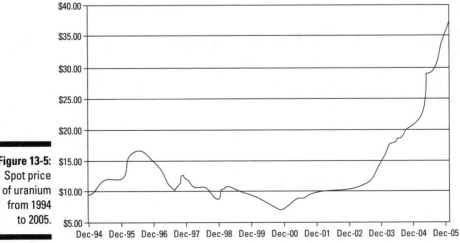

Figure 13-5: Spot price of uranium from 1994 to 2005.

Because uranium isn't a widely tradable commodity, the best way to profit from this trend is to invest in companies that specialize in the mining, processing, and distribution of uranium for civilian nuclear purposes. Here are a few companies I like in this sector:

- **Cameco Corporation (NYSE: CCJ):** Cameco is the marquee name in the uranium mining space. The company operates four uranium mines in the United States and Canada. The company mines uranium and is also involved in refining and converting the uranium into fuel that's sold to nuclear power plants to generate electricity.

- **UEX Corporation (Toronto: UEX):** UEX is a Canadian-based mining company that specializes in the exploration and mining of uranium in the Athabasca basin. The Athabasca basin in Canada is an important region in global uranium mining that accounts for about 30 percent of total world production. The company is currently still in exploration phases, but it could become a real money-maker if it comes across large deposits of uranium. The company trades on the Toronto Stock Exchange.

- **Strathmore Corporation (Toronto: STM):** While UEX is involved in the exploration of uranium ore, Strathmore — another Canadian company — specializes in the mining of uranium. The company, which trades on the Toronto Stock Exchange, operates in the Athabasca region in Canada as well as in the United States.

For more information on nuclear power, the Energy Information Administration (EIA) has an excellent Web site with all sorts of practical information on this industry at www.eia.doe.gov/fuelnuclear.html.

The Ux Consulting Company is a great resource for everything regarding uranium and nuclear power. Their Web site is located at www.uxc.com.

You've Been Zapped! Trading Electricity

Benjamin Franklin may not have imagined what his kite experiment would mean for the world, but his experimentation paved the way for developments in electricity, which is now a necessity of modern life. It is also a tradable commodity. In this section, I show you how to make money investing in electricity.

Current affairs

Have you ever wondered how that electricity that allows you to watch TV, use your air conditioner, or power your computer comes from? Before I show you how to profit from this electrifying resource, I want to take a quick moment to show you how it is generated.

Getting electricity to residential, commercial, and industrial consumers is a lengthy process. The electricity is first created in a generator at a power plant and is then sent through transmission lines at very high voltages to a substation near the consumers. The substation is equipped with a generator that transforms the high voltage electricity into low voltage form, which is then sent to consumers via distribution lines. So how can you profit from it? It's quite simple.

Most of the electricity in the United States is generated through steam turbines. The water used to generate steam is heated to very high temperatures using traditional energy sources such as coal, natural gas, and nuclear power, as well as other renewable sources (such as wind and solar). Look at Figure 13-6 for a breakdown of how electricity was generated in the United States in 2004.

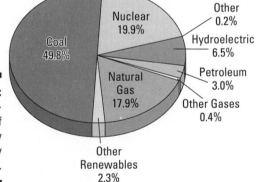

Figure 13-6:
U.S. production of electricity by energy source.

Electricity is measured in watts where one kilowatt is equal to 1000 watts and a megawatt equals 1 million watts. In the power industry, watts are expressed in terms of hours of operation where 1 kilowatt hour (1 kWh) is 1000 watts working for a period of 1 hour. Your electricity bill is measured in kWh and 1 kWh is the equivalent of 3412 Btu. To put it in perspective, the United States consumed a grand total of 3669 Billion kWh of electricity in 2003.

Power plays

As you can see from Figure 13-6, investing in coal, as well as nuclear power, is one way to invest in electricity. But there are also several ways you can invest directly in the power industry. I discuss these investment procedures in the following sections.

Charged and ready to go

The most direct way of investing in electricity is . . . by buying it! The New York Mercantile Exchange (NYMEX) offers a futures contract that tracks the price of electricity as administered by PJM Interconnection. PJM is a *Regional Transmission Organization* (RTO) that oversees the largest electric grid system in the world and services over 50 million customers in the United States. It is responsible for the generation of over 700 Million megawatt hours of electricity across 55,000 miles of transmission lines. Because of its dominance in the U.S. electricity market, the PJM electricity futures contract on the NYMEX provides you with a widely recognizable and tradable electricity benchmark. For more information on the NYMEX and other commodity exchanges, please flip to Chapter 8.

The PJM contract offers you the option of trading both *on-peak* and *off-peak* electricity hours. On-peak times are defined as Monday through Friday between 7:00 a.m. and 11:00 p.m., the times where the most electricity is consumed in the United States. Off-peak hours go from midnight to 7:00 a.m. local time, Monday through Friday, and include Saturdays and Sundays as well. On-peak hours are usually more liquid because that's when most of the electricity is consumed.

The PJM contract is traded in units of 40 mWh (megawatt-hours) under the ticker symbol JM. For more information on this specific contract, check out the NYMEX Web site at www.nymex.com/jm_desc.aspx. To find out more about futures contracts in general, please turn to Chapter 9.

Although most of the market participants in the electricity futures market are local and regional power providers and suppliers, the futures contract lends itself to being traded by individual speculators as well. In recent years, as interest in commodities as an asset class has increased, the number of speculative participants in the electricity market has grown as well.

Power to the people

You probably get a letter from them every month, but you may have never given too much thought about the investment opportunities they present. I'm talking of course about electric utilities. *Utilities* are the companies responsible for providing electricity to millions of folks in America and around the world.

I like utilities for a number of reasons, but particularly for their very high dividend payout. The industry has on average a 5 percent dividend yield, one of the highest of any industry. However, remember when you're investing for dividend income that dividends are subject to market fluctuations. I list in Table 13-3 some utilities you could consider, along with their dividend yield.

Table 13-3	Publicly Traded Utilities, 2006 Dividend Yields	
Utility	*Ticker*	*Dividend Yield*
Great Plains Energy	NYSE: GXP	6.00%
Consolidated Edison	NYSE: ED	5.20%
Duke Energy Corp.	NYSE: DUK	4.30%
Dominion Resources	NYSE: D	3.70%
PG & E Corp.	NYSE: PCG	3.40%
Entergy Corp.	NYSE: ETR	3.10%

Dividends are a taxable source of income. Because of recent tax relief legislation, taxes on income generated through dividends are capped at 15 percent. However, Congress is considering an overhaul of the dividend tax in 2008 that may result in an increase in the dividends tax rate. Make sure to keep a close eye on these dividend tax issues because they will have a direct impact on your utility investments.

Always Brand Spanking New! Renewable Energy Sources

As the price of traditional sources of energy such as oil, natural gas, and coal continues upward and the calls from environmentalists about the hazards of burning these fossil fuels grows louder, more attention will be paid to renewable sources of energy, such as solar and wind power.

Currently, renewable sources of energy make up about 8 percent of total energy use in the world (see Figure 13-2 for the breakdown). This figure pales compared to the 87 percent share of fossil fuels, but it has the potential to grow as nonrenewable energy sources are depleted. The field of renewable energy is getting a lot of attention and there is certainly potential to make some money in this field. I look at a couple of promising sectors in this field in the following sections.

If you're interested in keeping up-to-date on the latest developments in the renewable energy space, I recommend you check out the Department of Energy's Energy Efficiency and Renewable Energy (EERE) initiative. The Web site is www.eere.energy.gov.

Sunny delight: Solar energy

Solar power is the process by which energy from the sun is harnessed and channeled into a usable energy form, generally heat or electricity. Solar power can be transformed using two different processes:

- ✔ **Solar Thermal Energy:** This method transforms the sun's energy into heat, which may be used for a number of different purposes, such as interior space heating or water heating. If you've ever seen flat panel solar collectors mounted on homes or buildings, they are used for solar thermal energy purposes.

- ✔ **Solar Photovoltaic Energy:** Don't be intimidated by this high sounding name — it simply describes the method whereby energy from the sun is captured and transformed into electricity. A lot of companies are trying to turn these two methods of transforming solar energy into a commercially viable enterprise, but they face some challenges. One of the biggest impediments to the commercial success of solar power is the sun itself! Specifically, the sun isn't a resource that you can control. For one thing, you can't manipulate the weather, and you're therefore at the mercy of rain, fog, clouds, the Earth's rotation, and other natural external factors that block the sun. For this reason, solar power accounted for a little less than 0.06 percent of total energy consumed in the United States during 2005.

However, this doesn't mean you can't make any money investing in this sector. Because of technological advancements, the future looks bright for solar energy. Although a number of companies have entered the field of solar power, two companies stand out as well positioned to take advantage of the increased demand for solar energy:

- ✔ **Evergreen Solar (Nasdaq: ESLR):** Evergreen Solar has operations in Germany and the United States and is engaged in the production and distribution of photovoltaic cells. It has a patented system that allows for direct transformation from solar to consumable electricity. It sells its electricity directly to residential, commercial, and industrial consumers.

- ✔ **Suntech Power Holdings (NYSE: STP):** This company, with headquarters in China, launched its IPO in the Unites States in 2005. The company is also involved in producing photovoltaic cells and panels for electricity generation. This is an attractive company because it has a foothold in China, which could be a huge market for solar power.

Fast and furious: Wind energy

Wind energy is another renewable resource that is getting increasing attention from investors. Energy is generated by huge wind machines (similar to traditional wind mills), which are placed side by side in *wind farms*.

The challenge to wind energy is that it is dependant on the wind, a very unpredictable natural phenomenon. As a result, wind energy only accounted for 0.4 percent of electricity generation in the United States in 2004. That same year, total energy consumption from wind was 0.14 percent in the United States. As a result, it is extremely difficult to invest in wind energy at this stage. Currently there are very few publicly traded companies that deal specifically in wind power.

However, with rising energy prices, wind energy may get more focus. If you are interested in investing in wind power and want to keep on top of any emerging trend, check out the American Wind Energy Association. Their Web site is www.awea.org. They keep a database of private companies involved in wind energy that might go public one day.

What's up with ethanol?

Ethanol is an alcohol fuel that can be used as a transportation fuel. It can be made from corn, sugar, wheat, and other agricultural products. Because of its origins, it is a renewable source of energy. In Brazil, the world's largest producer of ethanol fuel, ethanol is the primary automotive fuel. The United States has seen an increase in the use of ethanol as a transportation fuel and that trend is likely to increase. One company involved in the production of ethanol that I recommend is Pacific Ethanol (NASDAQ: PEIX). If you're interested in getting exposure to ethanol, then PEIX is a good way to go.

Chapter 14

Totally Energized: Investing in Energy Companies

*O*ne way to play the energy markets is to invest in the companies involved in the production, transformation, and distribution of the world's most important energy commodities. In this chapter, I look at specialized energy and oil companies that are critical links in the global crude oil supply chain. This chain is long and convoluted, and these industries move in cycles, so identifying who does what will allow you to develop a targeted investment strategy.

I show you in the following sections how to profit from the first step of the oil industry (exploration and production), through the transformational process (refining), and finally through the delivery system (transportation). Each of the companies operating in these segments of the market offers unique money-making investment opportunities. (See Chapter 11 for the goods on the large integrated oil companies (often referred to as "the majors") that allow you to buy the market, so to speak, because they are involved in all facets of the global energy industry.)

Bulls Eye! Profiting from Oil Exploration and Production

The oil industry all starts in one place: at the oilfield. Actually, the birth of the modern oil industry began with the discovery of the first commercially viable oilfield by "Colonel" Edwin Drake in Titusville, Pennsylvania, in 1859. (The title Colonel is in quotations because Edwin Drake was not really a colonel. He simply called himself that in order to get permits from the local authorities to drill for oil!)

Ever since that day, individuals, companies, and countries have relentlessly pursued the discovery of oilfields and oil wells. This pursuit was perhaps best portrayed by James Dean in the classic movie *Giant,* where Dean portrays a Texas wildcatter who strikes it rich after discovering a *gusher,* a well that literally gushes oil.

Among industry insiders, exploring for oil and gas is affectionately called *wildcatting.* Most wildcatting expeditions end up without any oil discoveries. When wildcatters drill a hole in the ground and no oil comes out, that is known as having a *dry hole,* the unfortunate opposite of a gusher.

The exploration and discovery of oil is a very lucrative segment in the oil business. To this day, when someone strikes it rich, the metaphor "it's like she discovered oil" is still used. So how you can you strike it rich by discovering oil? Fortunately you won't have to roll up your sleeves and go prospecting for oil in the Texas heartland. You can invest in companies that specialize in the exploration and production of oilfields, known in the business as *E&P.*

Oil wells are found in one of two places: either on land or on sea. In recent years, offshore drilling has generated a lot of interest among investors, and a flurry of activity has been taking place in this sector as oil on land becomes more and more scarce. In this section, I introduce you to some of the companies involved in this exciting segment of the market.

Going offshore

Before I present the leading companies in the offshore drilling market, I need to go over some terminology with you. The offshore drilling business is a technology-heavy industry, and you have to be familiar with some of these technical terms in order to make the most out of your investments.

Going upstream

The oil business is effectively divided into three phases. The first phase is extracting the oil from the ground (or the sea). This is known in the industry as the *upstream* segment of the market. Next, the oil needs to be refined into consumable products such as gasoline and jet fuel. The companies involved in the refining process are known as *midstream* companies. Finally, the specific products must be delivered to consumers, either via pipeline or by ships (sometimes by other means, but these are the two dominant methods). This last phase is known as the *downstream* portion of the market.

Because offshore drilling activity may take place in unforgiving locations, companies have to deploy specific vessels for specific drilling projects. These vessels are among the most technologically advanced structures created by man. Some vessels are designed to withstand harsh winds and high waves. Others are more suited for shallow water exploratory projects and need to have the ability to move from location to location quickly.

Here are the names of some of these vessels you can expect to come across as you start investing in offshore drilling companies.

- **Drilling barge:** The drilling barge is one of the most nimble vessels in the market. The drilling barge is a floating device usually towed by tugboat to target drilling locations. It's primarily used in inland, in still, shallow waters such as rivers, lakes, and swamps.

- **Jack-up rig:** The jack-up rig is a hybrid vessel that is part floating barge, part drilling platform. The jack-up rig is towed to the desired location, usually in open, shallow waters where its three "legs" are lowered and "jacked" down to the seafloor. Once the legs are secured, the drilling platform is elevated to the desired levels to enable safe drilling.

- **Submersible rig:** The submersible rig is similar to the jack-up rig in that it is primarily used for shallow water drilling activity and is secured to the seabed.

- **Semi-submersible rig:** Sometimes referred to as a *semi,* this structure is a feat of modern technological development. It is similar to a submersible, except that it has the capacity to drill in deep waters under harsh and unforgiving weather conditions. The drilling platform is elevated and sits atop a floating structure that is semi-submerged in the water (hence the name) and is secured by large anchors that can weigh up to ten tons each.

- **Drill ship:** The drill ship is essentially a ship with a drilling platform. It is perhaps the most versatile drilling vessel because it can be easily dispatched to remote offshore locations, including drilling in very deep waters.

- **Offshore oil platform:** Once one of the previous vessels discovers a commercially viable offshore oil field, a company may decide to build a permanent platform to exploit this discovery. Enter the offshore oil platform. These structures are a sight to behold and they are truly manmade floating cities. They house personnel, include living quarters, and are often even equipped with heliports. They are ideally suited to withstand harsh, deepwater conditions.

You can get information on an offshore drilling company's fleet in its annual report. Companies will usually lease out these vessels to customers, which may include independent oil and gas companies, national oil companies, and the major integrated oil companies, for a premium. The company will also include this type of financial information regarding its fleet in the annual

---

In the public eye: Looking at a company's public disclosure forms

A publicly traded company in the United States is required by the *Securities and Exchange Commission* (SEC) to file annual and quarterly reports. The quarterly report, known as *Form 10Q*, contains information about the company's financial operations during each of the first three fiscal quarters in a given year. (A company doesn't need to file a quarterly report at the end of the fiscal year since that's when the annual report is released.) *Form 10K*, which is the annual report, contains a much more comprehensive overview of a company's financial operations. It is released at the end of the fourth quarter of the fiscal year, and it includes information on the company's structure, shareholders, business activities, assets, and liabilities.

An additional disclosure form you may want to look at is *Form 8K*. A company is required to file Form 8K with the SEC in the event that it undertakes structural changes, such as a merger or acquisition, bankruptcy, or election of new board members. Form 8K may contain important information regarding the company's future plans. So where can you check out a company's annual report or Form 8K? Perhaps the best resource for this type of information is EDGAR (www.edgar-online.com). They include the most comprehensive SEC filings I've ever come across. A subscription may be required.

---

report. (See more on annual reports and other important forms in the sidebar "In the public eye: Looking at a company's public disclosure forms.")

Here are some of the leading companies in the offshore drilling business:

- ✔ **Transocean Inc. (NYSE: RIG):** Transocean, whose company motto is "We're never out of our depth," is the Exxon Mobil of the offshore drillers. It's the largest company in terms of its market capitalization as well as the size and scope of its operations. The company has over 90 offshore drilling units at its disposal and is an expert in operating under harsh and extreme weather conditions. It has offshore operations in the U.S. Gulf of Mexico, Brazil, South Africa, the Mediterranean Sea, the North Sea, Australia, and Southeast Asia. If you're looking for the most diversified company in the group, then this is it.

- ✔ **GlobalSantaFe Corp. (NYSE: GSF):** GSF is a truly global offshore drilling contractor. It operates a fleet of over 60 vessels in locations stretching from Canada to the Middle East. It operates in three major segments: the leasing of drilling equipment, services, and crews (contract drilling); engineering and project services where it teams up with clients to provide offshore engineering solutions; and turnkey services where it assumes full control and responsibility of drilling projects from the design to the implementation phase.

GSF offers an array of full offshore services to its clients, which include independent and integrated oil companies as well as foreign governments and oil companies.

✔ **Noble Corporation (NYSE: NE):** Founded in 1921 in Texas, Noble is one of the oldest drilling contractors in the world. While it has a fleet of over 60 vessels and operations stretching from Brazil to the North Sea, it has an edge in implementing technologically oriented solutions to meet customer demands.

Noble Corporation actually has a subsidiary, Noble Technology Services Division, which is a sort of technological think-tank dedicated to generate technical solutions for customers.

If you'd like to dig deeper into this sector, you can check out the following Web site: www.rigzone.com, which includes up-to-date information on the offshore industry as well as the oil industry as a whole.

Staying on dry land

A large part of E&P activity takes place on dry land. Actually, the first commercially viable oil wells were first discovered on land. While most industry insiders agree that a majority of onshore oil wells have been discovered, you can still benefit by investing in companies that are involved in the exploitation and production of onshore oilfields.

Here are a couple of companies you could consider to invest in this segment of the *drilling* market:

✔ **Nabors Industries (NYSE: NBR):** Nabors is one of the largest land drilling contractors in the world. It has a division that is able to perform heavy-duty and horizontal drilling activities.

✔ **Patterson-UTI Energy Inc. (NASDAQ: PTEN):** Patterson-UTI is an onshore oilfield drilling contractor that has extensive operations in North America. It operates in a number of segments, including the drilling of new wells, as well as the servicing and maintenance of existing oil wells. It is part of the *S&P 400 MidCap* stocks.

Servicing the oilfields

Another area that I recommend taking a close look at is companies that focus on oilfield maintenance and services. The oilfield services sector is dominated by technology oriented and labor-intensive companies that seek to maximize an oilfield's output through the use of sophisticated technological techniques, such as horizontal drilling and 3-D mapping and imaging.

The oilfield services companies are generally hired by the major integrated oil companies or national oil companies for general oilfield and oil well maintenance and extraction solutions. For example, Saudi Aramco, the largest oil company in the world in terms of proven reserves, may turn to an oilfield services company for the maintenance of a particular oilfield. The services company may get involved in the actual extraction of crude from the oil well; provide data and statistics on current and past usage as well as on potential future output; use technologically oriented techniques to extract hard-to-recover oil; and perform other specific and general oilfield management services.

The added value of the oilfield services companies is that they can improve oil recovery rates on existing fields and recover previously untapped oil pockets in old fields. As fewer and fewer oilfields are discovered, the world's major oil companies are looking for ways to maximize existing oilfields. Therefore the role of the oilfield services companies will become increasingly important in the future.

Perhaps the most well-known oilfield services company is *Halliburton* (NYSE: HAL). A lot of people are familiar with the name because it's a high-profile Defense Department contractor that was once headed by Vice President Dick Cheney. Because of the nature of its political contracts, Halliburton is often a lightning rod for criticism. I would recommend going beyond some of this criticism and directly analyzing the company's balance sheet, income statement, and other metrics to get a more accurate sense of the company's scope of operations. Although some of its work is political in nature (government contracts), this only represents a fraction of its operational activities. More importantly, although Halliburton is the most notorious of the oilfield services companies, it is certainly not representative of the other companies in the field. Many of the other players in this space are focused exclusively on oilfield maintenance and services and aren't involved in work that's of a political nature.

Here is your hit list of top companies if you're looking to invest in the oilfield services space:

- **Schlumberger Ltd. (NYSE: SLB):** Schlumberger may not be a household name, but it's well known and well regarded in the oil industry. The company is one of the most technologically savvy services companies out there and can provide solutions regarding all aspects of oilfield management services, from exploration and extraction to maintenance and abandonment. It provides evaluations to help customers identify the short-term and long-term viability of an oilfield and specializes in maximizing oilfield output through technologically advanced solutions.

- **Halliburton Co. (NYSE: HAL):** The Houston, Texas, based company makes a lot of headlines (sometimes not very positive ones) because of the political nature of its work with the U.S. government and military. Besides its governmental contracts — which only make up a fraction of its revenues — the company is a leader in oil and gas field maintenance. It helps customers extract as much energy from existing wells as possible while maintaining low costs. This makes Halliburton a knowledgeable company in the petroleum services sector.

- ✔ **Baker Hughes Inc. (NYSE: BHI):** Like most oilfield services companies, Baker Hughes is headquartered in Houston, Texas. The company operates both in the United States as well as internationally, with operations stretching from the Persian Gulf to West Africa. Baker Hughes provides technologically oriented solutions to its customers to maximize oilfield output efficiency. Baker Hughes is not the biggest company in the group, but it's certainly a nimble competitor.

For more information on the oilfield services sector and all the companies involved in it, I recommend checking out the Yahoo! Finance Web site at: `http://biz.yahoo.com/ic/124.html`.

Oh My, You're So Refined! Investing in Refineries

Crude oil by itself doesn't have many useful applications — it needs to be refined into consumable products such as gasoline and jet fuel. Refineries are a critical link in the crude oil supply chain because once crude oil is discovered, it needs to be transformed into products before being sent to consumers.

Here is a list of some of the products that refineries derive from refining crude oil. You may recognize some of them (tongue-in-cheek):

- ✔ Gasoline
- ✔ Heating oil (commercial and residential)
- ✔ Diesel fuel
- ✔ Jet fuel (military and commercial aviation)
- ✔ Kerosene
- ✔ Automotive lubricating oil
- ✔ Propane
- ✔ Petrochemicals
- ✔ Asphalt

Given the importance of these derivative products, you can imagine that you can make a lot of money investing in refineries. But before I give you a few company options, I want to get a few technical terms you should be familiar with out of the way.

Here are three criteria you need to look at when considering investing in companies that operate refineries:

- **Refinery throughput:** The capacity for refining crude oil over a given period of time, usually expressed in barrels.
- **Refinery production:** Actual production of crude oil products, such as gasoline and heating oil.
- **Refinery utilization:** The difference between production capacity, the throughput, and what's actually produced.

You can find this information in a company's annual or quarterly reports. Table 14-1 presents an example of a refinery's earnings.

Table 14-1   Throughput and Yield Data for the Two Months Ended March 31, 2006, and March 31, 2005

	2006 Bpd	2006 %	2005 Bpd	2005 %
Refinery throughput:				
Sour crude	62,720	88.9	41,096	86.6
Sweet crude	3,191	4.5	2,829	6.0
Blendstocks	4,618	6.6	3,522	7.4
Total refinery throughput	**70,529**	**100.0**	**47,447**	**100.0**
Refinery production:				
Gasoline	32,846	47.2	21,562	45.8
Diesel/jet	23,701	34.1	15,232	32.4
Asphalt	6,444	9.3	4,297	9.1
Petrochemicals	4,266	6.0	3,617	7.7
Other	2,346	3.4	2,352	5.0
Total refinery production (17)	**69,603**	**100.0**	**47,060**	**100.0**
Refinery utilization (18)		**94.2%**		**88.9%**

The largest refinery in the United States is located in Baytown, Texas, and is operated by Exxon Mobil. It has a refining capacity of 557,000 bbls/day. Most major integrated oil companies have large refining capacity. These include some of the majors like Exxon Mobil and BP. One way to get exposure to the refining space is by investing in these major companies. I discuss the majors, their scope of activity, and how to invest in them in Chapter 11.

Another, more direct, way to profit from refining activity is by investing in independent refineries. The marquee name in this area is a company called *The Valero Energy Corporation* (NYSE: VLO). Valero is the largest independent refining company in North America. It has a throughput capacity of 3.3 Million bbls/day and operates the largest number of refineries in North America.

I like Valero because if you want to play the refinery card, it provides you with one of the most direct ways to do so. The major integrated companies are a good play, but they are so big that you don't get the same kind of direct exposure you do from Valero. In addition, Valero is a consistent performer in a very cyclical industry. Check out the long-term performance of Valero's stock in Figure 14-1.

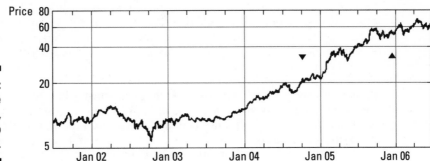

Figure 14-1: Stock price of Valero, June 2001 to June 2006.

Although Valero is the goliath in the refinery space, a number of smaller companies exist that could offer you a lot of value.

Here are a couple of these companies:

- **Sunoco Inc. (NYSE: SUN):** Sunoco is the second largest refiner in terms of total refinery throughput. It refines approximately 1 Million Barrels of crude a day into refined products, which it distributes primarily in the eastern United States.

  Sunoco, with headquarters in Philadelphia, operates refineries in Pennsylvania, Ohio, and New Jersey and has a wide distribution network across the East Coast.

> ✔ **Tesoro Corp. (NYSE: TSO):** Tesoro, headquartered in San Antonio, Texas, is one of the leading refiners in the mid-continental and western United States. Its refineries transform crude oil into gasoline that is distributed through a network of about 500 retail outlets in the western United States. This is a good regional play.
>
> It operates refineries in Utah, California, Washington, Alaska, and even Hawaii.

The Energy Information Administration compiles data on all U.S. refineries at www.eia.doe.gov/neic/rankings/refineries.htm.

How to Become an Oil Shipping Magnate

Commodities, such as oil and gas, would be useless if there was no way of transporting them to consumers. In fact, transporting commodities to consumers is probably as important as finding and processing them in the first place. Fortunately, as an investor, this provides you with fertile ground to make money in the transportation of commodities.

Here's a statistic to put things in perspective for you: Two out of every three barrels of oil that are transported are moved around in ships. The remaining one-third is transported via pipelines. (For more on how to invest in pipeline infrastructure, you should consider Master Limited Partnerships, which I discuss in Chapter 6.) Therefore the shipping industry plays a crucial role in the integrated oil business.

Perhaps no one person embodies the shipping industry like Aristotle Onassis, the Greek shipping magnate. Onassis built one of the largest fortunes in the world by shipping oil and other commodities around the world. Although I don't promise to make you as rich as Onassis, I am confident that investing in the seaborne transportation business can give your portfolio a big boost.

In this section, I provide you with tools to help you invest in the oil shipping business. I introduce you to the types of vessels that make up a modern oil tanker fleet, present you to some of the major companies involved in the business, and offer you advice on pinpointing the right entry and exit points.

Swimming in oil: Transportation supply and demand

Before I show you how to start investing in oil shipping, I want to make a couple of important points about the shipping industry. One of the most common questions I get asked about the oil shipping industry is the following: What is the relationship between the price of crude oil and oil tanker profit margins? Like many good questions, there is no straight answer. It depends on a lot of factors. My short answer is this: The relationship between the price of crude oil and tanker spot rates is not easily quantifiable.

Tanker spot rates — the bread and butter of the shipping industry — are determined by supply and demand. The supply side, in this case, consists of how many ships are available to transport crude and products to the desired destinations around the world. On the demand side is how much crude oil and products need to be shipped from point A to point B. In the global shipping business, these are the two factors that you need to watch closely.

For example, recently there has been some supply-side pressure on tanker spot rates. Because of a series of environmental incidents, the *International Maritime Organization* (the global regulatory body of the shipping industry — www.imo.org) ordered the phasing out of all single hull ships in 1997 in order to help prevent further oil spills.

Single hull ships have just one layer of protection. *Double hull ships* provide more protection against oil leaks because they are composed of two layers, one exterior and one interior.

Because of this regulation, the number of ships in the open sea transporting oil and products has decreased. This created a supply-side crunch that has contributed to the increase in tanker spot rates during the 2002–2004 period, the largest run-up in tanker spot rates in recent memory. (See Figure 14-2 at the end of the chapter.) The program to phase out all single hull ships from open waters is scheduled to end before 2010.

Shipping companies are planning on replacing these single hull ships with double hull ships, but like almost anything that has to do with the commodities business, the construction of these ships takes time. Therefore the supply side pressure on tanker spot rates will remain until these newly designed double hull ships are brought on board.

On the demand side of the equation, demand for crude oil and products on a worldwide basis remains robust. In 2006, the world consumed on average 85 Million Barrels of oil *a day*, and that number is growing.

Another important demand factor, sometimes overlooked by many industry onlookers, is *oil import dependency*. While crude oil demand is critical, if oil could be produced and consumed without the need to transport it across long distances on seaborne voyages, the oil shipping industry would be out of business. The lifeblood of the global oil tanker business is the international flow of oil across countries and continents, or the dependence on oil imports. One key metric to help you gauge the level of activity in this area is global import and export data, which is monitored by the Energy Information

Administration's energy statistics division. Their Web site is www.eia.doe.gov/oil_gas/petroleum/info_glance/petroleum.html.

As long as the supply of ships remains tight and the demand for crude oil seaborne transportation remains high, tanker spot rates will stay elevated. Now, to the extent that crude oil prices affect the demand of crude oil world-wide, crude oil prices will have an effect on tanker spot rates. Specifically, if crude oil prices go so high that folks are no longer willing to buy crude, thus causing demand destruction, the demand for shipping crude oil worldwide will also decrease (this is the notion of *elasticity,* which I cover in Chapter 2), causing tanker spot rates to go down as well. However, this rate drop is an indirect effect of rising oil prices and that's why the relationship between crude oil prices and tanker spot rates is not easily quantifiable. There are simply too many variables at play.

At the end of the day, as long as there is a demand for crude to be transported from producers to consumers, you can rest assured that oil shippers will remain in business.

Ships ahoy!

One factor you need to consider as you're planning investments in the oil shipping industry is the ships themselves. Before you invest in a tanker stock, closely examine the fleet of vessels it operates.

To help you with this examination, I list some of the types of vessels used in the global crude oil shipping industry:

- **Ultra Large Crude Carrier (ULCC):** This type of vessel, known in the industry as the ULCC, is the largest vessel in the market. It's used for long haul voyages. It offers economies of scale because it can carry large amounts of oil across long distances.

- **Very Large Crude Carrier (VLCC):** The VLCC is the vessel of choice for long distance seaborne voyages. It's ideally suited for intercontinental maritime transportation; its areas of operation include the Persian Gulf to East Asia and West Africa to the United States, among other routes.

- **Suezmax:** This vessel is named thus because its design and size allows it to transit through the Suez Canal, in Egypt. The Suezmax is among the vessels used to transport oil from the Persian Gulf to Europe, as well as to other destinations. It is ideally suited for medium haul voyages.

- **Aframax:** The Aframax, whose first four letters are an acronym for Average Freight Rate Assessment, is considered the "workhorse" in the tanker fleet. Because of its smaller size, it is ideally suited for short haul voyages and has the ability to transport crude and products to most ports around the world.

✔ **Panamax:** Like the Suezmax, the Panamax gets its name from its ability to transit through a canal, in this case the Panama Canal. This vessel is sometimes used for short haul voyages between the ports in the Caribbean, Europe, and the United States.

Besides their catchy names, these vessels are also identified by how much crude oil and products they can transport on sea. The unit of measurement used to capture this capacity is known as the *Dead Weight Ton*, or DWT. DWT measures the weight of the vessel including all cargo it is carrying. Most ships are constructed in such a way that one DWT is the equivalent of 6.7 Barrels of oil.

I list in Table 14-2 the DWT capacity of the vessels listed previously, along with their equivalent in barrels of oil.

Table 14-2	Vessel Capacity in DWT and Oil Equivalents	
Vessel Type	*Dead Weight Tons*	*Oil Equivalent (Barrels)*
ULCC	320,000 and up	2+ million
VLCC	200,000 – 320,000	2 million
Suezmax	120,000 – 200,000	1 million
Aframax	80,000 – 120,000	600,000
Panamax	50,000 – 80,000	300,000

Masters of the sea: Petroleum shipping companies

The companies responsible for transporting crude oil and petroleum products are an essential link in the global energy supply chain. This group is a diverse bunch, and each company provides a necessary and important service to this crucial industry. Some companies concentrate their operations regionally, such as in the Gulf of Mexico or the Persian Gulf. Others have extensive transportation capabilities with operations in all four corners of the globe. Some operate a small group of VLCC vessels, while others operate a large number of smaller vessels. And still others specialize in shipping only crude oil, while others focus primarily on petroleum products such as gasoline.

With so many options to choose from, it can be confusing trying to identify which company to invest in. In this section, I give you a list of all the major publicly traded oil shipping companies, and I go through their operations and scope of activities so you can decide which one is right for your investment needs.

✔ **Teekay Shipping Corp. (NYSE: TK):** Teekay Shipping is one of the world's largest seaborne transporters of crude oil and crude oil products. It operates a fleet of over 130 vessels, including one VLCC (2 Million Barrel capacity) that transports crude from the Persian Gulf and West Africa to Europe, the United States, and Asia; about 15 Suezmax vessels (1 Million Barrel capacity) that connect producers in North Africa (Algeria) and West Africa to consumers in Europe and the United States; and over 40 Aframax vessels (0.6 Million Barrel capacity) that operate in the North Sea, the Black Sea, the Mediterranean Sea, and the Caribbean.

In addition to conventional tankers, Teekay operates a fleet of offshore tankers that are constructed to transport crude from offshore locations to onshore facilities. If you're interest in a truly global and diversified oil shipping company, you can't go wrong with Teekay Shipping.

✔ **Frontline Ltd. (NYSE: FRO):** Founded in 1948, Frontline is one of the oldest shipping companies in the world. It also operates one of the world's largest fleets of VLCC vessels with over 44 VLCCs. In addition to its VLCCs, Frontline owns over 35 Suezmax vessels (1 Million Barrel capacity), making it one of the largest tanker companies in the world in terms of transportation capacity. Cumulatively, it has the capacity of 18 Million Dead Weight Tons. With operations in the Persian Gulf, Europe, the United States, and Asia, Frontline runs a very tight ship indeed!

In addition to its tanker fleet, Frontline offers shareholders one of the highest dividend payouts I have ever seen: an eye-popping $6 per share! At current market prices, that's a yield of over 18 percent! (See Table 14-3 for more on dividend yields.)

✔ **Overseas Shipholding Group, Inc. (NYSE: OSG):** OSG, unlike many of its competitors that are incorporated in offshore locations such as Bermuda and the Bahamas, is headquartered in New York City. Although it has an international presence, it is the only company with a large presence in the American shipping market. Its U.S. vessels are mainly engaged in the transportation of crude oil from Alaska to the continental United States, and products from the Gulf of Mexico to the East Coast.

Additionally, OSG has one of the highest profit margins in the industry: a whopping 45 percent profit margin (2006 figures)! If you're interested in the domestic crude oil transportation market, then take the plunge with OSG.

✔ **General Maritime Corp. (NYSE: GMR):** General Maritime focuses on the small and mid-size segment of the tanker market. They operate a fleet of Suezmax and Aframax vessels with operations primarily focused in the Atlantic basin. General Maritime links producers and consumers from Western Africa, the North Sea, the Caribbean, the United States, and Europe. If you're looking for exposure to the trans-Atlantic oil seaborne trade, then GMR is a good bet.

Also, the fact that they offer a $5 dividend per share makes this an attractive tanker stock.

✔ **OMI Corporation (NYSE: OMM):** OMI Corporation specializes in the transport of crude products on smaller vessels such as the Handysize and Handymax vessels. It has a nice niche market in the transportation of refined products from refineries to consumer markets. In addition, it also operates over ten Suezmax vessels and two Panamax vessels. OMI is a lean and mean competitor in this highly competitive industry.

I've given you here a snapshot of global tanker activities. If you do decide to invest in the global oil shipping business, I recommend you dig deeper into a target company's operations. Most of the information you need is found in a company's annual report (Form 10K) or quarterly report (Form 10Q). Additional information can also be obtained through third parties, such as analyst reports.

One of the best-kept secrets in this industry is the high dividend payout these companies issue. I'm a huge fan of dividends because they provide you with certainty in an uncertain investment world. And oil tanker stocks offer some of the highest dividend payouts out there. Table 14-3 gives you a group of shipping company stocks that offer some remarkable dividend payouts.

Table 14-3	Oil Tanker Stocks, 2006 Dividend Yields	
Company	*Ticker*	*Dividend Yield*
Nordic American Tankers	NYSE: NAT	18.1%
Frontline	NYSE: FRO	17.6%
General Maritime	NYSE: GMR	16.7%
Knightsbridge Tankers	NASDAQ: VLCCF	15.9%

Calculating dividend payouts can be tricky because a company isn't obligated to give back money to shareholders in the form of dividends. Some companies will pay out high dividends one year but not the next, while for others paying dividends may only be a one-time event. One way to determine future dividend payouts is by examining the company's dividend payout history. Any good stock screener should have this information handy. I personally find that the Yahoo! Finance Web site does the job: www.finance.yahoo.com.

Swimming with sharks: Avoiding industry risk

As with most things that have to do with commodities, tanker spot rates and fixed rates, which provide the bulk of a shipping company's revenue stream, are highly cyclical. It's not out of the ordinary for shipping rates to fluctuate by 60 or 70 percent on a daily basis. Take a look at the tanker spot rate volatility in Figure 14-2.

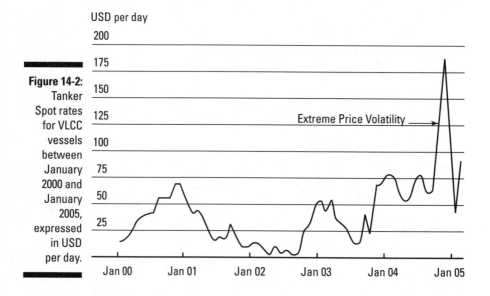

Figure 14-2:
Tanker Spot rates for VLCC vessels between January 2000 and January 2005, expressed in USD per day.

So how do you protect yourself from these extreme price volatilities? One way to hedge your positions is by investing in one of the large oil tanker stocks that I mentioned in the previous section. These companies have been in the business a long time and have substantial experience managing these wild price swings.

Another factor you need to consider is global economic growth. The oil shipping industry is dependent on a strong global economy with a healthy appetite for crude oil and crude oil products. If the global economy is thrown in a recession, you can expect that the tanker stocks will take a hit. Everything else equal, if the world demand for oil products slows down, I recommend getting out of these tanker stocks.

For the more adventurous investor, there's always the option of shorting the stock of companies you know aren't going to do well. You can short a company's stock through various means, such as buying a put option or even selling a call option. I discuss short selling in Chapter 9.

To find out more about the oil shipping industry, I recommend you check out Martin Stopford's excellent book on the subject, *Maritime Economics* (Routledge).

Part IV
Pedal to the Metal: Investing in Metals

The 5th Wave   By Rich Tennant

"Precious metals? Energy futures? Pork bellies? I say we stick the money in the ground like always, and then feed this guy to the sharks."

In this part . . .

People have always been fascinated by precious metals such as gold. In this part, I cover not only precious metals such as gold, silver, and platinum, but also important base and industrial metals like copper, aluminum, zinc, and steel. I provide you with an in-depth look at these markets and introduce you to some of the world's best mining companies to help you profit in this market.

Chapter 15

Getting the Glitters: Investing in Gold, Silver, and Platinum

. . . .

In This Chapter

▶ Investing in gold

▶ How to make money in silver

▶ Making investments in platinum

. . . .

Metallurgy and civilization go hand in hand. Man's ability to control metals has enabled him to develop modern society and civilization. As a matter of fact, human prehistory is classified using a three-age system based on man's ability to control metals: the stone age, the bronze age, and the iron age. Societies that have mastered the use of metals in weaponry and tool-making have been able to thrive and survive. Those without this ability have faced extinction.

Similarly, investors who have been able to master the fundamentals of the metals markets have been handsomely rewarded. In this chapter, I introduce you to the fascinating world of precious metals, which include gold, silver, and platinum. These metals can play a role in your portfolio because of their precious metal status, their ability to act as a store of value, and their potential to provide a hedge against inflation. In this chapter, you discover all you need to know to incorporate precious metals into your portfolio.

As a general rule, metals are classified into two broad categories: *precious metals* and *base metals*. This classification is based on a metal's resistance to corrosion and oxidation: Precious metals have a high resistance to corrosion, whereas base metals (which I cover in Chapter 16) have a lower tolerance.

Going for the Gold

Perhaps no other metal — or commodity — in the world has the cachet and prestige of gold. For centuries, gold has been coveted and valued for its unique metallurgical characteristics. It was such a desirable commodity that

The golden boy from the gold rush

The California gold rush was a defining moment in the history of the United States. When word spread that gold had been discovered in the San Francisco area, a large number of young men rushed out West with a burning desire to strike it rich. A number of success stories emerged from this era. However, one of the greatest *untold* stories of the California Gold Rush is the story of Samuel Brannan, who was California's first millionaire. Sam Brannan was the third man to find out that gold had been discovered in California. Not surprisingly, the first two people who knew about the gold — John Sutter and James Marshall — wanted to keep the discovery a secret. Sam Brannan had other plans.

Instead of keeping quiet about the discovery, Sam Brannan quickly got the word out that gold had been discovered in California. What's remarkable is that Sam Brannan made a fortune during the California Gold Rush without ever digging a single hole or prospecting for a single nugget of gold. How did he make his money? By selling shovels to the large number of people who were interested in digging for the gold! Before telling the world about the California gold, Sam Brannan quietly bought almost all the shovels in Northern California. When the prospectors flooded in, the price of shovels went through the roof, and Sam was the only man in town to sell them. He reaped untold fortunes selling shovels during the gold rush.

One of the lessons of Sam Brannan's story is that you don't have to actually dig for gold to profit from it. You need to keep your mind open to creative investment ideas that will allow you to profit creatively from the commodities boom.

it developed monetary applications, and a number of currencies were based on the value of gold. In 1944, for example, 44 of the world's richest countries decided to peg their currencies to the yellow metal; this is known as the *Bretton Woods Agreement*, and it included such major currencies as the US Dollar. Although President Nixon removed the dollar from the gold standard in 1971, a large number of countries still use gold as a global currency benchmark.

In addition, gold has a number of applications in industry and jewelry that have resulted in increased demand for this precious metal. Check out the price of gold between 1997 and 2006 in Figure 15-1.

The gold standard

The increased demand for gold is due to a number of reasons. In order to profit from this increased demand, you need to be familiar with the fundamentals of the gold market. I go through these market fundamentals in this section.

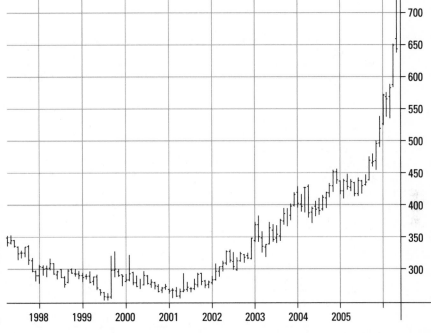

Figure 15-1:
Historical
price levels
of Gold on
the COMEX
from 1997
to 2006
(Dollars per
Troy Ounce).

First, you should know what gold is used for. You may not be surprised to find out that jewelry accounts for a large portion of gold demand. However, did you know that dentistry also represents a significant portion of the gold market? Here are some of the uses of gold:

✔ **Jewelry:** Since it was first discovered by man thousands of years ago, gold has been used as an ornament and in jewelry. The ancient Egyptian king Tutankhamen was so enamored with gold that he was buried in a gold coffin. Today, jewelry is the most important consumer use of gold in the world, accounting for over 70 percent of total consumption.

✔ **Electronics:** Because of its ability to efficiently conduct electricity, gold is a popular metal in electronics. It is used as a semiconductor in circuit boards and integrated boards in everything from cellphones and TVs to missiles.

✔ **Dentistry:** Because gold resists corrosion, it has wide application in dentistry. It is alloyed with other metals such as silver, copper, and platinum to create dental fixtures.

✔ **Monetary:** Many central banks hold reserves of gold. In addition, gold is one of the only commodities that is held in its physical form for investment purposes by the investing public. (See section "Getting physical.") Another monetary use of gold aside from central bank reserves and investor portfolios is the use of gold in coinage. In countries such as Canada and South Africa, some gold coins are actually legal tender.

A large number of countries and banks hold reserve assets of gold. I list in Table 15-1 the top ten holders of gold around the world.

Table 15-1	World Gold Holdings in Tons, 2006 Figures
Country/Entity	*Reserves (Tons)*
USA	8135
Germany	3427
International Monetary Fund	3217
France	2790
Italy	2451
Switzerland	1290
Japan	765
European Central Bank	720
Netherlands	654
China	600

In gold we trust

Why is gold such an important metal? Here are some traits that will help you get an understanding of where gold derives its value:

- ✔ **Quasi-indestructibility:** Gold has high resistance levels and doesn't easily corrode. Corrosive agents such as oxygen and heat have almost no effect on gold, which can retain its luster over long periods of time (think thousands of years). The only chemical that is able to affect gold is cyanide, which dissolves gold.

- ✔ **Rarity:** Gold is one of the rarest natural resources on Earth. A lot of people don't realize this, but only about 150,000 tons of gold have ever been produced since humans first began mining gold over 6,000 years ago. To give you an idea of how little that is, if you were to take all the gold in the world it would not even fill up four Olympic size swimming pools! And because most gold is recycled and never destroyed, a majority of gold is still in use today. As a matter of fact, about 15 percent of gold is recycled every year.

- ✔ **Malleability:** Pure gold (24 karat) is a very malleable metal and is prized by craftsmen around the world who enjoy shaping it into jewelry and other objects of beauty. One ounce of gold can be transformed into over 96 square feet of gold sheet!

✔ **Ductility:** Gold is a very ductile metal. In metallurgy, *ductility* measures how much a metal can be drawn out into a wire. For example, one ounce of gold can be converted into over 50 miles of gold wire! This gold wire can then be applied in electronics and used as an electric conductor.

The wizard of oz: How to measure gold

Gold, like most metals, is measured and weighed in *troy ounces* (oz). One troy ounce is the equivalent of 31.10 grams. (Despite the common misperception, the troy ounce does not take its name from the mythic ancient Greek city of Troy. Rather it is named after the French town of Troyes, which was an important center of trade and commerce with a thriving precious metals market during the Middle Ages.) When you buy gold for investment purposes, such as through an Exchange Traded Fund (ETF) or gold certificates, troy ounces is the measurement of choice.

When you want to refer to large quantities of gold, such as the amount of gold a bank holds in reserves or the amount of gold produced in a mine, then the unit of measurement you use is *metric tons*. One metric ton is equal to 32,150 troy ounces.

If you've bought gold jewelry, you may have come across the following measurement: karats. *Karats* (sometimes spelled carats) measures the purity of gold. The purest form of gold is 24 karat gold (24K). Everything below that number denotes that the gold is alloyed, or mixed, with another metal.

Table 15-2 shows you what the different numbers of karats translate to in terms of gold's purity.

Table 15-2	Purity of Gold, Measured in Karats
Karats	*Purity (percentage)*
24K	100%
22K	91.67%
18K	75%
14K	58.3%
10K	41.67%
9K	37.5%

If you buy physical gold either for adornment purposes (jewelry) or for investment purposes (gold coins/bars), you want to get the purest form of gold, 24K. If you can't get 24K gold, then you should aim to get the purest form of gold you can get your hands on. Remember that the purer the gold, the higher its value. Pure gold (24K) is always a yellow color. However, you've probably encountered white gold or even red gold — these other colors are created by alloying gold with metals such as nickel or palladium for a white color or with copper to create *red gold*. By definition, white and red gold aren't pure gold.

While purity measures how precious gold is in a percentage basis, *fineness* measures gold's purity expressed as a whole number. Fortunately, fineness and purity are so similar that gold with 91.67% purity has a fineness of 0.9167.

Good as gold

In this section, I introduce you to the different ways you can invest in gold: physical gold, gold ETFs, gold mining companies, and gold futures contracts.

Getting physical

Gold is unlike any other commodity because it is one of the few commodities that can be physically stored to have its value preserved or increased over periods of time. One investment method unique to gold is to actually buy it — hard, physical gold. You can purchase gold bars, bullion, and coins and store them in a safe location as an investment. Perhaps no other commodity offers you this unique opportunity. (Storing physical coal or uranium for investment purposes just doesn't work, believe me!) In some countries, folks will actually buy gold jewelry for the dual purpose of adornment and investment. Here are some different forms of gold you can get your hands on:

- **Gold coins:** One of the easiest ways to invest in physical gold is by buying gold coins. I like gold coins because they give you a lot of bang for your buck. Unlike large gold bars, gold coins allow you to purchase the yellow metal in smaller quantities and units. This means two things: First, you don't have to put up as much money to buy a gold coin compared to buying a gold bar; second, if you want to sell part of your gold holdings, you can easily sell five gold coins and keep five — that's not possible when you only have one gold bar. Another reason I like gold coins is that they can be easily and safely stored; they're more discreet than having large gold bullion. The third reason I like gold coins is that they're actually issued by a federal government and are instantly recognized as such; in some countries (Canada and South Africa), they are even considered legal tender. I list the most popular types of gold coins, by country of issuance, here:

  - **Gold Eagle:** The gold eagle coin is issued by the United States government; it has the full backing of Congress and the U.S. Mint. It comes in various sizes including 1 oz., ½ oz., ¼ oz. and ⅟₁₀ oz. At 22 karats, it's a high quality coin that can actually be used towards funding an IRA account.

- **Gold Maple Leaf:** The gold maple leaf, you guessed it, is backed by the Canadian government. It is issued by the Royal Canadian Mint and, at 24 karats, is the purest gold coin on the market.

- **Gold Krugerrand:** The gold krugerrand is issued by the South African government and is one of the oldest gold coins issued in the world. It has a fineness of 0.916.

✔ **Gold bars:** Gold bars have an undeniable allure. In pop culture, for example, gold is usually depicted as large gold bars. Think of the movies *Goldfinger* and *Die Hard 3,* for instance. Much more than great movie props, gold bars are also a great investment. While gold coins are more suited for smaller purchases, gold bars are ideal if you're interested in purchasing larger quantities of gold. Despite popular depictions, gold bars come in all shapes and sizes. They can be as small as 1 gram or as large as 400 troy ounces. Despite the size, most gold bars are high quality with a fineness of 0.999 and above (24 karats). For a comprehensive listing of gold bars, I recommend *The Industry Catalogue of Gold Bars Worldwide,* which you can find at www.grendon.com.au/goldbarscat.htm. Perhaps the only drawback of gold bars is their size, which makes them harder (and more expensive) to store.

✔ **Gold certificates:** Gold certificates are a hybrid instrument that allows you to own physical gold without actually taking possession of it. Gold certificates, like the name implies, certify that you own a certain amount of gold, which is usually stored in a safe location by the authority who issues the gold certificates. Owning gold certificates is my favorite way of owning physical gold because it is safe and easy to store. When you own gold bars or coins, safety is always a concern — someone could literally steal your gold. Storage is another concern, particularly if you have large quantities of the stuff, because it can end up costing you a lot to store your gold (such as in a bank vault or personal safe). The gold standard of gold certificates is the *Perth Mint Certificate Program* (PMCP).

The PMCP is administered by the Perth Mint, Australia's oldest and most important mint. At one point, the Perth Mint had as much gold as Fort Knox. The PMCP is the only certificate program that is guaranteed by a government, in this case the Government of Western Australia. The PMCP issues you a certificate and it stores your gold in a secure government vault. You may retrieve or sell your gold at any point. For more on this program check out the Perth Mint's Web site at www.perthmint.com.au.

Gold bullion is nothing more than large gold bars.

If you want to purchase gold coins, bars, or even certificates, you need to go through a gold dealer. One gold dealer I recommend is Kitco (www.kitco.com).

Before doing business with any gold dealer, though, make sure you find out as much information about the business (and business history) as possible. You can check out different gold dealers by going through the Better Business Bureau at www.bbb.org.

Gold ETFs

Exchange Traded Funds offering exposure to commodities are a popular investment gateway for folks who don't want to mess around with futures contracts. Signaling gold's importance, one of the first commodity ETFs is, you guessed it, a gold ETF. Currently you have two gold ETFs to choose from:

- ✔ **StreetTracks Gold Shares (NYSE: GLD):** The StreetTracks gold ETF is the largest gold ETF on the market today. Launched in late 2004, it holds about 12 Million Ounces of physical gold in secured locations. (That's more than $7 Billion worth of gold in 2006 bullion prices). The price per ETF unit is calculated based on the average of the bid/ask spread in the gold spot market. This fund is a good way of getting exposure to physical gold without actually owning it.

- ✔ **iShares COMEX Gold Trust (AMEX: IAU):** The iShares gold ETF holds a little more than 1.3 Million Ounces of gold in its vaults. The per unit price of the ETF seeks to reflect the current market price in the spot market of the ETF gold.

Make sure to find out about the fees and expenses associated with each of the ETFs mentioned. Because these ETFs actually hold physical gold, they have to pay a number of entities to make this possible, so make sure to inquire about any storage fees. This is in addition to the general fund expenses such as registration and administration fees. Carefully consider all expenses and fees because these will have a direct impact on your bottom line.

Because both the *StreetTracks* and *iShares* ETFs track the price of gold on the spot market, their performance is remarkably similar — at times, it's actually identical. Therefore, if you can't decide between the two, I recommend *StreetTracks* because it holds more physical gold and, more importantly, it offers you more liquidity than the *iShares* ETF.

Stocks in gold companies

Another way to get exposure to gold is by investing in gold mining companies. A number of companies specialize in mining, processing, and distributing this precious metal. Here are a few companies I recommend:

- ✔ **Newmont Mining Corporation (NYSE: NEM):** Newmont, which is headquartered in Colorado, is one of the largest gold mining companies in the world. It has operations in Australia, Indonesia, Uzbekistan, the United States (Nevada and California), Canada, Peru, and Bolivia. It is actually the largest gold producer in South America. Additionally, it has exploration programs in Ghana that could turn out to be very promising for the company. If you're looking for a truly global and diversified gold producer with real growth potential, then you can't go wrong with Newmont.

✔ **Barrick Gold Corporation (NYSE: ABX):** Barrick is a Canadian company with headquarters in Toronto. It is a premier player in the gold mining industry and has operations in Canada, the United States, Argentina, Peru, Chile, Tanzania, South Africa, Australia, and Papua New Guinea. It also has a foothold in the potentially lucrative Central Asian market, where it has joint operations in Turkey, Russia, and Mongolia. Another reason I like Barrick is that it has one of the lowest production costs per ounce of gold in the industry.

✔ **AngloGold Ashanti Ltd. (NYSE: AU):** AngloGold, which is listed in five different stock exchanges around the world, is a truly global gold company. Based in South Africa, it operates over 20 mines and has significant operations in Africa and South America, particularly in South Africa, Namibia, Tanzania, Ghana, Mali, Brazil, Argentina, and Peru, which all have major gold deposits. It has additional operations in Australia and North America. It is a wholly owned subsidiary of *Anglo-American*, the global mining giant (which I cover in Chapter 18).

A number of other mining companies have gold mining operations that are part of a general mining program that includes other metals, such as silver, copper, and so on. I selected these companies because their sphere of operations revolve almost exclusively on gold mining.

The performance of these companies is not directly proportional to the spot or future price of gold. These companies don't give you the direct exposure to gold that gold certificates or bars do, for example. Also, by investing in these stocks you're exposing yourself to regulatory, managerial, and operational factors.

Gold contracts

Gold futures contracts provide you with a direct way to invest in gold through the futures markets. You can choose from two gold futures contracts that are widely traded in the United States (see Chapter 9 for the goods on futures contracts):

✔ **COMEX Gold (COMEX: GC):** The COMEX gold futures contract was the first such contract to hit the market in the United States (back in the 1970s). It is traded on the COMEX division of the New York Mercantile Exchange (NYMEX), and it's the most liquid gold contract in the world. It is used primarily by large commercial consumers and producers, such as jewelry manufacturers and mining companies, for price hedging purposes. However, you can also purchase the contract for investment purposes. Each contract represents 100 Troy Ounces of gold.

> ✔ **CBOT Mini-Gold (CBOT: YG):** Launched in 2004, the Chicago Board of Trade (CBOT) gold contract is a relative newcomer to the North American gold futures market. However, it's a very popular contract because you can trade it online through the CBOT's electronic trading platform. In addition, at a contract size of 33.2 Troy Ounces, the mini is popular with investors and traders who prefer to trade this smaller size contract than the larger 100-ounce contract offered by CBOT or COMEX.

Although the CBOT also offers the more traditional, full size 100-ounce gold contract, the COMEX's 100-ounce contract is the more liquid of the two. However, this may change in the future.

When investing in the futures markets, always trade in the most liquid markets. *Liquidity* is an indication of the number of contracts that are traded on a regular basis. The higher the liquidity, the more likely you are to find a buyer or seller to close out or open a position. You can get information on the volume and open interest of contracts traded in the futures markets through the Commodity Futures Trading Commission's (CFTC) Web site at www.cftc.gov.

Get the Tableware Ready: Investing in Silver

Creating and designing silverware and jewelry isn't the only use for silver. As a matter of fact, silverware is only a small portion of the silver market. A large portion of this precious metal goes towards industrial uses, such as conducting electricity, creating bearings, and welding, soldering, and brazing (the process by which metals are permanently joined together). Because of its numerous practical applications and its status as a precious metal, investing in silver can bolster your portfolio. In this section, I introduce you to the ins and outs of the silver market, and then show you how to actually include silver in your portfolio.

Checking out the big picture on the silver screen

Silver has a number of uses that make it an attractive investment. Here are the most important ones, which account for more than 95 percent of total demand for silver:

> ✔ **Industrial:** The industrial sector is the single largest consumer of silver products, accounting for almost 45 percent of total silver consumption in 2005. Silver has a number of applications in the industrial sector,

including creating control switches for electrical appliances and connecting electronic circuit boards. Because it's a good electrical conductor, silver will keep playing an important role in the industrial sector.

✔ **Jewelry and silverware:** A large number of people believe (incorrectly) that the largest consumer of silver is the jewelry industry. Although silver does play a large role in creating jewelry and silverware, demand from this sector accounted for 27 percent of total silver consumption in 2005, the latest year for which data is currently available.

✔ **Photography:** Did you know that the photographic industry is also a major consumer of silver, accounting for about 20 percent of total consumption. In photography, silver is compounded with halogens to form *silver halide,* which is used in photographic film. Almost 200 Million Troy Ounces of silver was used by the photography industry in 2003. That number is slowly decreasing, however, because digital cameras, which don't use silver halide, are becoming more popular than traditional cameras. Keep this decrease in demand in mind as you consider investing in silver.

Monitor the commercial activity in each of these market segments, looking for signs of strength or weakness in these areas because a demand increase or decrease in one of these markets will have a direct impact on the price of silver.

Knowing where the silver comes from is always important to an investor, so I list the top producers of silver in the world in Table 15-3.

Table 15-3	Top Silver Producers, 2006 Figures
Country	*Production (Millions of ounces)*
Peru	102.6
Mexico	92.3
Australia	77.4
China	64.7
Chile	44.3
Russia	42.2
Poland	40.5
United States	39.2
Canada	34.1
Kazakhstan	25.9

If you're interested in finding out more about silver and its investment possibilities, the *Silver Institute* maintains a comprehensive database on the silver market. The Silver Institute is a trade association for silver producers and consumers. Its Web site is www.silverinstitute.org.

A sliver of silver in your portfolio

Silver can play an important role in your portfolio. Because of its precious metal status, you can use it as a hedge against inflation and to preserve part of your portfolio's value. In addition, because it has important industrial applications, you can use it to provide you with capital appreciation opportunities. Whether for capital preservation or appreciation purposes, I believe there is room in any portfolio for some exposure to silver. In this section, I introduce you to the different ways you can invest in silver.

Buying physical silver

One of the unique characteristics of silver is that you can invest in it by actually buying the stuff, as you would buy gold coins and bars for investment purposes. Most dealers that sell gold generally offer silver coins and bars as well. Here are a few silver coins to consider as investments:

- **Silver Maple Coins:** These coins, which are a product of the Royal Canadian Mint, are the standard for silver coins around the world. Each coin represents 1 oz. of silver and has a purity of 99.99 percent, making it the most pure silver coin on the market.

- **100 oz. Silver Bar:** If you're interested in something a little more substantial than 1 oz. silver coins, you could buy the 100 oz. silver bar. Before buying it, check the bar to make sure it's pure silver (you want 99 percent purity or above).

The term *sterling silver* refers to a specific silver alloy that contains 92.5 percent silver and 7.5 percent copper (other base metals are occasionally used as well). Pure silver is sometimes alloyed with another metal, such as copper, in order to make it stronger and more durable. Just remember that if you're considering some silver jewelry as an investment, sterling silver won't provide you with as much value in the long term as buying pure silver.

Buying the silver ETF

One of the most convenient ways of investing in silver is by going through an Exchange Traded Fund (ETF). Until recently, there were no ETFs to track silver. However, Barclays Global Investors (a subsidiary of the investment bank) launched an ETF through its *iShares* program in April 2006 to track the price of silver. The iShares Silver Trust (AMEX: SLV) holds silver bullion in a vault and seeks to mirror the spot price of that silver based on current market prices. This new silver ETF is a testament to the increased demand by investors to include silver in their portfolios.

Looking at silver mining companies

Another alternative investment route is to go through companies that mine silver. Although some of the larger mining companies (which I cover in Chapter 18) have silver mining operations, you can get a more direct exposure to the silver markets by investing in companies that *specialize* in mining this precious metal. These companies may not be household names, but they are a potentially good investment nevertheless. Here are a couple of companies that focus exclusively on mining silver:

✔ **Pan American Silver Corporation (NASDAQ: PAAS):** Pan American Silver, based in Vancouver, has extensive operations in the Americas. It operates six mines in some of the most prominent locations in the world, including Peru, Mexico, and Bolivia. If you're interested in a well-managed company to provide you with exposure to Latin American silver mines, you won't go wrong with Pan American Silver.

✔ **Silver Wheaton Corp. (NYSE: SLW):** Silver Wheaton is one of the only mining companies that generates all of its revenues from silver mining activity. While other mining companies may have smaller interests in other metals, Silver Wheaton focuses exclusively on developing and mining silver. It has operations in geographically diverse areas that stretch from Mexico to Sweden. If you're looking for a geographically diverse company to provide you with direct access to silver mining activities, then Silver Wheaton is your best bet.

Silver futures contract

The silver futures contracts, like gold futures, provide you with the most direct access to the silver market. I list the most liquid silver futures contracts below:

✔ **COMEX Silver (COMEX: SI):** The COMEX silver contract is the standard futures contract for silver. It is traded on the COMEX division of the New York Mercantile Exchange (NYMEX), and represents 5000 Troy Ounces of silver per contract.

✔ **CBOT Mini-Silver (CBOT: YI):** The Mini-Silver contract that trades on the Chicago Board of Trade (CBOT) represents a stake in 1000 Troy Ounces of silver with a purity of 99.9 percent. This contract is available for electronic trading.

To give you an idea of the performance of the NYMEX/COMEX silver futures contract, I list its price in Figure 15-2.

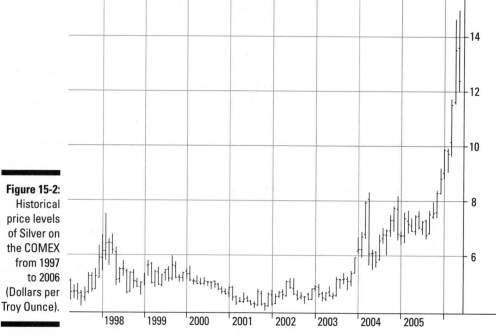

Figure 15-2:
Historical
price levels
of Silver on
the COMEX
from 1997
to 2006
(Dollars per
Troy Ounce).

Bling Bling: Investing in Platinum

Platinum, which is sometimes referred to as "the rich man's gold," is one of the rarest and most precious metals in the world. Perhaps no other metal or commodity carries the same cachet as platinum, and for good reason. It is by far the rarest metal in the world: If you were to put all the platinum that has ever been mined in an Olympic size swimming pool, that platinum would not even cover your ankles! As a matter of fact, while precious and base metals such as gold and copper have been exploited for thousands of years, man's interest in platinum only developed in the 17th century when the Conquistadors discovered large amounts of the metal in South America. It was soon discovered that platinum had superior characteristics to most metals: It is more resistant to corrosion, doesn't oxidize in the air, and has stable chemical properties. Because of these characteristics, platinum is a highly desirable metal and can play an important role in your portfolio.

Platinum is also the name of the group of metals that includes platinum, palladium, rhodium, ruthenium, osmium, and iridium. In this section, I talk about the metal and not the group of metals, although I cover palladium in Chapter 17.

Platinum facts and figures

Deposits of platinum ore are extremely scarce and, more importantly, are geographically concentrated in a few regions around the globe, primarily in South Africa, Russia, and North America. South Africa has the largest deposits of platinum in the world and, by some accounts, may contain up to 90 percent of the world's total reserve estimates. Russia is also a large player in the production of platinum, currently accounting for 20 percent of total global production (2006 figures). North America also contains some commercially viable platinum mines, located mostly in Montana.

Platinum's rarity is reflected in its price per troy ounce. For example, the price of platinum in June 2006 was $1,230.25 *per* troy ounce! By comparison, silver during the same period cost $11.55 per troy ounce.

So who uses platinum? Platinum has several uses. Here are the most important ones:

- **Catalytic converters:** You may be surprised to find out not only that platinum is used in catalytic converters in transportation vehicles, but also that this accounts for over 45 percent of total platinum demand. Platinum's unique characteristics make it a suitable metal in the production of these pollution-reducing devices. As environmental fuel standards become more stringent, expect the demand from this sector to increase in the future.

- **Jewelry:** At one point jewelry accounted for over 50 percent of total demand for platinum. Although that number has decreased, the jewelry industry is still a major purchaser of platinum metals for use in highly prized jewelry.

- **Industrial:** Because it's a great conductor of heat and electricity, platinum has wide applications in industry. It is used in the creation of everything from personal computer hard drives to fiber optic cables. Despite its relative value, platinum will continue to be used for industrial purposes.

A change in demand from one of these industries will affect the price of platinum. The International Platinum Association maintains an updated database of the uses of platinum. Check out their Web site for more information on platinum supply and demand at www.platinuminfo.net.

Going platinum

Platinum's unique characteristics as a highly sought-after precious metal with industrial applications makes it an ideal investment. Fortunately, you can invest in platinum in a number of ways. I list a couple of these methods in the following sections.

Platinum futures contract

The most direct way of investing in platinum is by going through the futures markets. The New York Mercantile Exchange (NYMEX) offers a platinum futures contract. Because of increased demand from the industrial sector and other fundamental supply and demand reasons, the price of the NYMEX platinum futures contract has experienced significant upward shift in recent years. Check out the price of platinum in Figure 15-3.

The NYMEX platinum futures contract represents 50 Troy Ounces of platinum and is available for trading electronically. It trades under the ticker symbol PL.

Platinum mining companies

Here are a couple of companies you can check out that will give you direct exposure to platinum mining activities:

- ✔ **Stillwater Mining Company (NYSE: SWC):** Stillwater Mining is headquartered in Billings, Montana, and owns the rights to the Stillwater mining complex in Montana, which contains one of the largest commercially viable platinum mines in North America. This is a good play on North American platinum mining activities.

- ✔ **Anglo-American PLC (NASDAQ: AAUK):** Anglo-American is a diversified mining company that has activities in gold, silver, platinum, and other precious metals. I recommend Anglo-American because it has significant interests in South African platinum mines, the largest mines in the world. If you're looking for an indirect exposure to South Africa's platinum mining industry, then Anglo-American does the trick.

Investing in companies that mine precious metals, or any other commodity for that matter, does not provide you with direct exposure to the price fluctuations of that commodity. You need to be familiar with the fluctuations and patterns of the equity markets in order to be able to profit from this investment methodology. You also need to take into consideration any external factors that will impact the performance of the company, such as management effectiveness, total debt levels, areas of operation, and other metrics that are specific to companies. That said, investing in the equity markets still gives you access to the commodities markets.

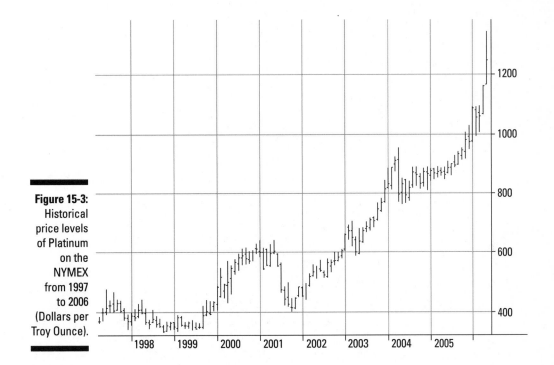

Figure 15-3:
Historical
price levels
of Platinum
on the
NYMEX
from 1997
to 2006
(Dollars per
Troy Ounce).

Chapter 16

Metals That Prove Their Mettle: Steel, Aluminum, and Copper

• •

In This Chapter

▶ Mapping out a strategy to invest in steel

▶ Evaluating opportunities in the aluminum market

▶ Examining the ins and outs of the copper industry

• •

Steel, aluminum, and copper may not be as glamorous as their precious metals counterparts — gold, silver, and platinum, covered in Chapter 15 — but they are perhaps even more precious to the global economy. Gold, silver, and platinum do have industrial applications, but their primary value is derived from their ability to act as stores of value, in addition to their use in jewelry. Steel, aluminum, and copper are the most important *industrial* components of the metals complex, used to build everything from railcars to bridges. You may be surprised to find out that steel is the most widely used metal in the world — over 1.1 Billion Tons of it was produced in 2005. Steel is closely followed by aluminum, which itself is closely followed by copper in terms of total global output. So steel, aluminum, and copper — in that order — rank at the top of the metals complex based on total output.

Without these metals, which are literally the building blocks of modern societies, life as you and I know it wouldn't exist. Buildings couldn't be built without steel, cars wouldn't be as lightweight and efficient without aluminum, and you probably wouldn't be able to get any electricity in your home without copper, which is the electrical conductor of choice. Due in part to rapid industrialization in China (which happens to be the largest steel producer), India, and other leading developing countries, demand for these three building block metals is strong and will remain robust for the medium to long term. The future looks bright for these metals, and in this chapter I help you develop a game plan to invest in these powerhouse metals.

Building a Portfolio That's As Strong As Steel

The development of steel, alongside iron, has changed the course of human history. In fact, the last stage of prehistoric times, the *iron age,* is named thus because humans mastered the iron and steel making process. This development allowed societies to build tools and weapons, which speeded advancements in construction and technology. Steel was responsible for another revolution in the 19th century — the Industrial Revolution. Today, in a high-tech world dominated by software and technological gadgets, this age-old metal is still as reliable as ever. In fact, steel is making a resurgence as advanced developing countries — China, India, and Brazil — barrel down a path towards rapid industrialization not unlike the one the West experienced in the 19th century (see Chapter 2). *Steel,* which is iron alloyed with other compounds (usually carbon), is still the most widely produced metal in the world today.

Steel is measured in *Metric Tons,* sometimes abbreviated as MT. For *global* production and consumption figures, *Million Metric Tons* (MMT) is used.

Steely facts

Before I introduce the best ways to invest in steel, take a look at the dynamics of the broader steel industry. Steel production is dominated by China, which has generous subsidies in place for its steel manufacturers. China now produces three times more steel than Japan, the second largest producer. For a long time, the United States was the number one producer of steel, but its

---

Andrew Carnegie: Man of steel

Perhaps no one individual has had as much impact on the modern, global steel industry as Andrew Carnegie, the self-made industrialist. Carnegie single-handedly established the steel industry in Pittsburgh, Pennsylvania, which would dominate the steel industry for decades. He established the Carnegie Steel Corporation, which would eventually become U.S. Steel, in the 1890s and played a decisive role in the industrialization of the young nation. His steel was used in everything from building bridges to railroads. Another contribution to the steel industry, which is perhaps less known, is

Carnegie's pioneering business philosophy of "counter-cyclical investing". Many business executives at the time invested their profits to upgrade facilities when business was booming; this was a costly endeavor. Carnegie, identifying the cyclical nature of the industry, would undertake capital expenditures when the industry was in decline — this was less expensive. By investing when the industry was in a down cycle, his cost upgrades would be less expensive than during up cycles. This greatly helped increase his company's profitability, and it is a business practice still used today.

dominance eroded in large part due to competition from Asia (especially China and Japan) and partly due to internal reasons (such as high costs of running a steel mill in the United States). The United States is still an important player in the steel industry, and other countries worth mentioning include Russia, Germany, and South Korea. I list in Table 16-1 the top steel producers in the world.

Table 16-1	Top Steel Producing Countries, 2005 Figures
Country	*Production (Million Metric Tons)*
China	349.4 MMT
Japan	112.5 MMT
United States	94.9 MMT
Russia	66.1 MMT
South Korea	47.8 MMT
Germany	44.5 MMT
Ukraine	38.6 MMT
India	38.1 MMT
Brazil	31.6 MMT
Italy	29.3 MMT

Source: International Iron and Steel Institute

To put things in perspective, total global steel production in 2005 stood at 1131.8 MMT.

If you're interested in exploring additional statistical information relating to steel production and manufacturing, I recommend checking out the following resources:

- **International Iron and Steel Institute:** www.worldsteel.org
- **Iron and Steel Statistics Bureau:** www.issb.co.uk
- **Association for Iron and Steel Technology:** www.aist.org

Investing in steel companies

Although futures contracts are available for everything from crude oil to coffee, there is no underlying futures contract for steel. However, a number of exchanges have expressed interest in developing a steel futures contract, so keep an eye out for such a development.

But for now, the best way to get exposure to steel is by investing in companies that produce steel, specifically globally integrated steel companies. The companies I list in Table 16-2 are global leaders in the steel industry.

Table 16-2	Top Steel Producing Companies, 2005 Figures
Company	*Production (Million Metric Tons)*
Mittal Steel (Worldwide)	63 MMT
Arcelor (Europe)	46.7 MMT
Nippon Steel (Japan)	32 MMT
POSCO (South Korea)	30.5 MMT
JFE Group (Japan)	29.9 MMT
Shanghai Baosteel (China)	23.8 MMT
U.S. Steel (USA)	19.3 MMT
Nucor Steel (USA)	18.4 MMT
Corus Group (Europe)	18.2 MMT
Riva Group (Europe)	17.5 MMT

Source: International Iron and Steel Institute

The companies in Table 16-2 are the world leaders in the industry. However, not all are available for investment. Some of them are private, and others trade on foreign exchanges that don't issue *American Depository Receipts* (ADRs). (Turn to Chapter 18 for more on ADRs, which essentially allow you to invest in foreign companies through U.S. financial institutions.) The following list, however, represents good investments that not only are the best-run companies, but also display the greatest potential for future market dominance:

✔ **U.S. Steel (NYSE: X):** U.S. Steel, which was formed as a result of the consolidation of Andrew Carnegie's steel holdings in the early 20th century, is one of the oldest and largest steel companies in the world. U.S. Steel represents by itself the whole history of the modern steel industry. At one point it was the largest producer of steel in the world. While it has scaled down its operations, it is still a significant player in the industry today, and is the seventh largest steel producing company worldwide (see Table 16-2). U.S. Steel is involved in all aspects of the steel-making process from iron ore mining and processing to the marketing of finished products.

- **Nucor Corp. (NYSE: NUE):** The American steel industry remains a robust competitor on the global stage, despite the dominance of Asian (particularly Chinese) companies. Nucor operates almost exclusively in the United States and, if you're interested in getting exposure to the American steel market, you should consider an investment in it. Nucor is also one of the only companies to operate *mini-mills* domestically, which many argue are more cost-efficient than the traditional blast furnaces.

- **Arcelor-Mittal** (Newly combined entity is not yet listed on an exchange, pending merger approval): While I was writing this book, the two largest steel companies in the world entered into a merger agreement after months of contentious talks. The newly-formed company will have control over 10 percent of the world's steel market (in terms of output) and produce approximately 120 MMT of steel annually. The merger could result in cost-cutting synergies across both companies. I recommend considering an investment in this new steel behemoth in part due to its size and the resulting economies of scale. I examine the prospects of this new company in Chapter 18.

Aluminum: Everything Is Illuminated

Aluminum is one of the most ubiquitous metals of modern society. It's not just all those aluminum soda cans that account for its widespread use — aluminum is also used in transportation (cars, trucks, trains, and airplanes), construction, and electrical power lines, to name just a few end-uses. As a matter of fact, aluminum is the second-most widely used metal in the world, right after steel. Because of its indispensability, there is room to include this metal in your portfolio. In this section, I show you how to do just that.

Aluminum is generally measured in *Metric Tons* (MT).

Just the aluminum facts

Aluminum is a lightweight metal that is resistant to corrosion. Because of these characteristics, it is widely used to create a number of products, from cars to jets. Here are a few items that are made out of aluminum. You may recognize a few of them:

- **Transportation:** Aluminum is used to create the body, axles, and, in some cases, engines of cars. In addition, large commercial aircrafts are built using aluminum because of its light weight and sturdiness.

- **Packaging:** Almost a quarter of aluminum is used to create aluminum wrap and foil, along with beverage cans and rivets.

✔ **Construction:** Aluminum has industrial uses as well that include usage in the construction of buildings, oil pipelines, and even bridges. Building constructors are attracted to it because it is lightweight, durable, and sturdy.

Check out in Table 16-3 the breakdown of total aluminum consumption by sector.

Table 16-3	Aluminum Consumption by Sector, 2005 Figures
Industry	*Aluminum Consumption (Percentage of Total)*
Transportation	26%
Packaging	22%
Construction	22%
Electrical	8%
Machinery	8%
Consumer Goods	7%
Miscellaneous Uses	7%

Source: London Metal Exchange (LME)

If you're interested in finding out more about the aluminum industry, I recommend checking out the following organizations:

✔ **International Aluminium Institute:** www.world-aluminium.org

✔ **The Aluminum Association:** www.aluminum.org

✔ **aluNET International:** www.alunet.net

Aluminum futures

You can invest in aluminum through the futures markets. Currently, two major contracts for aluminum are available. The first one is through the London Metal Exchange (LME), while the second one is traded in the COMEX division of the New York Mercantile Exchange (NYMEX).

✔ **LME Aluminum:** The London Metal Exchange's (LME) aluminum contract is the most liquid in the world. The LME aluminum contract represents a size of 25,000 tons and its price is quoted in US Dollars.

✔ **COMEX Aluminum:** The aluminum contract traded on the COMEX division of the NYMEX trades in units of 44,000 pounds, with a 99.7 percent purity. The contract is tradable during the current calendar month as well as for the next 25 consecutive months. It trades under the symbol AL and is also available for trade electronically.

Because the NYMEX is located in the United States, it is regulated by the Commodity Futures Trading Commission (CFTC). However, because the LME is located in the United Kingdom, it falls under the jurisdiction of the Financial Services Authority (FSA), the British regulator. (For more on commodity exchanges and regulatory bodies, please turn to Chapter 8.) This information is crucial because if you start investing in futures, and something goes wrong, you need to know who to turn to. These regulatory bodies are well equipped to handle customer complaints and questions.

To give you an idea of the performance of aluminum in recent years, Figure 16-1 shows you the chart of COMEX aluminum. As you can see, the underlying demand from rapidly industrializing nations such as China and India has resulted in upward price pressures on the metal.

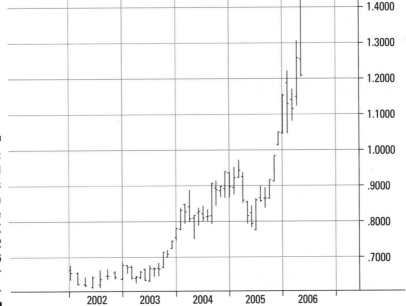

Figure 16-1: Historical price levels of aluminum on the COMEX from 2002 to 2006 (Dollars per Pound).

Aluminum companies

Another way I recommend investing in aluminum is by investing in companies that produce and manufacture aluminum products. Here are a few companies that make the cut:

- **Alcoa (NYSE: AA):** Alcoa is the world leader in aluminum production. It is involved in all aspects of the aluminum industry and produces primary aluminum, fabricated aluminum, as well as alumina. The company has operations in over 40 countries and services a large number of industries, from aerospace to construction. If you're looking to get the broadest exposure to the aluminum market, then you can't go wrong with Alcoa.

- **Alcan (NYSE: AL):** Alcan, which is headquartered in Canada, is a leading global manufacturer of aluminum products. It has operations that cover the spectrum of aluminum processing, from mining and refining to smelting and recycling. Like Alcoa, Alcan provides you with wide exposure to aluminum.

- **Aluminum Corporation of China (NYSE: ACH):** Like its name implies, ACH is primarily engaged in the production of aluminum in the Chinese market. I recommend this company, which trades on the New York Stock Exchange (NYSE), because it provides you with a foothold in the aluminum Chinese market, which has the potential to be the biggest such market in the future. Besides this competitive advantage, ACH is a well-run company with profit margins that, during the writing of this book, were in excess of 20 percent.

A Visit to Dr. Copper

Copper, the third-most widely used metal in the world, has applications in many sectors, including construction, electricity conduction, and engineering large-scale industrial projects. Copper is sought after because of its high electrical conductivity, resistance to corrosion, and malleability. Copper played a huge role during the Industrial Revolution and in connecting and wiring the modern world. Because of the current trends of industrialization and urbanization across the globe (see Chapter 2), demand for copper has been — and will remain — very strong, making it a good investment.

Quick copper facts

Copper is used for a wide variety of purposes, from building and construction to electrical wiring and engineering. To get a better idea of its wide usage, check out the breakdown of copper use by sector in Table 16-4.

Table 16-4	Copper Consumption by Sector, 2005 Figures
Sector	*Copper Consumption (Percentage of Total)*
Building/Construction	48%
Electrical	17%
Engineering	24%
Transportation	7%
Miscellaneous Uses	4%

Source: Copper Development Association (CDA)

You probably come across items made from copper on a daily basis but may have never given too much thought about its ubiquity. Here are everyday items that are made from copper:

✔ Electrical wiring

✔ Construction tubes, pipes and fittings

✔ High-speed internet cables

✔ Industrial sleeve bearings

✔ Doorknobs

✔ Plumbing tubes

✔ Artistic (bronze statues such as the Statue of Liberty)

✔ Coinage (US coins like the quarter and dime are over 90 percent copper)

✔ Musical instruments (brass instruments such as the trumpet and the tuba)

Copper is often alloyed with other metals, usually with nickel and zinc (both covered in Chapter 17). When copper and nickel are alloyed, the resulting metal is *bronze;* when copper is alloyed with zinc it results in *brass.* It's kind of ironic but the US penny, which is the only US coin that's a reddish/brown color (the color of copper), is the only coin that only uses 2.5 percent copper — 97.5 percent of the penny is made from zinc. The other coins in US currency — which are all silvery/white colors — contain more than 90 percent copper.

If you're interested in finding out more about copper usage, I recommend you consult the *Copper Development Association.* Their Web site is www.copper.org.

Copper futures contracts

Like most of the other important industrial metals, there is a futures market available for copper trading. Most of this market is used by large industrial producers and consumers of the metal, although you can also use it for investment purposes. You have two copper contracts to choose from:

- ✔ **LME Copper (LME: CAD):** The copper contract on the London Metal Exchange (LME) accounts for over 90 percent of total copper futures activity. It represents a lot size of 25 tons. *Note:* Because the LME is located in the United Kingdom, it is regulated by the British Financial Services Authority (FSA).

- ✔ **COMEX Copper (COMEX: HG):** This copper contract trades in the COMEX division of the New York Mercantile Exchange (NYMEX). COMEX copper, which trades during the current month and subsequent 23 calendar months, is traded both electronically and through the open outcry system. It represents 25,000 pounds of copper and trades under the symbol HG.

Demand for copper from China, India, and other advanced developing countries is increasing, and that has put upward pressure on the price of copper. Check out in Figure 16-2 the price of copper futures on the COMEX division of the NYMEX.

Figure 16-2: Historical price levels of Copper on the COMEX from 2002 to 2006 (Dollars per Pound).

Copper companies

Another investment vehicle I recommend is getting involved in companies that specialize in mining and processing copper ore. The companies I list here are leaders in their industry and are involved in all aspects of the copper supply chain. The only drawback of investing in companies is that you don't get direct exposure to the price fluctuations of the metals. Still, they're a good option if you don't want to venture into the futures markets.

- **Phelps Dodge Corporation (NYSE: PD):** Founded in 1834, Phelps Dodge is one of the oldest mining companies in the United States. It is also one of the largest manufacturers and producers of copper and copper products in the world. The company has a global presence in copper mining, with operations in the United States, South Africa, the Philippines, and Peru, among others. Because of its size and experience in the industry, Phelps Dodge is in a good position to capitalize from the increased demand for copper.

- **Freeport-McMoRan Inc. (NYSE: FCX):** One of the reasons why I like Freeport-McMoRan is that it's one of the lowest cost producers of copper in the world. It has copper mining and smelting operations across the globe and has a significant presence in Indonesia and Papua New Guinea. The company specializes in the production of highly concentrated copper ore, which it then sells on the open market. FCX also has some operations in gold and silver.

I cover copper companies in-depth in Chapter 18. I also examine integrated and diversified mining companies to help you design an investment strategy that effectively allows you to "buy the market."

Chapter 17

Weighing Investments in Heavy and Not-So-Heavy Metals

*I*n this chapter, I go over a diverse group of metals: palladium, a precious metal, and two industrial metals, zinc and nickel. These metals are important components of the metals complex in their own right: palladium because of its precious metal status and as a part of the *Platinum Group Metals* (PGM), and nickel and zinc for their wide usage in industry. These metals may not get much attention from the financial press, but you should still consider including them in your portfolio because they're essential building blocks of the global economy. I outline the market characteristics of each of these metals, so that you can determine whether they're right for you.

Palladium: Metal for the New Millennium

Palladium, which belongs to the Platinum Group Metals (PGM), is a popular alternative to platinum in the automotive industry and the jewelry industry. Its largest use is in the creation of pollution-reducing catalytic converters. Palladium's malleability and corrosion resistance make it the perfect metal for such usage. In addition, because palladium is less expensive on a troy ounce basis than platinum ($315/oz. vs. $1235/oz., 2006 figures), it is increasingly becoming the metal of choice for the manufacture of these devices.

Besides its usage in catalytic converters and jewelry, palladium is also used in dentistry and electronics. I list in Table 17-1 the main consumers of palladium.

Table 17-1	Palladium Consumption by Industry, 2005 Figures	
Sector	**Consumption (Million Ounces)**	**Percentage Of Total**
Auto Industry (Catalytic Converters)	3.37	48%
Jewelry	1.47	21%
Electronics	0.98	14%
Dentistry	0.91	13%
Other	0.28	4%

Source: U.S. Geological Survey

Palladium has benefited from more stringent fuel emission standards established by the *Environmental Protection Agency* (EPA) and other international environmental organizations. When pollution-reducing regulation was established in the 1970s, demand for palladium skyrocketed as a direct result of these changes. All things equal, if emissions standards are further improved and require a new generation of catalytic converters, demand for palladium will increase. Another reason to be bullish on palladium is that the number of automobiles, trucks, and other vehicles equipped with platinum- and palladium-made catalytic converters is increasing, particularly in China. So if you invest in palladium, make sure you keep an eye out on automobile manufacturing patterns.

The palladium market is essentially dominated by two countries: Russia and South Africa. These two countries account for over 85 percent of total palladium production, as you can see in Table 17-2.

Table 17-2	Top Palladium Producing Countries, 2005 Figures	
Country	**Production (Million Ounces)**	**Percentage Of Total**
Russia	4.61	55%
South Africa	2.6	31%

Country	Production (Million Ounces)	Percentage Of Total
North America	0.92	11%
Other	0.25	3%

Source: U.S. Geological Survey

Because palladium production is dominated by these two countries, however, any supply disruption from either country has a significant impact on palladium prices. This was just the case in the beginning of the year 2000, when the Russian government announced that shipments of palladium and other platinum group metals would be halted for the year. As you can see in Figure 17-1, the price of palladium in the year 2000 almost doubled, partly in response to Russian supply-side disruptions.

The Russian government eventually announced a resumption of palladium mining activity and prices dropped back to normal levels in 2001. As a result of this price shock, mining companies have tried to diversify their activities beyond Russia and South Africa. However, there's just no way around the fact that most of the world's reserves of palladium ore are located in these two countries. As a matter of fact, perhaps no two countries dominate a commodity as much as Russia and South Africa dominate palladium.

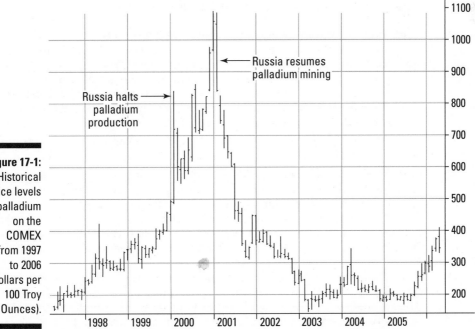

Figure 17-1: Historical price levels of palladium on the COMEX from 1997 to 2006 (Dollars per 100 Troy Ounces).

Make sure to keep in mind the unique market structure as you consider investing in this precious metal.

One of the best — albeit indirect — methods of getting exposure to the palladium markets is by investing in companies that mine the metal. A number of companies specialize in this activity, but here are a couple I recommend taking a look at:

- ✔ **Stillwater Mining Company (NYSE: SWC):** Stillwater Mining, based in Montana, is the largest producer of palladium outside South Africa and Russia. Although it is involved in platinum and other PGM, its primary mining output is palladium. It produces approximately 500,000 Ounces of palladium a year, primarily through North American mines.

- ✔ **North American Palladium (AMEX: PAL):** North American Palladium, headquartered in Toronto, has a significant presence in the Canadian palladium ore mining business. It is the largest producer of palladium in Canada, with production in 2005 totaling almost 200,000 Ounces. North American palladium is your entry into the lucrative Canadian palladium mining sector.

Although these are the two largest companies that trade publicly on American exchanges, several international companies have significantly larger palladium mining activities. Just make sure you're aware of the many regulatory differences between American and overseas markets before investing in companies that trade in overseas stock markets.

Here are a couple of international palladium companies to consider:

- ✔ **Anglo Platinum Group (South Africa):** While Anglo Platinum Group invests in platinum group metals, as the name suggests, it is also one of the largest producers of palladium in the world. The company produced over 2.5 Million Ounces of palladium in 2005 and is estimated to have reserves of over 200 Million Ounces (this includes other platinum group metals). With its operations located primarily in South Africa, Anglo Platinum Group is your gateway to South African palladium. Its shares are traded in the Johannesburg Stock Exchange (JSE), as well as the London Stock Exchange (LSE).

- ✔ **Norilsk Nickel (Russia):** Norilsk Nickel may not be a household name, but it is the largest producer of palladium in the world. It dominates the Russian palladium industry, which is the largest in the world (see Table 17-2). While the company has large palladium mining activities, it's also a major player in copper and nickel ore mining. The company's shares are available through the Moscow Inter-bank Currency Exchange (MICEX).

For folks who are comfortable in the futures markets, the New York Mercantile Exchange (NYMEX) offers a futures contract that tracks palladium. This contract represents 100 Troy Ounces of palladium and trades both electronically and during the open outcry session. It trades under the symbol PA.

Zinc and Grow Rich

Zinc is the fourth-most widely used metal, right behind iron/steel, aluminum, and copper (which I cover in Chapter 16). Zinc, which has unique abilities to resist corrosion and oxidation, is used for metal *galvanization,* the process of applying a metal coating to another metal to prevent rust and corrosion. As you can see from Table 17-3, galvanizing metals (particularly steel) is by far the largest application of zinc.

Table 17-3	Zinc Consumption by Sector
Sector	*Percentage of market consumption*
Galvanization	47%
Brass and bronze coatings	19%
Zinc alloying	15%
Other	14%

Source: London Metal Exchange

The best way to invest in zinc is by going through the futures markets. The London Metal Exchange (LME) offers a futures contract for zinc, which has been trading since the early 1900s and is the industry benchmark for zinc pricing. The contract trades in lots of 25 Tons and is available for trading during the current month and the subsequent 27 months. Figure 17-2 charts zinc's recent performance.

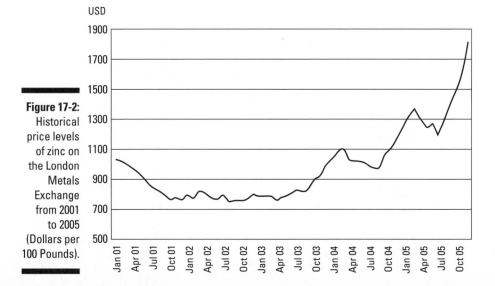

Figure 17-2:
Historical price levels of zinc on the London Metals Exchange from 2001 to 2005 (Dollars per 100 Pounds).

You Won't Get Nickel and Dimed by Investing in Nickel

Nickel is a *ferrous metal,* which means it belongs to the iron group of metals. It is an important industrial metal that is used as an alloy with metals such as iron and copper, and it is sought-after because of its ductility, malleability, and resistance to corrosion.

One of nickel's primary applications is in the creation of stainless steel. When steel is alloyed with nickel, its resistance to corrosion increases dramatically. Because stainless steel is a necessity of modern life, and a large portion of nickel goes toward the creation of this important metal alloy, you can rest assured that demand for nickel will remain strong. As you can see from Table 17-4, although there are a number of important uses for nickel, the creation of stainless steel remains its primary application.

Table 17-4	Nickel Consumption by Sector
Sector	*Percentage of market consumption*
Stainless Steel	65%
Non-ferrous alloys	12%
Ferrous alloys	10%
Electroplating	8%
Other	5%

Source: London Metal Exchange

Australia has the largest reserves of nickel, and its proximity to the rapidly industrializing Asian center — China and India — is a strategic advantage. Another major player in the nickel markets is Russia; the Russian company Norilsk Nickel (covered in the section on palladium) is the largest producer of nickel in the world. Nickel mining is a labor-intensive industry, but those countries that have large reserves of this special metal are poised to do very well. Check out the countries with the largest reserves of nickel in Table 17-5.

Table 17-5	Largest Nickel Reserves, 2004 Figures	
Country	*Reserves (Thousand Tons)*	*Percentage of Total*
Australia	48,611	25.1%
Russia	24,625	12.7%

Country	Reserves (Thousand Tons)	Percentage of Total
Indonesia	22,491	11.6%
New Caledonia	13,863	7.1%
Canada	13,074	6.7%
Cuba	11,640	6.0%
Philippines	9860	5.1%
Papua New Guinea	8903	4.6%
Brazil	6960	3.6%
China	550	2.8%

Source: U.S. Geological Survey

The London Metal Exchange (LME) offers a futures contract for nickel. The nickel futures contract on the LME provides you with the most direct access to the nickel market. It trades in lots of 6 Tons, and its tick size is $5.00 per ton. As with zinc, it trades during the first month, in addition to 27 subsequent months.

Check out the historical performance of nickel on the LME in Figure 17-3.

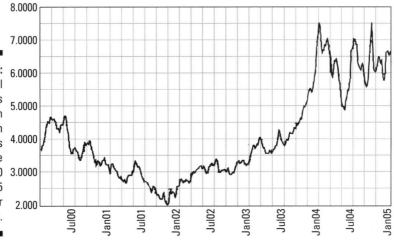

Figure 17-3: Historical price levels of nickel on the London Metals Exchange from 2000 to 2005 (Dollars per Pound).

The term *nickel,* used to denote the five-cent coin, is misleading because the coin is actually primarily composed of copper (75 percent). Nickel, the metal, only makes up 25 percent of nickel, the coin.

The London Metal Exchange

The *London Metal Exchange* (LME), where the nickel and zinc contracts are traded, is one of the oldest futures exchanges in the world. It traces its origins back to the late 19th century, during Britain's Industrial Revolution. The Industrial Revolution was in part fueled by large consumption of metals, and metals producers and consumers needed a place to establish benchmark prices and transact with each other. That's where the LME came to play an important role. Today, the LME is one of the only exchanges dedicated to trading non-ferrous metals. Besides nickel and zinc, the exchange offers futures contracts for aluminum, copper, lead, and tin. The LME still has open outcry trading sessions, although it has introduced electronic trading as well.

Chapter 18

Mine Your Own Business: Unearthing the Top Mining Companies

*T*rading metals outright — through the futures markets — can be tricky for the uninitiated trader. You have to keep track of a number of moving pieces, such as contract expiration dates, margin calls, trading months, and other variables. In addition, metals on the futures markets can be subject to extreme price volatility, and you can set yourself up for disastrous losses. So it's understandable if you'd rather not trade metals futures contracts. But this doesn't mean that you should ignore the whole metals sub-asset class altogether because you could be missing out on some tasty returns.

One possible avenue for opening up your portfolio to metals is investing in companies that specialize in mining metals and minerals. A number of such companies exist, and their performance has been stellar recently. For example, Rio Tinto (NYSE: RTP), a mining conglomerate — which I discuss in this chapter — saw its stock price surge from $60 in 2002 to over $200 in 2006. Although not all mining companies have had similar performances, ignoring such a large group of the market is not advisable.

In this chapter, I look at the top mining companies — both the conglomerates and the specialized ones — to help you identify the best ones to include in your portfolio.

Diversified Mining Companies

Like the large integrated energy companies — ExxonMobil and BP, covered in Chapter 11 — diversified mining companies are involved in *all* aspects of the metals production process. These companies, which often employ tens of thousands of people, have operations in all four corners of the globe. They are involved in the excavation of metals — both *precious* and *base* metals, *ferrous* and *non-ferrous* — as well as the transformation of these metals into finished products and subsequent distribution of the end products to consumers.

Investing in one of these companies gives you exposure not only to a wide variety of metals, but also to the whole mining supply chain. I've selected the "best of breeds" and evaluate their investment suitability in the following sections.

BHP Billiton

BHP Billiton (formed as a result of the merger between *Broken Hill Proprietary* — an Australian company — and *Billiton* — an Anglo-Dutch company — in 2001) is one of the largest mining companies in the world. BHP Billiton, headquartered in Melbourne, Australia, has mining operations in over 25 countries including Australia, Canada, the United States, South Africa, and Papua New Guinea. The company processes a large number of metals, including aluminum, copper, silver, and iron; it also has small oil and natural gas operations in Algeria and Pakistan. The company is listed on the New York Stock Exchange (NYSE) under the symbol BHP.

One of the reasons I like BHP Billiton is that it offers economies of scale. This is a large company, by any standard. Here's a snapshot of the company's financial performance. (All figures are for 2006.)

- **Market Capitalization:** $125 Billion
- **Revenues:** $32.30 Billion
- **Net Income:** $7.80 Billion
- **Free Cash Flow:** $8.27 Billion
- **Profit Margins:** 24.22%

I'm providing you here only a snapshot of recent financial performance. Before you make an investment in Billiton, or any other company, you want to look at a number of metrics to determine its financial health. You should go through the balance sheet, income statement, and statement of cash flows — among other key financial statements — with a fine-toothed comb. Once you determine that the company has a clean financial bill of health and is poised for growth, only then should you proceed with your investment. Make sure to read Chapter 6 for more on the due diligence process.

The company has benefited handsomely from the increasing prices of commodities such as copper and aluminum. As a result, BHP Billiton's profit increased by a staggering 90 percent between 2004 and 2005. This increase is reflected in its stock price, illustrated in Figure 18-1.

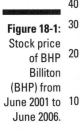

Figure 18-1:
Stock price of BHP Billiton (BHP) from June 2001 to June 2006.

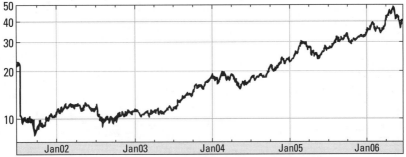

Remember that past results do not guarantee future performance. Commodity prices are cyclical in nature and prices for metals such as copper, silver, and aluminum cannot go up in a straight line forever. Make sure you take into account the cyclicality factor as you move forward with your commodity investments.

Rio Tinto

Rio Tinto is a mining company rich in both minerals and history. The company was founded in 1873 by the Rothschild banking family to mine ore deposits in Spain. Today, Rio Tinto boasts operations in Africa, Australia, Europe, the Pacific Rim, North America, Australia, and South America. It is a true mining conglomerate that is involved in all facets of the mining supply chain, from extraction to transformation and distribution.

The company is involved in the production of a number of commodities, including iron ore, copper, aluminum, and titanium. In addition, Rio Tinto has interests in diamonds, manufacturing almost 30 percent of global natural diamonds, processed primarily through its mining activities in Australia.

By investing in Rio Tinto, you not only get a company that has extensive operations across the mining complex but one that is in a solid financial position. Check out some numbers the company posted in 2006:

- **Market Capitalization:** $68 Billion
- **Revenues:** $19 Billion
- **Net Income:** $5.22 Billion

✔ **Free Cash Flow:** $3.20 Billion

✔ **Profit Margins:** 27.40%

These strong numbers, which reflect increased demand for the commodities the company is involved in, have had a positive mid- to long-term impact on the company's stock, as you can see in Figure 18-2. Rio Tinto trades on the New York Stock Exchange (NYSE) under the ticker symbol RTP.

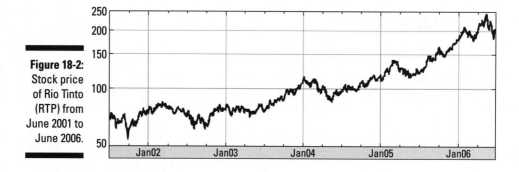

Figure 18-2:
Stock price of Rio Tinto (RTP) from June 2001 to June 2006.

Anglo-American

Anglo-American PLC began mining gold in South Africa in 1917. It was a venture by British and American entrepreneurs (hence the name), who saw an opportunity in developing South African mines. Ever since, it has played an important role in the development of South Africa's gold mining industry. Today, Anglo-American has operations in all four corners of the globe and operates in over 20 countries. It is involved in the production and distribution of a wide array of metals, minerals, and natural resources including gold, silver, and platinum but also diamonds and paper packaging (it actually owns 45 percent of DeBeers, the diamond company).

I recommend Anglo-American as a long-term investment because it has been in the business for almost a century, it's involved in almost all aspects of the mining industry, and the scale of its operations is global.

The company is listed in the London Stock Exchange under the ticker symbol AAL. In addition, it has American Depository Receipts listed in the NASDAQ National Market that trade under the symbol AAUK.

When a foreign company wants to access the American capital markets, it has the option of issuing its shares as *American Depository Receipts* (ADRs). ADRs are issued by a domestic bank (such as the Bank of New York, which is actually the largest issuer of ADRs) to the American investing public, while the bank holds shares of the foreign company overseas. The advantage of the ADR is that it allows American investors to invest in foreign companies without going through foreign exchanges. The ADRs trade in such a way that they reflect the daily price movements of the underlying stock as it is traded in a stock exchange overseas. For more information, you can check out the Bank of New York's Web site on ADRs at www.adrbny.com.

Making money during the mining merger mania

Profiting from the merger activity in the mining industry can be a good investment strategy. Since the year 2000, a number of large companies have entered into merger agreements (the marriage of the Australian BHP and the British Billiton, which resulted in BHP Billiton, is a good example), and this trend is likely to continue as mining companies seek to add new capacity by merging their activities and/or acquiring smaller rivals. In 2004, for instance, there were a total of 49 deals in the mining industry valued at $5.6 Billion; in 2005 the number of deals increased to 85 with a total value of $7.4 Billion.

Due to the sustained levels of high commodity prices, mining companies have large cash reserves and are looking to spend them to beef up their operations by acquiring other companies. Mergers and acquisitions present long-term value opportunities to these companies and their shareholders and are likely to continue in the years to come. During the writing of this book for example, Phelps Dodge (one of the largest copper mining companies) launched a simultaneous double bid to acquire Inco and Falconbridge, both independent Canadian mining companies, in a synchronized transaction valued at over $40 Billion.

The caveat of profiting from merger announcements, of course, is identifying the "hunter" and the "hunted," the acquirer and the target. This is not easy because, theoretically, there are an infinite number of merger and acquisition combinations in any given sector. The best way to do so is to regularly monitor the industry for news, special announcements, or unusual trading activity. Specifically, keep your eye out for any announcements by companies in Forms 8K (filings with the SEC that announce special situations); read news stories about the companies in the industry (I recommend reading the *Wall Street Journal's* "Heard On The Street" column); and remain alert to any sudden and unusual movements in the companies' stock activity, such as an unusual spike in volume. (Check out Chapter 10 for more on volume and other technical metrics.)

Identifying possible merger announcements is not an exact science, but it can yield some phenomenal returns. So much so that a lot of folks try to get insider information regarding merger deals, which is illegal and has led to some of the biggest financial scandals. If you trade on information that is not public, you could end up going to jail. So make sure you don't do it! Also remember that, as a general rule, you want to buy the "hunted" before any merger announcements because the stock price of a target company tends to increase with any merger announcement while that of the acquiring company decreases. The logic here is that the acquiring company is paying a premium for its acquisition and will have to bear the costs of incorporating this new entity within its corporate and operational structure.

Specialized Mining Companies

The benefit of investing in diversified mining companies, like those profiled in the previous section, is that you get to "buy the market" in one fell swoop. However, what if you spot a rally in gold, copper, or another individual metal and want to profit from this specific trend? In this case, the most direct exposure through the equity markets is by investing in companies that specialize in specific metals. I identify and evaluate some of these companies in this section.

Newmont Mining — Gold

Newmont is headquartered in Colorado but operates gold mines all over the world. It is the largest producer of gold in South America, one of the most important gold regions, and has wholly owned subsidiaries or joint ventures in Australia, Canada, and Uzbekistan.

I recommend Newmont because it is a premier player in the competitive gold mining industry. It has some competitive advantages, including its control of 50,000 square miles of land containing over 90 Million Equity Ounces of gold. (*Equity ounces* is the amount of gold measured in troy ounces multiplied by the current market price of gold as measured in US Dollars.) In addition, it has a strong balance sheet and is in strong financial condition. Check out some of Newmont's numbers (2006 Figures):

- **Market Capitalization:** $23.8 Billion
- **Revenues:** $4.6 Billion
- **Net Income:** $502 Million
- **Free Cash Flow:** $47.8 Million
- **Profit Margins:** 9.70%

If you're looking for a well-managed company with extensive experience and operations in the gold mining industry, then you can't go wrong with Newmont. (Make sure to read Chapter 15 for in-depth coverage of the gold industry.)

Silver Wheaton — Silver

Silver Wheaton focuses on one thing and one thing only: silver. While some mining companies may have small operations in secondary metals, Silver Wheaton generates *100 percent* of its revenues from silver mining. Specifically, the company operates mines primarily in Mexico and Sweden. The company's modus operandi is to purchase silver directly from the mines and sell it on the open market for a profit. As a result, the company has very little — if any — operating overhead. This results in strong revenues and cash flows, as you can see:

- ✔ **Market Capitalization:** $1.95 Billion
- ✔ **Revenues:** $80.53 Million
- ✔ **Net Income:** $33.89 Million
- ✔ **Operating Cash Flow:** $38.7 Million
- ✔ **Profit Margins:** 42.08%

Silver Wheaton may not generate the same kinds of revenues as Anglo-American or other large mining conglomerates, but it's a well-run company with high profit margins and stable revenues.

Silver Wheaton's numbers reflect a strong operating background. It is actually the second producer of silver, in terms of annual output measured in troy ounces. It produced over 15 Million Troy Ounces in 2005.

While I was writing this book, UBS (the Swiss investment bank) initiated research coverage of Silver Wheaton. It issued a "buy" rating for the stock, which is a good sign for the company.

For more information on the silver industry, including the top producers, the largest consuming segments, and an analysis of additional investment methodologies, please turn to Chapter 15.

Phelps Dodge — Copper

Phelps Dodge has been in the copper business for over 150 years. It started as a mining concern and played a key role in the industrialization of the United States. Copper was in high demand by the growing nation, and Phelps Dodge was there to supply it. Today, Phelps Dodge is still the market leader when it comes to copper production, and it also has significant operations in the production of molybdenum and molybdenum-based chemicals.

Molybdenum (pronounced mah-*lib*-den-um) is known as a transition metal because it's principally used as an alloy with a number of metals. It has wide applications in industry, used, for instance, in the construction of oil pipelines, aircraft engines, and missiles.

Phelps Dodge has two distinct entities that operate independently of each other: Phelps Dodge Mining and Phelps Dodge Industries. In addition, during the writing of this book, the company entered into a deal to acquire two mining companies: Inco and Falconbridge, both of Canada. This deal, which is still ongoing as of the writing, is sure to expand what is an already large company, as you can see from the company's 2006 figures:

- ✔ **Market Capitalization:** $15.86 Billion
- ✔ **Revenues:** $8.63 Billion
- ✔ **Net Income:** $1.55 Billion
- ✔ **Operating Cash Flow:** $800.2 Million
- ✔ **Profit Margins:** 17.43%

Because of the increasing price of copper, the company's primary commodity, the Phelps Dodge stock has performed well in recent years, as you can see in Figure 18-3.

Figure 18-3:
Stock price
of Phelps
Dodge (PD)
on the NYSE
from June
2001 to
June 2006.

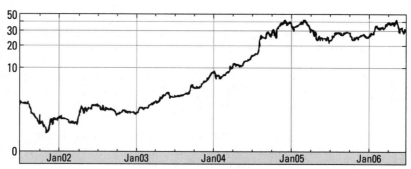

Phelps Dodge has an active hedging program, where it enters into agreements with other market participants through the futures markets in order to hedge against price risk. However, not all hedgers are created equal and Phelps Dodge has taken some hits in the past as a result of its hedging activities. During the second quarter of 2006, for instance, the company's net income fell to $471.1 Million from $682.3 Million the previous year-over-year quarter. This was a direct result of losses it incurred in hedging-related activity. So even though the price of copper was robust during this period, and the company would have benefited from these strong prices, its external activities were negatively affected. Always make sure you know what's going on with a company before investing in it.

You can find more information about the copper market and industry in Chapter 16.

Alcoa — Aluminum

Alcoa is a household name and for good reason: It is the largest producer of aluminum, which is the most ubiquitous metal in the modern world. Cars, soda cans, and fighter jets are all partly made from aluminum, and Alcoa is the primary supplier of this metal in the market today. Alcoa, whose acronym stands for the Aluminum Company of America, is involved in all phases of the aluminum supply chain. It provides aluminum-based products to a wide range of customers, including the aerospace and automotive industries, individual and commercial enterprises, the manufacturing sector, and the military.

Another reason I like Alcoa is that it is making some aggressive moves overseas and signing strategic, long-term pacts with some of the top aluminum producers. It recently entered into a partnership with the Aluminum Corporation of China (NYSE: ACH), China's largest aluminum producer, and is positioning itself to capitalize on the Chinese market, possibly the largest aluminum market in the future.

The following numbers are proof of Alcoa's influence in the market:

- ✔ **Market Capitalization:** $25.89 Billion
- ✔ **Revenues:** $28.45 Billion
- ✔ **Net Income:** $1.83 Billion
- ✔ **Free Cash Flow:** $289.38 Million
- ✔ **Profit Margins:** 6.56%

As you can see in Figure 18-4, the stock's performance has been choppy in recent years, so you want to make sure you research the company as much as possible before you take the plunge.

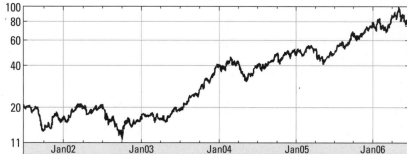

Figure 18-4: Stock price of Alcoa (AA) from June 2001 to June 2006.

Make sure to read Chapter 16 for a close examination of the aluminum market.

Arcelor-Mittal — Steel

While writing this book, I had the pleasure of watching one of the most heated takeover battles in recent memory involving two steel behemoths:

Mittal Steel and Arcelor. Mittal Steel, under the management of Indian-born steel magnate Lakshmi Mittal, launched an unsolicited bid to acquire Arcelor, the Luxembourg-based high-end steel manufacturer, in January 2006. After a long, protracted five-month takeover battle, which involved *poison pill* and *white knight* takeover defense strategies, the boards of both companies agreed to a merger of equals.

In Mergers & Acquisitions (M&A), companies use a number of strategies to fend off hostile takeovers. Two of the most popular defense strategies include pursuing a merger or acquisition with a "friendly" company, known as a *white knight*. The *poison pill strategy* involves making the company unattractive to the acquirer, such as increasing levels of debt or increasing the number of shares outstanding to dilute their value.

The new company combines the Number 1 and Number 2 steel producers in the world and will control over 10 percent of global steel output. Arcelor-Mittal is going to be a truly global steel manufacturer with operations in all four corners of the globe and across all stages of the steel-making process. If the performance of the new company is anything like the recent performance of Mittal stock, shown in Figure 18-5, then you would be missing out on some healthy returns.

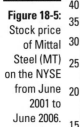

Figure 18-5:
Stock price of Mittal Steel (MT) on the NYSE from June 2001 to June 2006.

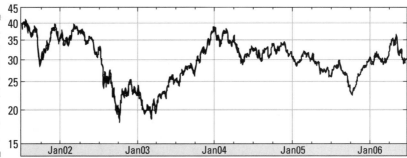

Turn to Chapter 16 for an in-depth examination of the global steel industry.

Part V
Going Down to the Farm: Trading Agricultural Products

The 5th Wave   By Rich Tennant

"Eat your cereal. Your father's heavily invested in grain."

In this part . . .

Food is the most essential resource in human life. Investing in this sector can also help improve your bottom line. In this part, I introduce the major sectors in this sub-asset class and show you how to profit from grains such as corn and wheat; tropical commodities like coffee and orange juice; and livestock that includes live cattle, feeder cattle, and frozen pork bellies. Get the scoop on this crucial sector.

Chapter 19

Breakfast of Champions: Profiting from Coffee, Cocoa, Sugar, and Orange Juice

The commodities I present in this chapter — coffee, cocoa, sugar, and frozen concentrated orange juice — are known as *soft commodities*. Soft commodities are those commodities that are usually grown, as opposed to those that are mined, such as metals, or those that are raised, such as livestock. The *softs,* as they are sometimes known, represent a significant portion of the commodities markets. They are indispensable and cyclical, just like energy and metals, but they are also unique because they're edible and seasonal. *Seasonality* is actually a major distinguishing characteristic of soft commodities because they can only be grown during specific times of the year and in specific geographical locations — usually in tropical areas. (This is why these commodities are also known as *tropical commodities.*) In this chapter, I show you that there's nothing soft about these soft commodities.

Give Your Portfolio a Buzz by Investing in Coffee

Coffee, which originated in Arabia sometime in the 15th century, is today the second-most widely traded commodity in terms of physical volume — behind only crude oil. Coffee is an important global commodity because folks just love a good cup of coffee. In this section, I show you how to stay grounded while investing in this market.

Coffee: It's time for your big break

Like a number of other commodities, coffee production is dominated by a handful of countries. Brazil, Colombia, and Vietnam are the largest producing countries, as you can see in Table 19-1.

Table 19-1	Top Coffee Producers, 2005 Figures
Country	*Production (Thousands of bags)*
Brazil	32,944
Colombia	11,550
Vietnam	11,000
Indonesia	6750
India	4630
Ethiopia	4500
Mexico	4200
Guatemala	3675
Honduras	2990
Uganda	2750

Source: International Coffee Organization

Large scale coffee production is measured in *bags*. One bag of coffee weighs 60 Kilograms or approximately 132 Pounds.

If you want to investigate the ins and outs of the coffee markets further, I recommend consulting the following resources:

- **International Coffee Organization:** www.ico.org
- **National Coffee Association of the USA:** www.ncausa.org

If you're interested in researching the coffee markets more thoroughly, I recommend Mark Pendergrast's excellent book *Uncommon Grounds: The History of Coffee and How It Transformed Our World* (Basic Books). This book will help you understand the mechanics of the global coffee trade; you may then capitalize on this information by applying it towards your trading strategy.

Brewing the right investment strategy

Just like choosing the right flavor when buying your cup of coffee, knowing the different types of coffees available for investment is important. The world's coffee production is pretty much made up of two types of beans:

- **Arabica:** Arabica coffee is the most widely grown coffee plant in the world, accounting for over 60 percent of global coffee production. Arabica is grown in countries as diverse as Brazil and Indonesia. It is the premium coffee bean, adding a richer taste to any brew, and, as a result, is the most expensive coffee bean in the world. Because of its high quality, it serves as the benchmark for coffee prices all over the world.

- **Robusta:** Robusta accounts for about 40 percent of total coffee production. Because it's easier to grow than Arabica coffee, it's also less expensive.

You have several ways to invest in coffee production. One way is by buying coffee in the futures markets, and the other is by investing in companies that specialize in running gourmet coffee shops.

The coffee futures contract: It could be your cup of tea

The coffee futures markets are used to determine the future price of coffee and, more importantly, to protect producers and purchasers of coffee from wild price swings (see Chapter 9 for more on futures contracts). In addition to the hedging opportunities, the coffee futures markets allow individual investors to profit from coffee price variations. The most liquid coffee futures contract is available on the New York Board of Trade (NYBOT).

The New York Board of Trade: The place for trading places and soft commodities

Besides being tropical commodities, the commodities I analyze in this chapter have another common characteristic: They all trade on the *New York Board of Trade* (NYBOT). The NYBOT is one of the oldest exchanges in the United States and is the premier location for the trade of agricultural commodities. The NYBOT also offers futures contracts that track cotton, ethanol, and wood pulp (*pulp* is used to make paper), as well as products that track several financial futures, such as the Euro (the currency), the New York Stock Exchange Composite Index, and the Reuters/Jefferies CRB Index. The NYBOT is also where the movie *Trading Places,* with Eddie Murphy and Dan Aykroyd, was shot. In the final scene of the movie, Murphy and Aykroyd corner the orange juice market and, in the process, wipe out Randolph and Mortimer Duke.

Launched in 1882, the NYBOT coffee futures contract is one of the oldest futures contract in the market today. Here are its contract specs:

- ✔ **Contract Ticker Symbol:** KC
- ✔ **Contract Size:** 37,500 Pounds
- ✔ **Underlying Commodity:** Pure Arabica Coffee
- ✔ **Price Fluctuation:** $0.0005/pound ($18.75 per contract)
- ✔ **Trading Months:** March, May, July, September, December

The price chart in Figure 19-1 gives you an idea of the performance of the coffee futures contract in recent years.

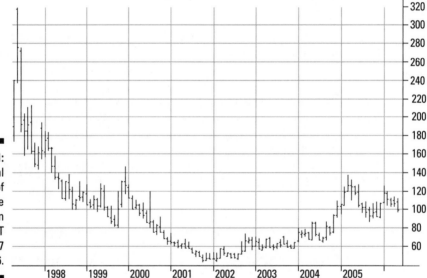

Figure 19-1:
Historical price of coffee futures on the NYBOT from 1997 to 2006.

Because of seasonality, cyclicality, and geopolitical factors, coffee can be a volatile commodity subject to extreme price swings. Make sure to research the coffee markets inside and out before investing.

Double tall iced white mocha valencia with sugar on top! Investing in gourmet coffee shops

In New York City, where I live, as in most other metropolitan areas, you can't walk a block without spotting two or three gourmet coffee shops, especially Starbucks. Coffee shops are nothing new — Arabian coffee shops sprang up in the Middle East as early as the 15th century. Today, coffee shops are still a place where you can enjoy a nice (and big) cup of coffee while socializing with friends.

But behind the relaxed, laid-back atmosphere is a complex money-making operation. Coffee is serious business and you can profit from the coffee craze that has gripped America (the largest consumer of coffee in the world) and is spreading throughout Europe and newly-developing countries like India and China by investing in the companies that are capitalizing on this trend. Find out where your $4.50 for a cup of coffee is going and profit from it.

While you're probably familiar with Starbucks, a number of other gourmet coffee shops and distributors provide you with a good investment opportunity. I list these purveyors of coffee here:

- ✔ **Starbucks Corp. (NASDAQ: SBUX):** Perhaps no other brand has come to represent an entire industry as Starbucks has coffee. (The only other brands that come to mind are Kleenex with tissues and Xerox with photocopiers.) Starbucks is a cultural phenomenon but, more importantly, it's also a financial Juggernaut. This is a $25 Billion company with over $7 Billion in revenue (2006 figures). Starbucks dominates the entire coffee supply chain, from purchasing and roasting to selling and marketing. It has over 10,000 stores worldwide, primarily in the United States and Europe but also in China, Singapore, and even one in Saudi Arabia.

- ✔ **Peet's Coffee and Tea, Inc. (NASDAQ: PEET):** Peet's Coffee only operates about 100 coffee shops, but their strength lies in distribution. The company sells a large selection of coffees, produced in countries as diverse as Guatemala and Kenya, to customers across the United States, including restaurants and grocery stores.

- ✔ **Green Mountain Coffee Roaster, Inc. (NASDAQ: GMCR):** Green Mountain Coffee, with headquarters in Vermont, operates in the distribution of specialized coffee products. It sells premium Arabica coffee to a number of entities, such as convenience stores, specialty retailers, and restaurants. It has a large presence in the East Coast and has a partnership with Paul Newman's *Newman's Own* company to provide organic coffee to customers. This is a good company if you want exposure to the high-end coffee distribution market in the Northeast.

Warming Up to Cocoa

Cocoa is a fermented seed from the cacao tree, which is usually grown in hot and rainy regions around the equator. The first cacao tree is said to have originated in South America, where cocoa beans were used for both consumption and monetary purposes. European traders came across the cacao tree and were so impressed with the tasty beverages made from cocoa beans that they brought some back to Europe, where cocoa beans were then turned into chocolate. From Europe, the cacao tree was introduced to Africa and, today, the cocoa trade is dominated by African countries, as you can see in Table 19-2.

Table 19-2	Top Cocoa Producers, 2005 Figures
Country	**Production (Thousands of Tons)**
Ivory Coast	1330
Ghana	736
Indonesia	610
Nigeria	366
Brazil	213
Cameroon	180
Ecuador	137
Colombia	55
Mexico	48
Papua New Guinea	42

Source: International Cocoa Organization

Cocoa production for import and export purposes is measured in metric tons. To put things in perspective, 3.3 Million Tons of cocoa were produced worldwide in 2005.

For a more nuanced understanding of the cocoa market and the companies that control it, check out these resources:

- ✔ **World Cocoa Foundation:** www.worldcocoafoundation.org
- ✔ **International Cocoa Organization:** www.icco.org
- ✔ **Cocoa Producer's Alliance:** www.copal-cpa.org

The New York Board of Trade (NYBOT) offers a futures contract for cocoa. Here is some useful information regarding this cocoa futures contract, which is the most liquid in the market:

- ✔ **Contract Ticker Symbol:** CC
- ✔ **Contract Size:** 10 Metric Tons
- ✔ **Underlying Commodity:** Generic Cocoa Beans
- ✔ **Price Fluctuation:** $1.0/ton ($10.00 per contract)
- ✔ **Trading Months:** March, May, July, September, December

Like coffee, the cocoa market is subject to seasonal and cyclical factors that have a large impact on price movements. Check out the price of the NYBOT cocoa futures contract in recent years in Figure 19-2. As you can see, it can be pretty volatile.

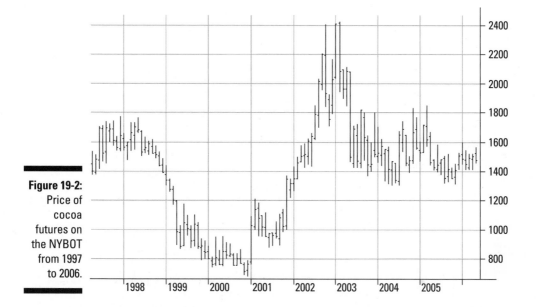

Figure 19-2:
Price of cocoa futures on the NYBOT from 1997 to 2006.

Invest in Sugar: It's Such a Sweet Move!

Sugar production is said to have started over 9000 years ago in southeastern Asia, where it was used in India and China for medicinal purposes. It then spread to southern Europe through Persia and Arabia around 400 B.C. In Europe and the Middle East, sugar became a popular food sweetener. From Europe, sugar spread to the New World in the fifteenth century and was particularly suitable for growing in Latin America. Today, Latin American countries dominate the sugar trade; Brazil is in fact the largest sugar producer in the world today, as you can see in Table 19-3.

Table 19-3	Top Sugar Producers, 2005 Figures
Country	*Production (Thousands of Tons)*
Brazil	27,665
India	25,945

(continued)

Table 19-3 *(continued)*

Country	Production (Thousands of Tons)
Brazil	27,665
China	12,757
United States	10,774
Mexico	7748
Russia	7280
Thailand	6027
Australia	5649
Indonesia	5020
Pakistan	4607

Source: United States Department of Agriculture

Total world sugar production for 2005 was 223 Million Tons.

If you're interested in investing in sugar, head over to the New York Board of Trade (NYBOT), which offers two futures contracts that track the price of sugar: *Sugar #11* (world production) and *Sugar #14* (U.S. production). Here are the contract specs for these two sugar contracts:

Sugar #11 (World):

- ✔ **Contract Ticker Symbol:** SB
- ✔ **Contract Size:** 112,000 Pounds
- ✔ **Underlying Commodity:** Global Sugar
- ✔ **Price Fluctuation:** $0.01/pound ($11.20 per contract)
- ✔ **Trading Months:** March, May, July, October

Sugar #14 (USA):

- ✔ **Contract Ticker Symbol:** SE
- ✔ **Contract Size:** 112,000 Pounds
- ✔ **Underlying Commodity:** Domestic (US) Sugar
- ✔ **Price Fluctuation:** $0.01/pound ($11.20 per contract)
- ✔ **Trading Months:** January, March, May, July, September, November

On a historical basis, Sugar #14 produced in the United States tends to be more expensive than Sugar #11. However, Sugar #11 accounts for most of the volume in the NYBOT sugar market. Check out the historical price of Sugar #11 on the NYBOT in Figure 19-3.

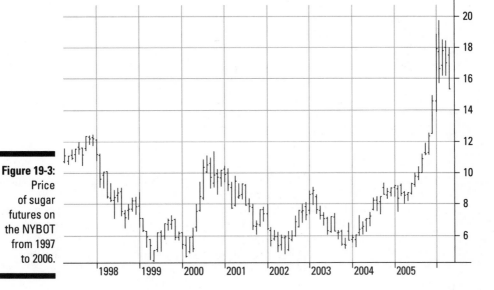

Figure 19-3:
Price
of sugar
futures on
the NYBOT
from 1997
to 2006.

Orange Juice: Refreshingly Good for Your Bottom Line

Orange juice is one of the only actively traded contracts in the futures markets that's based on a tropical fruit: oranges. Oranges are widely grown in the western hemisphere, particularly in Florida and Brazil. As you can see in Table 19-4, Brazil is by far the largest producer of oranges although the United States — primarily Florida — is also a major player.

Table 19-4	Top Orange Producers, 2005 Figures
Country	*Production (Tons)*
Brazil	17,804,600
USA	8,266,270
Mexico	3,969,810

(continued)

Table 19-4 *(continued)*

Country	Production (Tons)
India	3,100,000
Italy	2,533,535
China	2,412,000
Spain	2,149,900
Iran	1,900,000
Egypt	1,789,000
Indonesia	1,311,703

Source: United Nations Statistical Database

Because oranges are perishable, the futures contract tracks *frozen concentrated orange juice* (FCOJ). This particular form is suitable for storage and fits one of the criteria for inclusion in the futures arena — that the underlying commodity be deliverable. This contract is available for trade on the New York Board of Trade (NYBOT). The NYBOT includes two versions of the FCOJ contract: one that tracks the Florida/Brazil oranges and another one based on global production.

Here are the contract specs of FCOJ on the NYBOT:

FCOJ-A (Florida/Brazil):

- ✔ **Contract Ticker Symbol:** OJ
- ✔ **Contract Size:** 15,000 Pounds
- ✔ **Underlying Commodity:** FCOJ from Brazil and/or Florida only
- ✔ **Price Fluctuation:** $0.0005/pound ($7.50 per contract)
- ✔ **Trading Months:** January, March, May, July, September, November

FCOJ-B (World):

- ✔ **Contract Ticker Symbol:** OB
- ✔ **Contract Size:** 15,000 Pounds
- ✔ **Underlying Commodity:** FCOJ from any producing country
- ✔ **Price Fluctuation:** $0.0005/pound ($7.50 per contract)
- ✔ **Trading Months:** January, March, May, July, September, November

The production of oranges is very sensitive to weather. For instance, the hurricane season common in the Florida region can have significant impact on the prices of oranges both on the spot market and in the futures market. In Figure 19-4, you can clearly see a huge spike in the price of the FCOJ contract during the 2004–2005 period, which was a period of heavy hurricane activity. Make sure to take into consideration weather and seasonality when investing in FCOJ futures.

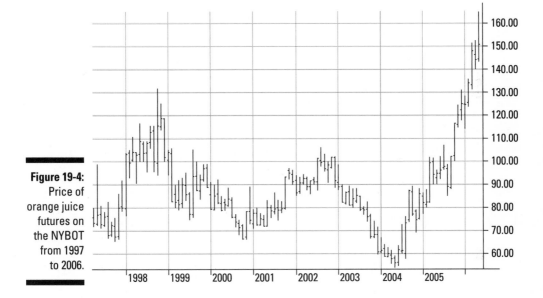

Figure 19-4:
Price of
orange juice
futures on
the NYBOT
from 1997
to 2006.

Chapter 20

How to Gain from Grains: Trading Corn, Wheat, and Soybeans

● ●

In This Chapter

▶ Exploring the corn markets

▶ Examining opportunities in the wheat markets

▶ Selecting the right strategy to trade soybeans

● ●

*I*n this chapter, I take a look at some of the major agricultural commodities that trade in the futures markets. These commodities, sometimes simply known as *ags,* are a unique component of the broader commodities markets. They are very labor intensive and are subject to volatility because of underlying market fundamentals, which I explore in the following sections. However, they also present solid investment opportunities. Corn, for example, is a major food staple; wheat is an absolutely necessary commodity and, according to archaeologists, may be the first commodity grown and traded by man; and soybeans have a growing number of applications, ranging from fuel additives to feedstock to trendy food products. I examine all three of these commodities and their investment opportunities in depth.

For additional information on agricultural commodities in general, I recommend checking out the following resources:

✔ **National Grain and Feed Association:** www.ngfa.org

✔ **U.S. Department of Agriculture (USDA):** www.usda.gov

✔ **USDA National Agriculture Library:** www.nal.usda.gov

✔ **USDA National Agricultural Statistics Service:** www.nass.usda.gov

Field of Dreams: How to Invest in Corn

In 2005, world corn production stood at about 700 Million Metric Tons. Approximately 35 Million Hectares of land are used exclusively for the production of corn worldwide, a business that the U.S. Department of Agriculture values at over $20 Billion a year. Corn is definitely big business, and I provide you with all the information you need in this section to help you invest in this major crop.

Corn, like other commodities such as crude oil and coffee, comes in different qualities. The most important types of corn you should be familiar with are *high-grade number 2* and *number 3 yellow corn*, which are both traded in the futures markets.

The most direct way of investing in corn is by going through the futures markets. A corn contract exists, courtesy of the Chicago Board of Trade (CBOT), to help farmers, consumers, and investors manage and profit from the underlying market opportunities. Here are the contract specs:

- **Contract Ticker Symbol:** C
- **Electronic Ticker:** ZC
- **Contract Size:** 5000 Bushels
- **Underlying Commodity:** High grade No. 2 or No. 3 Yellow Corn
- **Price Fluctuation:** $0.0025/bushel ($12.50 per contract)
- **Trading Hours:** 9:05 a.m. to 1:00 p.m. Open Outcry, 6:30 p.m. to 6:00 a.m. Electronic (Chicago Time)

  It's important to know the trading hours for corn and other commodities that trade both on the open outcry and through electronic trading.

- **Trading Months:** March, May, July, September, December

Corn futures contracts are usually measured in bushels (such as the corn contract offered by the CBOT). Large scale corn production and consumption is generally measured in metric tons.

Historically, the United States has dominated the corn markets, and still does due to abundant land and helpful governmental subsidies. China is also a major player and exhibits a lot of potential for being a market leader in the coming years. Other notable producers include Brazil, Mexico, Argentina, and France. I list the top producers in Table 20-1.

Table 20-1	Top Corn Producers, 2005 Figures
Country	**Production (Thousand Tons)**
United States	236,041
China	115,586
Brazil	34,179
Mexico	17,910
Argentina	14,860
France	14,791
India	10,504
Italy	9178
Romania	9102
South Africa	8382

Source: U.S. Department of Agriculture

Like other agricultural commodities, corn is subject to seasonal and cyclical factors that have a direct, and often powerful, effect on prices. Prices for corn can go through roller coaster rides, with wild swings in short periods of time, as you can see in Figure 20-1.

For more information on the corn markets, check out the following sources:

- ✔ **National Corn Growers Association:** www.ncga.com
- ✔ **Corn Refiners Association:** www.corn.org
- ✔ **Department of Agriculture Corn Research Service:** www.ers.usda.gov/briefing/corn

The Chicago Board of Trade

Established in 1848, the *Chicago Board of Trade* (CBOT) is the oldest commodity exchange in the world. All the commodities covered in this chapter trade on the CBOT, and it is the go-to exchange for grains and other agricultural products, such as oats, ethanol, and rice. The exchange has also branched out to include several metals contracts targeted towards individual investors, including the mini gold and mini silver contracts. On the financial product side of things, the CBOT offers the 30-year bond and the 10-year note. For more information on the CBOT, you can check out its Web site at www.cbot.com.

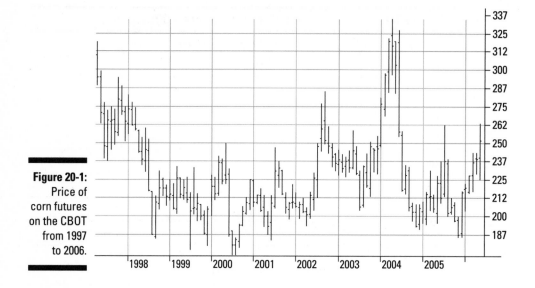

Figure 20-1:
Price of
corn futures
on the CBOT
from 1997
to 2006.

Welcome to the Bread Basket: Investing in Wheat

According archaeologists, wheat is one of the first agricultural products grown by man. Evidence suggests that wheat production developed in the Fertile Crescent region, an area that encompasses modern day Turkey and Syria. Today wheat is the second most widely produced agricultural commodity in the world (on a per volume basis), right behind corn and ahead of rice. World wheat production came in at 618 Million Metric Tons in 2005, according to the USDA.

Unlike other commodities that are dominated by single producers — Saudi Arabia and oil, the Ivory Coast and cocoa, Russia and palladium — no one country dominates wheat production. As a matter of fact, as you can see from Table 20-2, the major wheat producers are a surprisingly eclectic group. The advanced developing countries of China and India are the two largest producers, while industrial countries like Canada and Germany also boast significant wheat production capabilities.

Table 20-2	Top Wheat Producers, 2005 Figures
Country	*Production (Thousand Tons)*
China	108,712
India	65,856

(continued)

Table 20-2	Top Wheat Producers, 2005 Figures *(continued)*
Country	*Production (Thousand Tons)*
United States	62,550
France	35,062
Russia	34,656
Canada	25,717
Australia	19,290
Germany	19,203
Pakistan	17,628
Turkey	16,314

Source: U.S. Department of Agriculture

Wheat is measured in bushels for investment and accounting purposes. Each bushel contains approximately 60 pounds of wheat. As for most other agricultural commodities, metric tons are used to quantify total production and consumption figures on a national and international basis.

The most direct way of accessing the wheat markets, short of owning a wheat farm, is by trading the wheat futures contract. As with the other agricultural commodities discussed in this chapter, the Chicago Board of Trade (CBOT) offers a futures contract for those interested in capturing profits from wheat price movements — whether for hedging or speculative purposes. Here are the specs for the CBOT futures contract:

- **Contract Ticker Symbol:** W
- **Electronic Ticker:** ZW
- **Contract Size:** 5000 Bushels
- **Underlying Commodity:** Premium Wheat
- **Price Fluctuation:** $0.0025/bushel ($12.50 per contract)
- **Trading Hours:** 9:30 a.m. to 1:15 p.m. Open Outcry, 6:32 p.m. to 6:00 a.m. Electronic (Chicago Time)
- **Trading Months:** March, May, July, September, December

Wheat production, like that of corn and soybeans, is a seasonal enterprise subject to various output disruptions. Kazakhstan for instance, an important producer, has faced issues with wheat production in the past due to underinvestment in machinery and the misuse of fertilizers. This mismanagement of resources has an impact on the acreage yield, which in turn impacts prices. Such supply side disruptions can have a magnified effect on futures prices, as evidenced by the numbers in Figure 20-2.

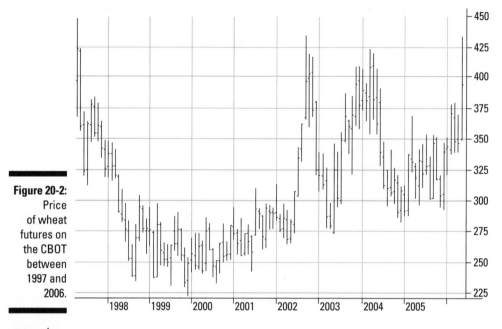

Figure 20-2:
Price
of wheat
futures on
the CBOT
between
1997 and
2006.

Interested in finding out more about the wheat market? I recommend the following sources:

- ✔ **Wheat Foods Council:** www.wheatfoods.org
- ✔ **National Association of Wheat Growers:** www.wheatworld.org
- ✔ **U.S. Wheat Associates:** www.uswheat.org

A number of organizations that offer information on specific commodities, such as corn and wheat, are specialized lobby groups whose agenda — alongside providing information to the public — includes promoting the consumption of the products they represent. Keep this in mind as you consult any outside resource for research purposes.

Trading Soybeans: It's Not Just Peanuts

The cultivation of soybeans, which developed in Asia, has been taking place for centuries. Soybeans are a vital crop for the world economy, used for everything from poultry feedstock to the creation of vegetable oil. In this section I introduce you to the different soybean extracts you can trade: soybeans themselves, soybean oil, and soybean meal.

If you're interested in getting more background information on the soybean industry, check out the following list:

- ✔ **American Soybean Association:** www.soygrowers.org
- ✔ **Iowa Soybean Association:** www.iasoybeans.com
- ✔ **Soy Stat Reference Guide:** www.soystats.com
- ✔ **Soy Protein Council:** www.spcouncil.org

Soybeans

Although most soybeans are used for the extraction of soybean oil (used as vegetable oil for culinary purposes) and soybean meal (used primarily as an agricultural feedstock), whole soybeans are also a tradable commodity. Soybeans are edible, and if you've ever gone to a sushi restaurant you might have been offered soybeans as appetizers, under the Japanese name *edamame*.

The United States dominates the soybean market, accounting for over 50 percent of total global production. Brazil is a distant second, with about 20 percent of the market. The crop in the United States begins in September, and the production of soybeans is cyclical, as you can see from the price patterns in Figure 20-3.

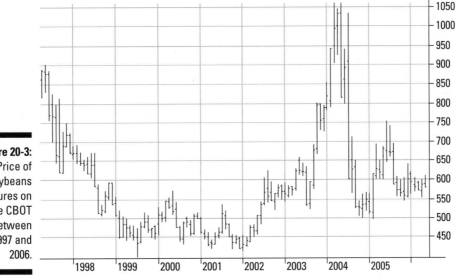

Figure 20-3: Price of soybeans futures on the CBOT between 1997 and 2006.

The most direct way for you to trade soybeans is through the Chicago Board of Trade (CBOT) soybean futures contract:

- ✔ **Contract Ticker Symbol:** S
- ✔ **Electronic Ticker:** ZS
- ✔ **Contract Size:** 5000 Bushels
- ✔ **Underlying Commodity:** Premium No. 1, No. 2 and No. 3 yellow soybean bushels
- ✔ **Price Fluctuation:** $0.0025/bushel ($12.50 per contract)
- ✔ **Trading Hours:** 9:30 a.m. to 1:15 p.m. Open Outcry, 6:31 p.m. to 6:00 a.m. Electronic (Chicago Time)
- ✔ **Trading Months:** January, March, May, July, August, September, November

Soybean oil

Soybean oil is an extract of soybeans that you and I know as vegetable oil. Soybean oil is the most widely used culinary oil in the United States and around the world, partly because of its healthy, nutritional characteristics. It contains about 85 percent unsaturated fat and very little saturated fat, which makes it appealing to health-conscious consumers.

In addition to its gastronomic uses, soybean oil is becoming an increasingly popular additive in alternative energy sources technology, such as bio-diesel. An increasing number of cars in the United States and abroad, for example, are being outfitted with engines that allow them to convert from regular diesel to soybean oil during operation. Because of their economic fuel mileage and low environmental impact, these soybean oil–enabled cars, known as *frybrids,* are becoming more popular.

Demand for soybean oil has increased in recent years as demand for these cleaner-burning fuels increases and as the automotive technology is more able to accommodate the usage of such bio-diesels. According to the Commodity Research Bureau (CRB), production of soybean oil increased from an average of 15 Billion Pounds in the mid-1990s to more than 22 Billion Pounds in 2003.

If you want to trade soybean oil, you need to go through the Chicago Board of Trade (CBOT), which offers the standard soybean oil contract. Here is the contract information:

- ✔ **Contract Ticker Symbol:** BO
- ✔ **Electronic Ticker:** ZL
- ✔ **Contract Size:** 60,000 Pounds

- ✔ **Underlying Commodity:** Premium Crude Soybean Oil
- ✔ **Price Fluctuation:** $0.0001/pound ($6.00 per contract)
- ✔ **Trading Hours:** 9:30 a.m. to 1:15 p.m. Open Outcry, 6:31 p.m. to 6:00 a.m. Electronic (Chicago Time)
- ✔ **Trading Months:** January, March, May, July, August, September, October, December

If you're wanting more info, take a look at the National Oilseed Processors Association, an industry group, www.nopa.org.

Soybean meal

Soybean meal, like soybean oil, is an extract of soybeans. Basically, whatever is left after soybean oil is extracted from soybeans can then be converted to soybean meal. Soybean meal is a high protein, high energy-content food that is used primarily as a feedstock for cattle, hogs, and poultry (see Chapter 21).

To invest in soybean meal, you can trade the soybean meal futures contract on the Chicago Board of Trade (CBOT). Here is the information to help you get started trading this contract:

- ✔ **Contract Ticker Symbol:** SM
- ✔ **Electronic Ticker:** ZM
- ✔ **Contract Size:** 100 Tons
- ✔ **Underlying Commodity:** 48% Protein Soybean Meal
- ✔ **Price Fluctuation:** $0.10/ton ($10.00 per contract)
- ✔ **Trading Hours:** 9:30 a.m. to 1:15 p.m. Open Outcry, 6:31 p.m. to 6:00 a.m. Electronic (Chicago Time)
- ✔ **Trading Months:** January, March, May, July, August, September, October, December

You can get more information regarding soybean meal from the Soybean Meal Information Center. Their Web site is www.soymeal.org.

Chapter 21

Alive and Kicking! How to Make Money Trading Livestock

According to the U.S. Department of Agriculture, consumers spend roughly 20 percent of their total food and beverage allowances on meat products, such as cattle and pork. Think of all those hamburgers and bacon sandwiches you've had over the years. Livestock, like the tropical and grain commodities, is a unique category in the agricultural commodities sub-asset class. It's not a widely followed area of the commodities markets — unlike crude oil, for example, you're not likely to see feeder cattle prices quoted on the nightly news — but this doesn't mean you should ignore this area of the markets.

That said, raising livestock is a time-consuming and labor-intensive undertaking, and the markets are susceptible and sensitive to minor disruption. These contracts are volatile (see the performance of frozen pork bellies in Figure 21-3), so you should venture into this area of the market only if you have an iron clad grasp on the concepts behind futures trading — and have a high tolerance for risk. In this chapter I analyze the markets for cattle (both live cattle and feeder cattle), lean hogs and frozen pork bellies.

Even by agricultural futures standards, livestock futures are notoriously volatile and should be traded only by traders with a high level of risk tolerance. Keep in mind that trading agricultural futures requires an understanding of the cyclicality and seasonality of the underlying commodity as well as large capital reserves to help offset any margin calls that may arise from a trade gone badly. If your risk tolerance is not elevated or you are not comfortable in the futures arena, then I recommend you don't trade these contracts because you could be setting yourself up for disastrous losses.

One resource I can recommend that provides fundamental data relating to the consumption and production patterns of pork bellies, livestock, and other commodities is the *Commodity Research Bureau Yearbook*. This book is compiled by the Commodity Research Bureau (CRB) and includes a large number of data on some of the most important commodities, including the identification of seasonal and cyclical patterns affecting the markets. For more information on this publication, you can visit the Web site www. crbtrader.com.

Holy Cow! How to Invest in Cattle

Some historians claim that cattle were the first animals domesticated by humans. Whether that is the case or not, one thing is for sure: Cattle have played a unique role in history. Throughout the ages, cows have been valued not only for their dietary value, but also monetary worth. Cows are literally a special breed because they are low maintenance animals with high products output: They eat almost nothing but grass yet they are used to produce milk, to provide meat, and, in some cases, to create leather goods. This input to output ratio means that cows occupy a special place in the agricultural complex.

The Chicago Mercantile Exchange

The *Chicago Mercantile Exchange* (CME), where all the commodities discussed in this chapter are traded, is the largest and most liquid futures exchange in the world. It has the heaviest trading activity — and open interest — of any exchange, partly because of the depth of its products offerings. Besides agricultural commodities, it also trades economic derivatives (contracts that track economic data such as U.S. quarterly GDP and non-farm payrolls); foreign currencies (it offers a broad currency selection ranging from the Hungarian forint to the South Korean won); interest rates (including the LIBOR — London Inter Bank Offered Rate); and even weather derivatives (contracts that track weather patterns in various regions of the world).

Because of its broad products listing, the CME is perhaps the most versatile of the commodity exchanges. In addition, the CME was one of the first exchanges to launch an electronic trading platform — the CME Globex — which has become an instant hit with traders. It now accounts for over 60 percent of the exchange's total volume. In 2006, the New York Mercantile Exchange (NYMEX) entered into an agreement with the CME to trade its marquee energy and metals contracts on the CME electronic platform (www.nymexoncmeglobex.com). The CME is also the first exchange to go public, and investors greeted the IPO with enthusiasm, raising the stock from $40 in 2003 to over $500 in 2006. (See Chapter 8 for more on the exchanges.) For more on the CME you should check out its Web site at www.cme.com, which also includes helpful tutorials on all its products.

Don't get mad: Considering the effect of mad cow disease on the livestock market

The live cattle and feeder cattle futures contracts are very sensitive to any supply-side disruptions or demand variations. When news broke out in the United Kingdom of a mad cow outbreak, this news had a major impact on U.S. live cattle futures prices. This event brought a lot of uncertainty in the markets and generated a lot of volatility. News of this sort is like a one-two punch to the markets because both demand and supply are affected simultaneously: Demand drops dramatically because folks no longer want to buy the products, and supply decreases as measures are taken to eliminate affected cattle.

For U.S. beef producers, the threat of mad cow disease also affects their bottom line because their exports decrease dramatically. For instance, when word came out of potential mad cow disease in U.S. herds, Japan — which buys over $1 Billion of U.S. beef a year — placed restrictions on the imports of U.S. beef. This caused a lot of pain to U.S. beef producers as they confronted declining demand both at home and abroad.

Two futures contracts exist for the cattle trader and investor: the live cattle and the feeder cattle contracts, which both trade on the Chicago Mercantile Exchange (CME).

Live cattle

The live cattle futures contract, traded on the Chicago Mercantile Exchange (CME), is unique because it was the first contract launched by the CME to track a commodity that's actually alive. Prior to the live cattle futures, all futures contracts were for storable commodities such as crude oil, copper, and sugar. The CME live cattle futures contract, launched in 1964, heralded a new era for the exchanges. This futures contract is now widely traded by various market players, including cattle producers, packers, consumers, and independent traders.

Here are the specs of this futures contract:

- **Contract Ticker Symbol:** LC
- **Electronic Ticker:** LE
- **Contract Size:** 40,000 Pounds
- **Underlying Commodity:** Live Cattle
- **Price Fluctuation:** $0.00025/pound ($10.00 per contract)

✔ **Trading Hours:** 9:05 a.m. to 1:00 p.m. (Chicago Time), Electronic and Open Outcry

✔ **Trading Months:** February, April, June, August, October, December

One of the reasons for the popularity of the live cattle contract is that it allows all interested parties to hedge their market positions in order to reduce the volatility and uncertainty associated with livestock production in general, and live cattle growing in particular. If you do trade this contract, keep the following market risks in mind: seasonality, fluctuating prices of feedstock, transportation costs, changing consumer demand, and the threat of diseases (such as mad cow disease).

As such, the market for the live cattle contract can be fairly volatile. Check out the performance of the live cattle futures contract on the CME in Figure 21-1.

Figure 21-1:
Price of
live cattle
futures on
the CME
from 1997
to 2006.

Feeder cattle

The CME launched a feeder cattle futures contract in 1971, only a few years after the launch of the groundbreaking live cattle contract. The feeder cattle contract is for calves that weigh in at the 650–849 Pound range, which are sent to the feedlots to get fed, fattened, and then slaughtered.

Because the CME feeder cattle futures contract is settled on a cash basis, the CME calculates an index for feeder cattle cash prices based on a 7-day average. This index, known in the industry as the *CME Feeder Cattle Index,* is an average of feeder cattle prices from the largest feeder cattle producing states in the United States, as compiled by the U.S. Department of Agriculture (USDA). These producing states are, in alphabetical order: Colorado, Iowa, Kansas, Missouri, Montana, Nebraska, New Mexico, North Dakota, Oklahoma, South Dakota, Texas, and Wyoming. You can get information on the CME Feeder Cattle Index through the CME Web site at www.cme.com.

To get livestock statistical information, you should check out the U.S. Department of Agriculture's statistical division. Their Web site is www.marketnews.usda.gov/portal/lg.

Here are the specs of this futures contract:

- ✔ **Contract Ticker Symbol:** FC
- ✔ **Electronic Ticker:** GF
- ✔ **Contract Size:** 50,000 Pounds
- ✔ **Underlying Commodity:** Feeder Cattle
- ✔ **Price Fluctuation:** $0.00025/pound ($12.50 per contract)
- ✔ **Trading Hours:** 9:05 a.m. to 1:00 p.m. (Chicago Time), Electronic and Open Outcry
- ✔ **Trading Months:** January, March, April, May, August, September, October, November

Lean and Mean: Checking Out Lean Hogs

The lean hog futures contract (which is a contract for the hog's carcass) trades on the Chicago Mercantile Exchange (CME) and is used primarily by producers of lean hogs — both domestic and international — and pork importers/exporters. Launched in 1997, the lean hog contract is a fairly new addition to the CME, launched as a replacement after the live hog futures contract was retired. The lean hog contract replaced the live hog contract since producers and consumers of these products don't transact the live animal (live hog), so it made more sense for the futures contract to track the product traded in the marketplace. Here are the contract specs for lean hogs:

- ✔ **Contract Ticker Symbol:** LH
- ✔ **Electronic Ticker:** HE
- ✔ **Contract Size:** 40,000 Pounds
- ✔ **Underlying Commodity:** Lean Hogs
- ✔ **Price Fluctuation:** $0.0001 per hundred pounds ($4.00 per contract)

✔ **Trading Hours:** 9:10 a.m. to 1:00 p.m. (Chicago Time), Electronic and Open Outcry

✔ **Trading Months:** February, April, May, June, July, August, October, December

Perhaps no other commodity, agricultural or otherwise, exhibits the same level of volatility as the lean hogs futures contract (see Figure 21-2). One of the reasons is that, compared to other products, this contract is not very liquid because it is primarily used by commercial entities seeking to hedge against price risk. Other commodities, say crude oil, that are actively traded by individual speculators as well the commercial entities are far more liquid and thus less volatile. If you are intent on trading this contract, keep in mind that you're up against some very experienced and large players in this market.

Figure 21-2:
Price of lean hogs futures on the CME from 1997 to 2006.

You Want Bacon with That? How to Trade Frozen Pork Bellies

Essentially, the term *pork bellies* is the traders' way of saying bacon. Physically, pork bellies come from the underside of a hog and weigh approximately 12 Pounds. These pork bellies are generally stored frozen for extended periods of time, pending delivery to consumers.

Man against machine: The battle over the future of trading

All of the contracts I discuss in this chapter are available for trading on the Chicago Mercantile Exchange's electronic trading platform, the CME Globex. Up until a few years ago, most of the trading taking place in the futures markets was done during the open outcry sessions by humans buying and selling contracts from each other. Recently, electronic trading — which matches buyers and sellers electronically — has overtaken the open outcry sessions as the main venue for trading. In the CME for example, over 60 percent of trading is now conducted electronically. The advantages of electronic trading are that it's more efficient and can be performed from remote locations.

The New York Mercantile Exchange (NYMEX) and the New York Board of Trade (NYBOT) are the only exchanges that still rely heavily on the open outcry sessions. However, that is on the decline, as the NYMEX recently signed an agreement to have its contracts offered on the CME Globex. And some exchanges, such as the Intercontinental Exchange, don't even own physical trading facilities — all the trading is done electronically through computer terminals. It seems that the age when humans interacted each other to establish prices for the world's most important commodities will soon be part of a bygone era.

As for most other livestock products, the Chicago Mercantile Exchange offers a futures contract for frozen pork bellies. This contract, which was launched by the CME in 1961, is the first ever contract on a commodity exchange where the underlying deliverable commodity is a meat — albeit dead meat. (The CME live cattle contract was the first contract based on a live animal. See live cattle section.)

Here are the specs for the CME frozen pork bellies futures contract:

- **Contract Ticker Symbol:** PB
- **Electronic Ticker:** GPB
- **Contract Size:** 40,000 Pounds
- **Underlying Commodity:** Pork Bellies, cut and trimmed
- **Price Fluctuation:** $0.0001/ pound ($4.00 per contract)
- **Trading Hours:** 9:10 a.m. to 1:00 p.m. (Chicago Time), Electronic and Open Outcry
- **Trading Months:** February, March, May, July, August

The pork bellies market is a seasonal market subject to wild price fluctuations. Although production of pork bellies is a major determining factor of market prices, other variables also have a significant impact on prices. A buildup in pork belly inventories usually takes place in the beginning of the calendar year, resulting in lower prices. But as inventories are depleted, the market moves to a supply side bias, thereby placing upward pressure on market prices. On the other side of the equation, consumer demand for bacon and other meats is not easily predictable and fluctuates with the seasons.

Because of the cyclicality of the supply side model, coupled with the seasonality of the demand model, pork belly prices are subject to extreme volatility. As a matter of fact, the pork bellies futures contract is one of the more volatile contracts trading in the market today. Check out the price of frozen pork bellies per pound in Figure 21-3.

Demand for bacon and other high-fat, high-cholesterol foods appears to be waning as a result of the health-conscious eating trends sweeping the nation. These dietary changes could have an impact on the prices of frozen pork bellies and other meats. Be aware of the impact of these dietary trends on the prices of pork bellies and other meats before investing.

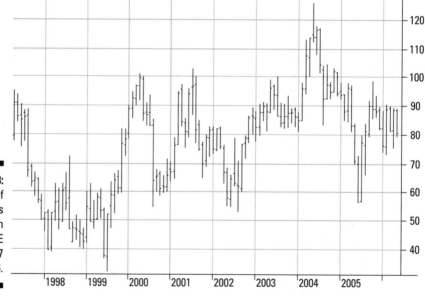

Figure 21-3:
Price of
pork bellies
futures on
the CME
from 1997
to 2006.

Part VI
The Part of Tens

The 5th Wave   By Rich Tennant

"My portfolio is gonna take a hit for this."

In this part . . .

1 include here the legendary *For Dummies* Part of Tens. In these three chapters, I uncover the best investment vehicles for commodities; pinpoint the major market indicators you should monitor to help you get a sense of where the markets are heading; and identify the top resources to use when you invest in the markets. This part includes invaluable advice that will help make you a better investor.

Chapter 22

Top Ten Ways to Invest in Commodities

In This Chapter

▶ Investing through the futures markets

▶ Getting exposure through equities

▶ Uncovering the benefits of fund investing

*B*ecause the commodities markets are so wide and deep, you have a number of investment vehicles to access these markets. A common misconception among investors is that you can only trade commodities by opening a futures account. While the futures markets certainly provide an avenue into the commodities markets, you have other tools at your disposal. I list the ten most important investment vehicles in this chapter.

Futures Commission Merchant

Opening an account with a *Futures Commission Merchant* (FCM) is the most direct way for you to invest in commodities through the futures markets. An FCM is registered with the National Futures Association (NFA) and its activities are monitored by the Commodity Futures Trading Commission (CFTC). When you open an account with an FCM, you can actually trade futures contracts, options, and other derivative products directly through the main commodity exchanges. Your orders are sometimes routed electronically or are placed during the open outcry trading session. However, you should only open an account with an FCM if you have a solid grasp of trading futures and options. For more on futures contracts, check out Chapter 9; I discuss FCMs in depth in Chapter 6.

Commodity Trading Advisor

A *Commodity Trading Advisor* (CTA) is authorized by the CFTC and the NFA to trade on behalf of individual clients in the futures markets. The CTA is a registered investment professional who has a good grasp of the concepts in the futures markets. However, before you invest through a CTA, you should research their track record and investment philosophy. Find out what you should be looking for when shopping for a CTA in Chapter 6.

Commodity Pool Operator

The *Commodity Pool Operator* (CPO) is similar to the CTA in that she has the authority to invest on behalf of clients in the futures markets. The biggest difference is that CPOs are allowed to "pool" client accounts under one giant account and enter the markets en masse. The pooling of client funds offers two advantages: It increases the purchasing power of the fund and it provides additional leverage. In addition, because a CPO is usually registered as a company, you can only lose your principal (in case things go wrong). In other words, you won't get any margin calls and owe the exchange money. Make sure to read Chapter 6 for more information on CPOs.

Integrated Commodity Companies

The equity markets offer a way for you to get exposure to commodities by investing in companies that process these natural resources. Some of these companies include large, integrated commodity-processing companies. In the energy space, these are companies like ExxonMobil (NYSE: XOM) and Total (NYSE: TOT) that have exposure to crude oil and natural gas in both the exploration and distribution phase of the supply chain. (I examine the integrated energy companies in Chapter 11.) In the metals complex, companies like Rio Tinto (NYSE: TRP) and BHP Billiton (NYSE: BHP) mine minerals and metals as varied as palladium and nickel. These integrated mining companies have operations throughout the globe. I cover them in Chapter 18.

Specialized Commodity Companies

If you want to get exposure to a specific commodity through the equity markets, you can always invest in *specialized* commodity companies. These companies focus on either one commodity or on one aspect of the supply chain. For example, oil tanker operators focus on transporting crude oil from Point

A to Point B — that's the extent of their activities, which I uncover in Chapter 14. Other such companies include Starbucks (NASDAQ: SBUX) (Chapter 19), which focuses strictly on selling and marketing coffee-related products. These are good companies to invest in if you want exposure to a specific commodity through the equity markets.

Master Limited Partnerships

Master Limited Partnerships (MLPs) are hybrid investment vehicles that invest in energy infrastructure. They are in fact private partnerships that trade on public exchanges, just like stocks. This unique combination provides several advantages. First, because the MLP is a partnership, it has tremendous tax advantages because it does not pay taxes on the corporate level, only on the individual level. It's therefore not subject to the double taxation that many corporations are subject to. Second, its mandate is to distribute practically all its cash flow directly to shareholders. It's therefore not uncommon to have an MLP return $3 or $4 per unit owned. Check out MLPs in Chapter 6.

Exchange Traded Funds

Since they first emerged on the scene a few years ago, the popularity of *Exchange Traded Funds* (ETFs) has soared. And for good reason. They're privately run funds that trade on a public exchange, just like stocks. This ease-of-use has directly contributed to their popularity among investors. A number of ETFs have been introduced in recent years, which track the performance of commodity-related assets, such as gold, silver, and crude oil. But it's not just individual commodities that are now tracked by ETFs. Commodity indexes, such as the Deutsche Bank Liquid Commodity Index (AMEX: DBC), also has an ETF that tracks its performance. Turn to Chapter 6 for a complete listing of ETFs on the market.

Commodity Mutual Funds

Investors who are used to investing in mutual funds will enjoy knowing that a number of mutual funds invest directly in commodities. Two of the biggest such mutual funds are the PIMCO commodity fund and the Oppenheimer fund, both covered in Chapter 6. Some funds seek to mirror the performance of various commodity benchmarks, while others invest in companies that process commodities.

Commodity Indexes

A commodity index acts a lot like a stock index: It tracks a group of securities for benchmarking and investing purposes. Commodity indexes are constructed and offered by different financial institutions, such as Goldman Sachs and Standard & Poor's, and they follow different construction methodologies. As such, the performance of the indexes — there are currently five — is different across the board. Most of these indexes can be tracked either through the futures markets or through ETFs. I devote all of Chapter 7 to these indexes.

Emerging Market Funds

Due to geographical happenstance, commodities are scattered across the globe. No single country dominates all commodities across the board. However, a few countries do dominate specific commodities. South Africa, for instance, has the largest reserves of gold in the world, Saudi Arabia has the largest oil reserves, and Russia has the biggest palladium reserves. As the demand for commodities increases, the economies of these emerging markets have been soaring. One way to play the commodities boom is by opening up your portfolio to emerging market funds, which I discuss in Chapter 6.

Chapter 23

Top Ten Market Indicators You Should Monitor

● ●

In This Chapter

▶ Understanding the importance of market indicators

▶ Identifying the major indicators

▶ Monitoring the indicators on a regular basis

▶ Applying the data to improve your bottom line

● ●

*T*he commodity waters can be perilous at times, and knowing how to navigate them is crucial. Keeping your eye on where the markets are heading — and where they've been — will help you develop a winning investment strategy. One way to identify where the markets are heading is by watching certain market indicators. These key metrics provide insight into what the markets are doing and help you design and calibrate an investment strategy based on the market fundamentals.

Consumer Price Index

The *Consumer Price Index* (CPI), compiled by the Bureau of Labor Statistics (BLS), is a statistically weighted average of a basket of goods and services purchased by consumers around the country. The CPI is the closest thing to a cost-of-living index and is sometimes used to gauge inflationary trends. If the CPI is rising, economists — especially the ones at the Federal Reserve — start worrying that inflation is creeping up. This may result in an increase in the *Federal Funds Rate* (see later in the chapter). The CPI is sometimes broken down further into the *Core CPI*, which excludes items like food and energy. Comparing the CPI with the Core CPI can give you a good idea of how much consumers, who account for two-thirds of economic activity, are spending on commodities such as energy and agricultural products. Visit www.bls.gov/cpi for the latest data on the CPI.

EIA Inventory Reports

Energy traders are glued to their Bloomberg terminals every Wednesday morning, at 10:30 a.m. EST to be precise, waiting for the latest inventory reports. The inventory reports are released by the Energy Information Administration (EIA), which is the statistical branch of the Department of Energy (DOE), and they detail activity in the country's energy sector. They include a summary of weekly supply estimates, crude oil supply, and disposition rates (consumer consumption), as well as production, refinery utilization, and any movement in stock changes. The EIA petroleum inventory reports may not get wide coverage in the press, but they have a direct impact on the price of crude oil and other energy products and should be monitored regularly. You can find all the information about these reports by going to the EIA Web site at www.eia.doe.gov.

Federal Funds Rate

Perhaps no other market indicator is as closely watched by investors as the *Federal Funds Rate*. When the financial press talks about interest rates going up or down, they're almost always referring to the Federal Funds Rate, which is established by the Federal Open Market Committee (FOMC). This is the short-term interest rate at which banks charge each other overnight for Federal Reserve balances. When the Fed wants to stimulate a sluggish economy, it tends to decrease this short term rate. On the other hand, if the Fed believes that the economy is overheating, and therefore subject to inflation, it increases this rate, which makes it more expensive to borrow money.

Gross Domestic Product

Gross Domestic Product (GDP) is one of the most closely watched economic indicators. GDP is essentially a measure of all the goods and services produced in a country by private consumers, the government, the business sector, and trade (exports - imports). GDP, especially *per capita GDP* — which essentially measures purchasing power on an individual level — is a good indication of the likely demand for and activity in commodities. The higher the GDP growth, the more likely a country is to spend more money on purchasing crude oil, natural gas, and other natural resources. Of course, GDP provides you with a big picture of the economic landscape and may not necessarily identify specific trends. That said, solid and growing GDP is a good measure of economic health and is a bullish indicator for commodities. While you could theoretically analyze the GDP of all countries, I recommend looking closely at U.S. GDP, the largest economy on the planet, and Chinese GDP, the fastest-growing economy in the world. These two countries are also the biggest purchasers of commodities such as crude oil and steel.

London Gold Fix

Gold is a special commodity because it's one of the only commodities that has a monetary role. For decades, many currencies — including the US Dollar and British Pound — were fixed to gold. Even though Nixon took the United States off of the gold standard in 1971, thereby heralding a floating exchange rate regime, gold is still used as a global monetary benchmark. The Federal Reserve and other central banks hold gold bullion in vaults for monetary purposes, and gold is sometimes used by economists as a measure of inflation. Monitoring gold, both as a possible measure of inflation and for its monetary stability, is a good idea. Spot gold prices are fixed in London daily — in what is known as *London Gold Fixing* — by five leading members of the financial community. The London Gold Fix is monitored closely by precious metals dealers and is used as a global benchmark for gold spot prices. You could also get an idea of where gold prices are heading by consulting the futures markets, specifically the COMEX gold futures prices provided by the New York Mercantile Exchange (NYMEX). Visit www.nymex.com for more on gold futures and www.goldfixing.com for the London Gold Fix.

Non-farm Payrolls

Like the Consumer Price Index, non-farm payrolls are compiled by the Bureau of Labor Statistics. Statistically speaking, *non-farm payrolls* includes the number of individuals with paid salaries employed by businesses around the country. It does not include government employees, household employees (homemakers), individuals who work in the non-profit sector, and those involved in agriculture. Non-farm payrolls include information on about 80 percent of the nation's total workforce, and this number is often used to determine unemployment levels. The non-farm payroll report is released monthly, on the first Friday of the month, and does not include total employment; rather it shows a change between the current employment levels and previous employment levels as measured by the *new* number of jobs that were added. The higher the number, the stronger the economy and the more people hired by businesses — which all means that consumers have more money to spend. Although the link is indirect, higher non-farm payroll numbers can be interpreted as a bullish sign for the commodities markets. Visit www.bls.gov/ces for more information on non-farm payrolls.

Purchasing Managers Index

The *Purchasing Managers Index* (PMI), released by the Institute of Supply Management (ISM), is a composite index and a good indicator of total manufacturing activity, which in turn is an important barometer of overall economic activity. The manufacturing sector is a large consumer of commodities, such as crude oil and natural gas, and a strong PMI signals that manufacturers are doing well and are likely to spend additional dollars on commodities. The PMI is released at 10 a.m. EST on the first business day of every month. You can view the reports at `www.ism.ws/ISMReport`.

Reuters/Jefferies CRB Index

The *Reuters/Jefferies CRB Index* is the oldest commodity index and is one of the most widely followed commodity benchmarks in the market. Although commodity indexes have their shortcomings — for example they only track commodities on futures contracts, thereby ignoring important commodities such as steel — they're the best measure of where the commodities markets as a whole are heading. The Reuters/Jefferies CRB Index tracks 19 commodities, everything from crude oil and silver to corn and nickel. Read Chapter 7 for more on commodity indexes.

US Dollar

Keeping your eye on what the US Dollar is doing is critical for a variety of reasons. As the world's de facto currency, most of the world's crucial commodities, from crude oil and gold to copper and coffee, are priced in USD. Any shift in the dollar will have an indirect impact on these important markets. For example, the integrated energy companies (the majors) have operations around the globe and often deal with the local currency in the area where they're operating. Any shift in the local currency/US Dollar exchange rate will have a direct impact on how the companies account for profits and expenses, as well as other metrics.

WTI Crude Oil

West Texas Intermediate (WTI) crude oil is one of the most widely followed benchmarks in the energy complex. WTI is a high-grade, low-sulfur, premium crude produced in West Texas. This light, sweet crude is traded on the New

York Mercantile Exchange (NYMEX) through a futures contract, which is widely quoted in the financial press and in analyst reports as a benchmark for global oil prices. More importantly, it is used by the industry players as a benchmark for global oil prices. Of course, because the price of the NYMEX WTI refers only to light, sweet crudes, the prices of heavy, sour crudes is going to be different. Currently, most heavy, sour crudes are priced relative to their lighter and sweeter counterparts. (Turn to Chapter 11 for more on the different grades of crude oil.)

An alternative global crude benchmark is the North Sea Brent, which is also a high-quality crude that's produced in the Norwegian/British North Sea. This contract trades on the Intercontinental Exchange (ICE). For more on the WTI contract please visit www.nymex.com, and visit www.theice.com for additional information on the North Sea Brent contract.

Chapter 24

Ten or So Resources You Can't Do Without

In This Chapter

▶ Using trade journals effectively

▶ Reading the financial press

▶ Getting help from the government

*L*iving in the information age can be both a curse and a blessing. The advantage of the information revolution is that you have so many sources of information to choose from; the drawback is how do you know which ones to use. It's easy to be overwhelmed with the amount of information that's out there.

In this chapter, I list the top ten or so resources you should use when investing in commodities. Although not all of these resources deal specifically with commodities, they are indispensable sources of information because they help you get a sense of where the financial markets are heading. Information and its application are what ultimately separate successful investors from the rest.

Using these resources will help you keep up to date on the major events that move markets and give you an edge over the competition.

The Wall Street Journal

For daily intakes of financial news, nothing beats *The Wall Street Journal*. If you want to be a successful trader, you need to keep abreast of all the information that's worth knowing. *The Journal* does a good job of presenting solid analysis and in-depth coverage of the day's main events. Its coverage of the commodities markets in its online edition at www.wsj.com is actually fairly extensive (a subscription is required), with interactive charts and graphs for both cash prices and futures markets. Also, keep an eye out for the section "Heard on the Street" because it includes a wealth of information to help you develop winning strategies that take advantage of the market fundamentals. I read *The Journal* every single day and couldn't imagine my day without it.

Bloomberg

The Bloomberg Web site at www.bloomberg.com is one of the best sources of raw information and data available to investors. Visiting this site once a day keeps you up on important developments in the markets. The Web site's commodity section at www.bloomberg.com/markets/commodities/cfutures.html contains comprehensive information on all the major commodities, from crude oil and cocoa to natural gas and aluminum, including regular price updates on the futures markets. If you trade futures, this is an indispensable resource.

Commodities-Investor.com

I set up this Web site, located at www.commodities-investor.com, to serve as an online companion to *Commodities For Dummies*. While the book provides you with a broad-based fundamental and technical approach to commodities, the Web site offers you up-to-date information on the markets. The world of commodities is fast-paced and staying on top of all the developments helps you improve your bottom line. So make sure to check out the Web site for regular updates, unique investment strategies and tips on trading techniques on a regular basis.

Nightly Business Report

I try to tune in every weeknight to my local PBS network to watch NBR's Paul Kangas, Susie Gharib, and the gang analyze the day's events. Their special features are insightful, and the market analysts they bring in are usually knowledgeable about the issues at hand. Plus, it's commercial free! Check your PBS station for local listings.

Morningstar

Morningstar is a heavyweight in the mutual fund analysis industry. Its Web site at `www.morningstar.com` includes a plethora of information on the latest mutual funds, exchange traded funds, and other investment vehicles popular with investors. If you want to invest in commodities through a managed fund, make sure you consult the Morningstar Web site before you do so.

Yahoo! Finance

Yahoo! Finance at `http://finance.yahoo.com` is my browser's default home page, and I don't plan on changing it anytime soon. I love this Web site because it includes so many different sources of information all conveniently located in one site. You have market analysis updated on an hourly basis, regular news alerts (you can sign up to receive these in your inbox), and one of the best chart services on the Web. If you're considering investing in companies that produce commodities, Yahoo! Finance is your one-stop-shop to get information on the stock's technical performance as well as its fundamental outlook.

Commodity Futures Trading Commission

The *Commodity Futures Trading Commission* (CFTC) is the federal regulatory body responsible for monitoring activities in the commodities markets. Before you do anything related to commodities, make sure you have at least one look at the Web site at `www.cftc.gov`. Before you invest, you need to know your rights as an investor and the CFTC does a magnificent job of informing you of your rights. Also make sure to check out their glossary, which is the most comprehensive one I've come across.

The Energy Information Administration

The *Energy Information Administration* (EIA) is part of the U.S. Department of Energy and is the official source of energy statistics for the U.S. government. The Web site, located at `www.eia.doe.gov`, is your number one source for information on energy markets. They cover everything from crude oil production and consumption to gasoline inventories and natural gas transportation activity. If you want to invest in energy, make sure you check out their *Country Analysis Briefs*, which give an overview of the global energy supply chain country by country. That section of the site is located at www.eia.doe.gov/emeu/cabs/contents.html.

Stocks and Commodities Magazine

If your desire is to become a serious commodity futures trader, then you can't go without reading *Stocks and Commodities* magazine. Its articles include market-tested trading strategies to help you place and execute trades. The Web site is www.traders.com.

Oil & Gas Journal

The *Oil & Gas Journal* is a subscription-based magazine that features in-depth articles about the energy industry. If you want to trade the energy markets, make sure to read O&G. Check it out at http://ogj.pennnet.com.

National Futures Association

The *National Futures Association* (NFA) is the industry's self-regulatory organization. If you are interested in investing in the futures markets, I highly recommend you check out the Web site www.nfa.futures.org before you start trading. Specifically, make sure to check out the database of registered investment advisors if you're going to go through a manager. NFA has comprehensive information on all managers (who are required to register with the NFA before handling client accounts) through its *Background Affiliation Status Information Center* (BASIC) service. BASIC is located at www.nfa.futures.org/basicnet.

Part VII
The Appendix

"Choosing the right mutual fund is like choosing the right hat. You find one that fits you best and then you stick with it."

In this part . . .

The appendix consists of a comprehensive glossary that explains all the technical terms I mention in the book. Having a grasp on the concepts behind the words is critical for your success as an investor, so make sure to familiarize yourself with this technical terminology.

Appendix

Glossary of Technical Terms

• •

*T*rading commodities requires mastery of a wide variety of technical terms. This glossary tells you what all those high-sounding financial terms actually mean, so you too can talk the talk!

Aframax: The Aframax tanker, whose first four letters are an acronym for Average Freight Rate Assessment, is considered the "workhorse" in the off-shore oil tanker fleet. Because of its smaller size, it is ideally suited for short haul voyages and has the ability to transport crude and products in most ports around the world.

Alpha coefficient: In portfolio allocation, *alpha* is used to measure the ability of an asset to generate returns independently of what the broader portfolio or market is doing.

Anthracite: Anthracite is the most valuable type of coal because it contains high levels of carbon and releases the most energy on a per unit basis.

Arbitrage: Arbitrage is a trading technique that seeks to exploit price discrepancies of a particular security that trades in different exchanges. Ideally, an arbitrageur will buy a security at a lower price on an exchange and sell it for a profit at a higher price in another trading venue.

Backwardation: Backwardation is a term used in the futures markets to refer to a situation where spot prices are higher than forward futures prices. This is the exact opposite of contango, where forward prices are higher than spot prices. See contango.

Base Metals: Base metals are metals that have low resistance to corrosion, unlike *precious metals* (See Precious Metals). Base metals include most of the industrial metals, such as copper, iron, nickel, and zinc.

Basis: the price difference between the actual (spot) commodity and the futures price.

Beta coefficient: In the *Capital Asset Pricing Model* (CAPM), *beta* measures the returns of an asset relative to the broader portfolio.

Bituminous: Bituminous is the second most valuable type of coal; it's used for both electricity generation and in the manufacturing of high quality steel.

Bollinger Bands: Bollinger bands consist of three "bands" that seek to measure a security's standard deviation from a moving average, usually the *Simple Moving Average* (which is one of the three bands). The upper and lower band track the price of the security on a simple moving average basis and attempt to determine whether a security is overbought or oversold based on its proximity to the two bands. If the price trend is flirting with the lower band, the security is oversold — — it's undervalued and it's expected to increase. On the other hand, if the security is approaching the upper band, it is overbought and may be ready for a downward price correction.

Brent, North Sea: North Sea Brent, Brent for short, is a premium grade of crude oil that's used as a global benchmark for crude oil prices.

British Thermal Unit (BTU): BTU is the standard unit of measurement for energy. Every bit of energy released from crude oil, natural gas, coal, or solar power can be quantified using BTUs. This is because one BTU refers to the amount of energy required to raise one pound of water by one degree Fahrenheit.

Buy in: A purchase that will offset a previous short sale. Covers or liquidates a short position.

Call option: A call option is a contract in the futures markets that gives the holder (buyer) of the contract the right, but not the obligation, to *purchase* an underlying asset at a specific point in time at a specific price. This is the opposite of a *put option*.

Candlestick: In technical analysis, a candlestick is a type of chart that's used to indicate crucial pieces of information regarding the performance of a security. Specifically, candlesticks indicate the security's opening price, closing price, daily high, and daily low.

Capital Asset Pricing Model (CAPM): In portfolio theory, CAPM helps calculate the amount of returns an investor can expect based on the amount of risk she is taking. The CAPM formula is fairly complex, but it stipulates that investors should be compensated based on how long they hold an investment (Time Value of Money) and on the amount of risk they take on.

Carrying charge: The cost to store and insure a physical commodity over a period of time.

Chicago Board of Trade (CBOT): Although the CBOT offers a broad products mix, this exchange dominates the grain markets, offering futures contracts for grains such as corn, wheat, soybeans, soybean oil, and soybean meal.

Chicago Mercantile Exchange (CME): The CME is the largest exchange in the world, based on total volume of contracts traded. It also offers the broadest product selection, providing contracts for commodities as varied as interest rates and butter. It's also the destination for folks who want to trade livestock because it has contracts for live cattle, feeder cattle, lean hogs, and frozen pork bellies.

Commodities Exchange (COMEX): A division of the New York Mercantile Exchange (NYMEX) that offers futures contracts and options on metals. Some of the metals on the COMEX include gold, silver, aluminum, and copper.

Commodity Futures Trading Commission (CFTC): The CFTC is the regulatory body of the futures markets. It is a federal agency that is responsible for the oversight of all the major commodity exchanges in the United States. In addition, it's responsible for monitoring the futures markets to make sure that the public is not subject to fraud or other unnatural market risks. It has the authority to investigate suspicious activity and prosecute cases.

Commodity Pool Operator (CPO): A CPO is like a futures fund manager, in that he can manage client assets under one fund for the purpose of investing in the futures markets.

Commodity Trading Advisor (CTA): A CTA could be a firm or individual, licensed by the Commodity Futures Trading Commission (CFTC), who's allowed to invest on behalf of individual clients in the futures markets.

Consumer Price Index (CPI): The CPI, compiled by the Bureau of Labor Statistics (BLS), is a statistically weighted average of a basket of goods and services purchased by consumers around the country. It's the closest indicator of how much consumers are spending on key products, including energy and agricultural products.

Contango: In the futures markets, contango refers to a specific situation where forward futures prices exceed spot prices, or where distant futures prices exceed nearer term futures prices. Essentially, contango means that prices are increasing across time in the futures markets. This is the opposite of *backwardation*. See backwardation.

Contract Month: The month in which a futures contract may be satisfied by making or accepting delivery.

Delivery: The tender and receipt of the actual commodity or the warehouse receipt in settlement of the future contract.

Delivery Notice: A notice of a clearing member's intentions to deliver a stated quantity of a commodity in settlement of a futures contract.

Derivative: A derivative is a financial instrument that derives its value from an underlying security. Examples of derivatives include futures contracts, forward contracts, and options on futures. The underlying security could be anything from an interest rate to a metal such as palladium.

Drill ship: The drill ship is essentially a ship with a drilling platform that's easily deployed to remote offshore locations for oil and gas drilling.

Drilling barge: The drilling barge is a floating device usually towed by tugboat in still, shallow waters — such as rivers, lakes, and swamps — used for offshore oil and natural gas drilling.

Energy Information Administration (EIA): The EIA is the statistical arm of the U.S. Department of Energy, which compiles information and statistics on all aspects of the global energy industry.

Enhanced Moving Average (EMA): In technical analysis, the EMA is a moving average that emphasizes a security's most recent prices. This is the opposite of the Simple Moving Average that follows an equal weight approach to all price closings. The EMA is also known as the Exponential Moving Average. See also *Simple Moving Average*.

Exchange Traded Fund (ETF): ETFs are funds that trade on public exchanges, just like stocks. The benefit of investing in ETFs is that you can invest in a fund — which could be investing in everything from commodity indexes to crude oil — by simply buying its shares on an exchange. A number of ETFs are available that cater specifically to the commodity trading community. ETFs are now available for crude oil, gold, silver, and commodity indexes such as the Deutsche Bank Liquid Commodity Index (DBLCI).

Federal Funds Rate: Commonly referred to in the financial press simply as "short-term interest rates", the federal funds rate is established by the Federal Reserve's Federal Open Market Committee (FOMC). It is the rate at which one depository institution charges another depository institution for borrowing balances at the Federal Reserve overnight.

Ferrous Metals: Ferrous — derived from the Latin *ferrum*, which means "iron" — is one method of classifying metals. Ferrous metals are metals that contain iron, such as nickel, steel, and iron itself. Metals that don't contain iron are known as *non-ferrous metals*. See Non-Ferrous Metals.

Financial Services Authority (FSA): The FSA is Britain's leading independent financial regulatory organization responsible for overseeing trading activity on UK stock and commodity exchanges. If you consider doing business in the UK, make sure you first consult the FSA.

Forward contract: A forward contract is similar to a futures contract except that it's an agreement entered into by two parties outside the scope of a regulated exchange. A futures contract is standardized and must meet specific standards and requirements established by the futures exchange it is traded on. The forward contract agreement is crafted by two parties and falls outside the jurisdiction of a regulated exchange. See *futures contract*.

Futures Commission Merchant (FCM): In the futures markets, an FCM is a licensed provider of derivative products. An FCM is similar to a stock broker and is allowed to act as a conduit between investors and the futures markets.

Futures contract: A futures contract is a highly standardized financial instrument where two parties enter into an agreement to exchange an underlying security at a specific time in the future at a mutually agreed-upon price. Both parties have the obligation of respecting the contractual obligations of the agreement.

Gross Domestic Product (GDP): GDP is a measure of all the goods and services produced in a country by private consumers, the government, the business sector, and through trade (exports–imports).

Intercontinental Exchange (ICE): ICE is one of the only exchanges that does not have physical trading floors with open outcry pits. All of its trading is done electronically via computer terminals. It offers the North Sea Brent crude oil contract and has recently added the WTI crude oil contract as well.

International Energy Agency (IEA): THE IEA, whose headquarters are in Paris, is an intergovernmental organization that's affiliated with the Organization for Economic Cooperation and Development (OECD). Besides compiling statistical information about global energy consumption and production, the IEA also acts as an energy advisor to member states.

Jack-up rig: The jack-up rig is a hybrid vessel that is part floating barge, part drilling platform used for offshore drilling purposes.

Last Trading Day: The final day in which trading may occur for a particular delivery month. After the last trading day any remaining commitment must be settled by delivery.

Lignite coal: Lignite is the least valuable type of coal because of its low energy value. It's sometimes known as brown coal.

London Metal Exchange (LME): The LME is one of the oldest exchanges in the world, and it specializes in non-ferrous metal trading. It includes contracts for aluminum, copper, nickel, lead, and zinc.

Master Limited Partnership (MLP): MLPs are hybrid investment vehicles because they are private partnerships that trade on public exchanges. This unique structure is advantageous to investors because the MLP has the tax advantages associated with partnerships while having the benefit of trading publicly like a corporation. In order for an entity to qualify as an MLP, it must generate over 90 percent of its revenues from activities in the commodities industry, such as operating gas storage facilities or crude oil pipelines.

Modern Portfolio Theory (MPT): MPT, the brainchild of economist Harry Markowitz, stipulates that investors stand to benefit through diversification. MPT emphasizes the importance of the portfolio (the whole) over individual assets (the parts).

Molybdenum: Molybdenum (pronounced mah-leb-dah-num) is known as a transition metal because it is primarily used as an alloying metal. Its resistance to corrosion and high melting points make it ideal as a coating for metals such as steel and cast iron.

National Association of Securities Dealers (NASD): The NASD is a private regulator of the securities industry in the United States. The NASD monitors virtually every security traded on American exchanges, from stocks and bonds to commodity futures and options. An individual who seeks to represent clients in the securities markets must pass rigorous qualification examinations administered by the NASD.

National Futures Association (NFA): The NFA is the future's industry self-regulatory body. Any individual or firm that seeks to transact in the futures markets on behalf of the public must be registered with the NFA. The NFA maintains a database on all its members.

New York Board of Trade (NYBOT): The NYBOT is a commodity exchange that focuses primarily on soft commodities, such as coffee, cocoa, sugar, and orange juice.

New York Mercantile Exchange (NYMEX): The NYMEX is one of the major commodities exchanges in the United States. It's headquartered in New York and offers a wide range of products to investors, from its marquee West Texas Intermediate (WTI) crude oil contract to palladium futures. Its Commodity Exchange (COMEX) division specializes in metals contracts.

Non-farm payrolls: Compiled by the *Bureau of Labor Statistics* (BLS), this measures the increase or decrease of the number of jobs added by the business sector during a given month. It's a useful measure of unemployment.

Non-Ferrous Metals: Non-Ferrous metals are metals that do not contain iron. These metals include gold, silver, and platinum but also aluminum, copper, and zinc. Metals that contain iron are known as *ferrous metals*. See Ferrous Metals.

North Sea Brent: See Brent, North Sea.

Open interest: In the futures markets, open interest represents the number of outstanding contracts held by market participants at the end of the trading day. While volume measures the amount of trading activity, open interest provides a measure of the amount of capital moving in and out of a specific security or market. See *volume*.

Option: Like a futures contract, an option is another type of derivative instrument traded in the futures markets. Options on futures are an agreement between a buyer and a seller. The buyer of the option, known as the holder, has the right but not the obligation of exercising the contract. On the other hand, the seller of the option, known as the underwriter, has both the right and the obligation of fulfilling the contract's terms if the holder exercises her rights. See *futures contract*.

Organization of Petroleum Exporting Countries (OPEC): OPEC is an organization that includes 11 of the world's top oil exporting countries. As an organization, OPEC is responsible for making sure that member states adhere to specific production and export quotas. Because OPEC's members collectively hold 60 percent of the world's total crude reserves, the organization has significant influence in the oil markets.

Over-The-Counter (OTC): The OTC market is where a majority of transactions involving commodity futures contracts, options, and other derivatives take place. The transactions involved in the OTC are, by definition, outside the purview of regulated commodity exchanges. One of the benefits of OTC deals is that the parties that enter into these agreements can create specific deals to suit specific needs (which regulated exchanges might not be able to offer). The drawback is that the regulated exchanges do offer regulatory oversight to all market participants. Despite this lack of oversight, or because of it, the OTC market is huge. To give you an idea, there are trillions of dollars of transactions conducted by the regulated exchanges, and that accounts for only 20 percent of total activity. The other 80 percent of trading is done through the OTC markets.

Panamax: The Panamax oil tanker gets its name from its ability to transit through the Panama Canal. This vessel is sometimes used for short haul voyages between the ports in the Caribbean, Europe, and the United States.

Photovoltaic: In solar energy, this is the process whereby solar power is captured and converted into electricity.

Precious Metals: One method of categorizing metals is based on their resistance to *corrosion*. Metals that are highly resistant to corrosion, and therefore don't rust easily, are known as precious metals. These metals include gold, silver, and the Platinum Group Metals such as platinum and palladium. Metals that easily corrode are known as *base metals*. See Base Metals.

Purchasing Managers Index (PMI): The PMI, released by the Institute of Supply Management (ISM), is a composite index that's a good indicator of total manufacturing activity, which in turn is an important barometer of overall economic activity.

Put option: In the futures markets, a put option gives the holder the right, but not the obligation, of selling a security at a predetermined price at a specific point in the future. This is the opposite of a *call option*.

Refinery production: Actual production of crude oil products in a refinery, such as gasoline and heating oil.

Refinery throughput: The capacity for refining crude oil over a given period of time, usually expressed in barrels.

Refinery utilization: The difference between production capacity, the throughput, and what's actually produced.

Relative Strength Index (RSI): RSI is a metric used in technical analysis that helps measure the price velocity and momentum of a security. In other words, it quantifies the momentum at which a security is increasing or decreasing and offers insight into how long an investor can expect that security to keep going on the price trajectory it is in.

Resistance: In technical analysis, resistance is where the number of sellers of a security is so large that price cannot move beyond a certain level. The number of sellers causes resistance to the security's upside. See *support*.

Securities and Exchange Commission (SEC): The SEC is the main regulatory organization of U.S. capital markets. It has oversight over all aspects of the capital markets, and its primary mandate is monitoring and regulating all the transactions that take place in the securities industry.

Semi-submersible rig: Sometimes referred to as a "semi", this structure has the capacity to drill in deep waters for energy under harsh and unforgiving conditions.

Simple Moving Average (SMA): In technical analysis, the SMA is a moving average that follows an equal weighted approach to all trading days, which the average tracks for a particular security. For example, a 50 Day SMA will place the same emphasis on the price of the security in Day 15 as it does on Day 48. See *Enhanced Moving Average*.

Sub-bituminous: This type of coal is the second least valuable in the coal family. It's used primarily for electricity generation.

Submersible rig: The submersible rig is similar to a jack-up rig in that it is primarily used for shallow water drilling activity. It is secured to the seabed.

Suezmax: This vessel is named thus because its design and size allow it to transit through the Suez Canal in Egypt. The Suezmax, ideally suited for medium haul voyages, is used to transport oil from the Persian Gulf to Europe as well as to other destinations.

Support: In technical analysis, support is where demand for a security is strong enough that prices for that security remain at or above a certain level. Thus the price is supported by buying activity. See *resistance*.

Troy Ounce: Troy ounce is the unit of measurement used to measure gold, silver, and other metals. It is the equivalent of 31.10 grams.

Ultra Large Crude Carrier (ULCC): This type of vessel is used to carry large amounts of oil across long distances.

Very Large Crude Carrier (VLCC): The VLCC is ideally suited for intercontinental maritime transportation of crude oil.

Volume: In finance, volume refers to the total number of shares, units, or contracts traded in a security or market during a specific period of time. See *open interest*.

West Texas Intermediate (WTI): The WTI is a premium type of crude oil that's used as a benchmark for global oil prices. Like its name implies, WTI is extracted from a region in West Texas that produces high-grade, low-sulfur crude. The NYMEX crude oil futures contract, widely quoted in the financial press as a standard for crude oil prices around the world, tracks the price of WTI crude.

Index

• _G_ •

BUSINESS, CAREERS & PERSONAL FINANCE

0-7645-5307-0

0-7645-5331-3 *†

Also available:
- Accounting For Dummies †
  0-7645-5314-3
- Business Plans Kit For Dummies †
  0-7645-5365-8
- Cover Letters For Dummies
  0-7645-5224-4
- Frugal Living For Dummies
  0-7645-5403-4
- Leadership For Dummies
  0-7645-5176-0
- Managing For Dummies
  0-7645-1771-6

- Marketing For Dummies
  0-7645-5600-2
- Personal Finance For Dummies *
  0-7645-2590-5
- Project Management For Dummies
  0-7645-5283-X
- Resumes For Dummies †
  0-7645-5471-9
- Selling For Dummies
  0-7645-5363-1
- Small Business Kit For Dummies *†
  0-7645-5093-4

HOME & BUSINESS COMPUTER BASICS

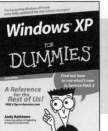

0-7645-4074-2

0-7645-3758-X

Also available:
- ACT! 6 For Dummies
  0-7645-2645-6
- iLife '04 All-in-One Desk Reference
  For Dummies
  0-7645-7347-0
- iPAQ For Dummies
  0-7645-6769-1
- Mac OS X Panther Timesaving
  Techniques For Dummies
  0-7645-5812-9
- Macs For Dummies
  0-7645-5656-8

- Microsoft Money 2004 For Dummies
  0-7645-4195-1
- Office 2003 All-in-One Desk Reference
  For Dummies
  0-7645-3883-7
- Outlook 2003 For Dummies
  0-7645-3759-8
- PCs For Dummies
  0-7645-4074-2
- TiVo For Dummies
  0-7645-6923-6
- Upgrading and Fixing PCs For Dummies
  0-7645-1665-5
- Windows XP Timesaving Techniques
  For Dummies
  0-7645-3748-2

FOOD, HOME, GARDEN, HOBBIES, MUSIC & PETS

0-7645-5295-3

0-7645-5232-5

Also available:
- Bass Guitar For Dummies
  0-7645-2487-9
- Diabetes Cookbook For Dummies
  0-7645-5230-9
- Gardening For Dummies *
  0-7645-5130-2
- Guitar For Dummies
  0-7645-5106-X
- Holiday Decorating For Dummies
  0-7645-2570-0
- Home Improvement All-in-One
  For Dummies
  0-7645-5680-0

- Knitting For Dummies
  0-7645-5395-X
- Piano For Dummies
  0-7645-5105-1
- Puppies For Dummies
  0-7645-5255-4
- Scrapbooking For Dummies
  0-7645-7208-3
- Senior Dogs For Dummies
  0-7645-5818-8
- Singing For Dummies
  0-7645-2475-5
- 30-Minute Meals For Dummies
  0-7645-2589-1

INTERNET & DIGITAL MEDIA

0-7645-1664-7

0-7645-6924-4

Also available:
- 2005 Online Shopping Directory
  For Dummies
  0-7645-7495-7
- CD & DVD Recording For Dummies
  0-7645-5956-7
- eBay For Dummies
  0-7645-5654-1
- Fighting Spam For Dummies
  0-7645-5965-6
- Genealogy Online For Dummies
  0-7645-5964-8
- Google For Dummies
  0-7645-4420-9

- Home Recording For Musicians
  For Dummies
  0-7645-1634-5
- The Internet For Dummies
  0-7645-4173-0
- iPod & iTunes For Dummies
  0-7645-7772-7
- Preventing Identity Theft For Dummies
  0-7645-7336-5
- Pro Tools All-in-One Desk Reference
  For Dummies
  0-7645-5714-9
- Roxio Easy Media Creator For Dummies
  0-7645-7131-1

SPORTS, FITNESS, PARENTING, RELIGION & SPIRITUALITY

0-7645-5146-9

0-7645-5418-2

Also available:

- Adoption For Dummies
  0-7645-5488-3
- Basketball For Dummies
  0-7645-5248-1
- The Bible For Dummies
  0-7645-5296-1
- Buddhism For Dummies
  0-7645-5359-3
- Catholicism For Dummies
  0-7645-5391-7
- Hockey For Dummies
  0-7645-5228-7

- Judaism For Dummies
  0-7645-5299-6
- Martial Arts For Dummies
  0-7645-5358-5
- Pilates For Dummies
  0-7645-5397-6
- Religion For Dummies
  0-7645-5264-3
- Teaching Kids to Read For Dummies
  0-7645-4043-2
- Weight Training For Dummies
  0-7645-5168-X
- Yoga For Dummies
  0-7645-5117-5

TRAVEL

0-7645-5438-7

0-7645-5453-0

Also available:

- Alaska For Dummies
  0-7645-1761-9
- Arizona For Dummies
  0-7645-6938-4
- Cancún and the Yucatán For Dummies
  0-7645-2437-2
- Cruise Vacations For Dummies
  0-7645-6941-4
- Europe For Dummies
  0-7645-5456-5
- Ireland For Dummies
  0-7645-5455-7

- Las Vegas For Dummies
  0-7645-5448-4
- London For Dummies
  0-7645-4277-X
- New York City For Dummies
  0-7645-6945-7
- Paris For Dummies
  0-7645-5494-8
- RV Vacations For Dummies
  0-7645-5443-3
- Walt Disney World & Orlando For Dummies
  0-7645-6943-0

GRAPHICS, DESIGN & WEB DEVELOPMENT

0-7645-4345-8

0-7645-5589-8

Also available:

- Adobe Acrobat 6 PDF For Dummies
  0-7645-3760-1
- Building a Web Site For Dummies
  0-7645-7144-3
- Dreamweaver MX 2004 For Dummies
  0-7645-4342-3
- FrontPage 2003 For Dummies
  0-7645-3882-9
- HTML 4 For Dummies
  0-7645-1995-6
- Illustrator CS For Dummies
  0-7645-4084-X

- Macromedia Flash MX 2004 For Dummies
  0-7645-4358-X
- Photoshop 7 All-in-One Desk Reference For Dummies
  0-7645-1667-1
- Photoshop CS Timesaving Techniques For Dummies
  0-7645-6782-9
- PHP 5 For Dummies
  0-7645-4166-8
- PowerPoint 2003 For Dummies
  0-7645-3908-6
- QuarkXPress 6 For Dummies
  0-7645-2593-X

NETWORKING, SECURITY, PROGRAMMING & DATABASES

0-7645-6852-3

0-7645-5784-X

Also available:

- A+ Certification For Dummies
  0-7645-4187-0
- Access 2003 All-in-One Desk Reference For Dummies
  0-7645-3988-4
- Beginning Programming For Dummies
  0-7645-4997-9
- C For Dummies
  0-7645-7068-4
- Firewalls For Dummies
  0-7645-4048-3
- Home Networking For Dummies
  0-7645-42796

- Network Security For Dummies
  0-7645-1679-5
- Networking For Dummies
  0-7645-1677-9
- TCP/IP For Dummies
  0-7645-1760-0
- VBA For Dummies
  0-7645-3989-2
- Wireless All In-One Desk Reference For Dummies
  0-7645-7496-5
- Wireless Home Networking For Dummies
  0-7645-3910-8

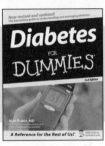

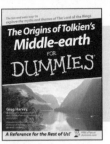

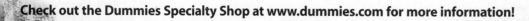